Appalachian Trail Guide
SHENANDOAH NATIONAL PARK
With Side Trails

1986
Ninth Edition

THE POTOMAC APPALACHIAN TRAIL CLUB
1718 N Street, N.W.
Washington, D.C. 20036

Ninth Edition
Edited
by
Molly Taber Denton
Floral Photos by Molly Denton, others by Dede Bauer

Printing History

The area covered in this GUIDE was originally part of a more comprehensive publication known as the *Guide to Paths in the Blue Ridge*. The first version was issued in 1931, and referred to Virginia only. In a second edition in 1934, the area covered was extended to include Pennsylvania and Maryland; supplements were issued in 1935 and 1937. The third edition was published in 1941 and the fourth in 1950. In 1959, the comprehensive Guidebook was divided into three sections, one of which covered the area represented by this GUIDE. The fifth edition was followed by the sixth in 1967, the seventh in 1973, and the eighth in 1977. All of the trails described were personally checked by the author and information rewritten in order to bring the descriptions completely up-to-date. This edition, the ninth, revises the Guide to take into account the changes that have occurred in the past nine years.

Copyright © 1986 by the Potomac Appalachian Trail Club

The Potomac Appalachian Trail Club

1718 N Street, N.W.

Washington, D.C. 20036

Library of Congress Catalog Number 86-61071

ISBN 0-915746-31-X

All rights reserved. No part of this book may be used or reproduced in any manner whatsoever without written permission except for brief quotations in reviews or articles.

In a GUIDE this size it is inevitable that errors, both typographical and factual, will occur. Please report any you find to the editor, in care of PATC Headquarters, so that they may be corrected in future editions.

Introduction and Acknowledgements

The ninth edition of the Guide has been made necessary because of major changes in the Shenandoah National Park's system of trails. The establishment of a number of Wilderness Areas covering 80,000 acres or approximately 40% of the entire park resulted in many fire roads being permanently blocked to vehicular use. Also some trails were eliminated to strengthen the wilderness ambiance of the areas.

Other trail changes have resulted from changes in SNP administrative policy. The system of yellow-blazed "fire foot trails" has been discontinued as obsolete. There has been a new emphasis on developing more trail circuits and over-the-mountain routes for horse travelers. Last, but not least, since the 8th edition of the Guide was published, the PATC has taken over the maintenance of the 95 miles of the Appalachian Trail within the Park as well as most of the other foot-trails, including many of the former fire foot trails.

In the early years a system of three-sided shelters was built along the *AT* for the use of backpackers. By the 70's these shelters were being overused by campers and misused by "car" campers. So the SNP administration closed them to all campers and demolished many of them. Under present policy seven of the remaining shelters have been designated as "huts" to be used only by backpackers having a 3 day camping permit.

Inevitably there will be trail changes within the Park in years to come—new trails built, old ones relocated or discontinued. Let us hope the changes won't come too fast and furiously.

In the preparation of this edition I must again acknowledge the wonderful cooperation of Shenandoah Park personnel—Supt. Robert Jacobson, Karen Wade, Dennis Carter, and the many rangers—who alerted me to trail alterations, who went through the 8th edition indicating corrections needed, and who scrutinized the manuscript for the 9th edition, helping me eliminate many potential errors.

All of the trail-checking for this edition has been a team-work affair, with husband, Jim, the principal member of my team.

M.T.D. Front Royal, Va. Jan. 1986

ABBREVIATIONS

AT or Trail	Appalachian Trail
ATC or Conference	Appalachian Trail Conference
km	kilometers
m. or mi	miles
NPS	National Park Service
Quad	quadrangle map with contours
PATC	Potomac Appalachian Trail Club
SNP or Park	Shenandoah National Park
SDMP	Skyline Drive milepost
USGS	United States Geological Survey

USE OF MILEAGE NUMBERS

In Chap. 4, under detailed Trail data, mileages are given in bold face type.

In Chap. 5, wherever two series of mileages are given (Example 0.0-9.2), the lefthand figures are the mileages in the direction as described, the figures to the right are the mileages in the reverse direction.

"Leave nothing but footprints, take nothing but pictures, kill nothing but time."

—Author unknown

TABLE OF CONTENTS

Printing History	ii
Introduction and Acknowledgments	iii
Abbreviations	iv
Use of Mileage Numbers	iv
Chapter 1: Use of the Guide and Trail	**1**
Format of Guidebook	1
The Trails	3
Trail Maps	3
Picnic Shelters, Huts and Cabins	3
Park Regulations-General	4
Camping Regulations	4
Accommodations in SNP	5
Backcountry Camping Regulations	6
Clothing and Equipment	9
Poison Ivy and Snakes	10
Distress Signal	11
Emergencies	11
Chapter 2: The Appalachian Trail	**13**
Early History	13
The Trail Route	14
The Appalachian Trail Conference	15
Guidebooks	15
Legislative Developments	16
National Trails System Act	17
Potomac Appalachian Trail Club	18
New Challenges	19
Chapter 3: The Shenandoah National Park	**21**
History of the Park	21
Natural History of the Park	23
Geology of the Shenandoah Park	24
Park Fauna	27
Park Flora	29
Heights of Waterfalls in SNP	34
Chapter 4: Appalachian Trail Data	**35**
North to South	
Section VI Northern Shenandoah Park	
U.S. 522 to Thornton Gap	35

v

  U.S. 522 to Gravel Springs Gap 35
  Gravel Springs Gap to Thornton Gap 39
 Summary of Distances Along the *AT*,
  Northern 45
 Summary of Distances by Skyline Drive to
  Points on *AT* 46

Section VII Central Shenandoah Park
 Thornton Gap to Swift Run Gap 47
  Thornton Gap to Skyland 49
  Skyland to Fishers Gap 54
  Fishers Gap to Swift Run Gap 59
 Summary of Distances Along the *AT*,
  Central 67
 Summary of Distances by Skyline Drive to
  Points on *AT* 68

Section VIII Southern Shenandoah Park
 Swift Run Gap to Rockfish Gap 69
  Swift Run Gap to Simmons Gap 70
  Simmons Gap to Browns Gap 72
  Browns Gap to Jarman Gap 74
  Jarman Gap to Rockfish Gap 81
 Summary of Distances Along the *AT*,
  Southern 83
 Summary of Distances by Skyline Drive to
  Points on *AT* 85

South to North
Section VIII Southern Shenandoah Park
 Rockfish Gap to Swift Run Gap 86
  Rockfish Gap to Jarman Gap 87
  Jarman Gap to Browns Gap 89
  Browns Gap to Simmons Gap 93
  Simmons Gap to Swift Run Gap 97
 Summary of Distances Along the *AT*, Southern ... 100
Section VII Central Shenandoah Park
 Swift Run Gap to Thornton Gap 101
  Swift Run Gap to Fishers Gap 103
  Fishers Gap to Skyland 110
  Skyland to Thornton Gap 114
 Summary of Distances Along the *AT*, Central 119

Section VI Northern Shenandoah Park
    Thornton Gap to U.S. 522 120
        Thornton Gap to Gravel Springs Gap 121
        Gravel Springs Gap to U.S. 522 126
    Summary of Distances along the AT, Northern 131

Chapter 5: Side Trails **133**
    List of Side Trails 133
    Introduction to Side Trails 139
    Northern Section 139
    Central Section 173
    Southern Section 230

Chapter 6: Picnic Shelters, Huts and Cabins **257**
    Picnic Shelters 257
    Huts 257
    Cabins 258

Index **265**

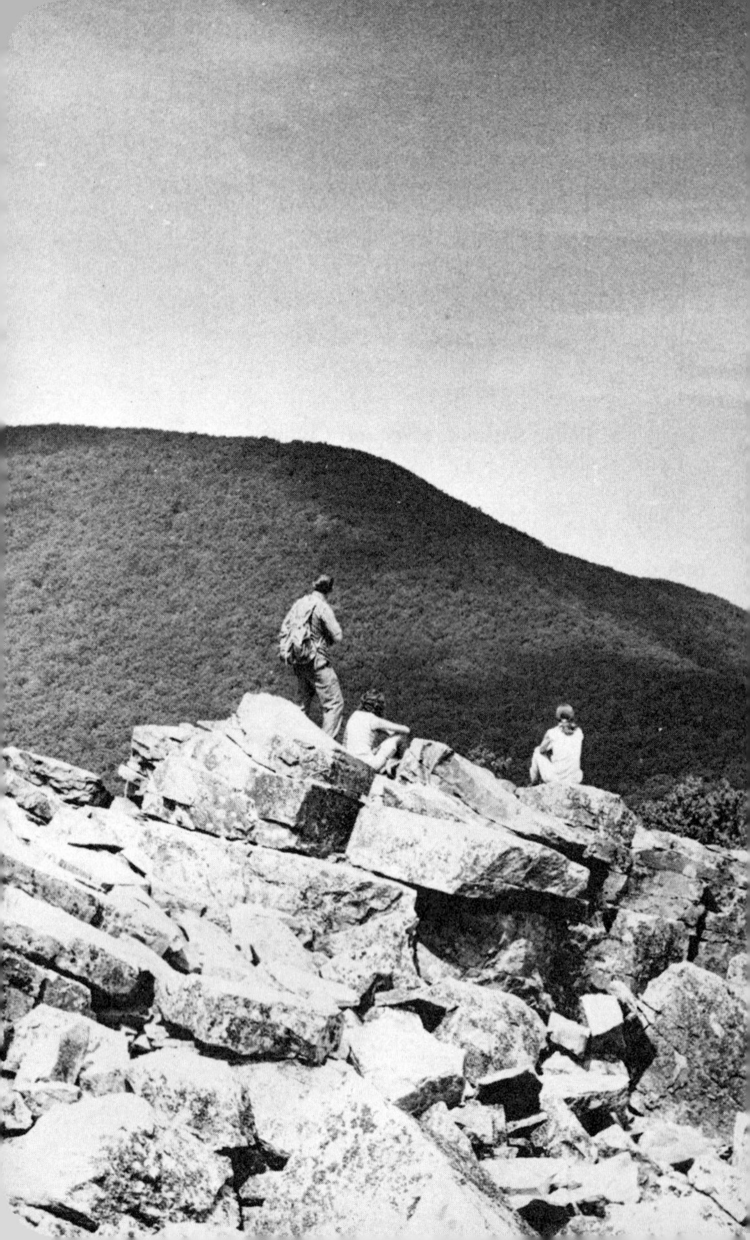

GUIDE TO THE APPALACHIAN TRAIL AND SIDE TRAILS IN THE SHENANDOAH NATIONAL PARK

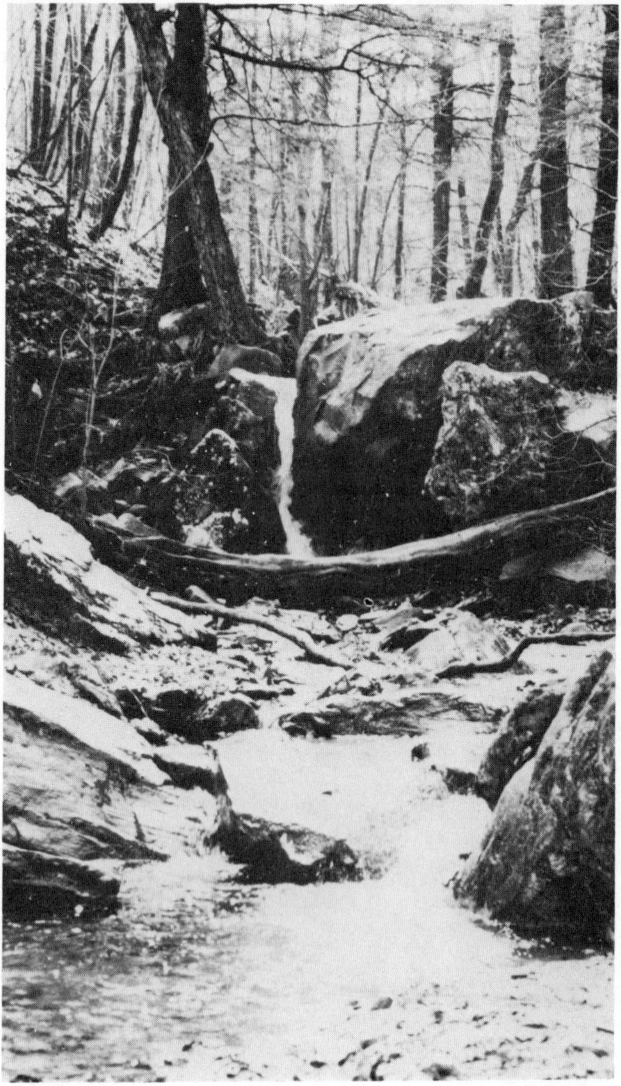

CHAPTER 1
USE OF THE GUIDE AND THE TRAIL

This GUIDE is one of a series of guidebooks covering the entire Appalachian Trail (*AT*) from Maine to Georgia. The Potomac Appalachian Trail Club is responsible for preparing this GUIDE plus a separate one for the area extending north from the Shenandoah National Park to the Maryland-Pennsylvania border. A complete list of *AT* guidebooks is provided in Chapter 2.

Format of Guidebook

The format of this GUIDE is suggested by the Table of Contents. A distinctive feature is that *AT* information is given in both directions, north to south, and south to north (though for certain short sections the respective directions may be more westerly or easterly).

The Trail data are broken down by the three major sections of the Park: VI northern, VII central and VIII southern. Within each section the *AT* descriptions are divided into subsections demarcated by Blue Ridge gaps.

For each section, both general information and detailed Trail data are provided:

- The general information includes a brief description of the overall route and notes features of particular scenic or historic interest; it also lists side trails, accommodations in the form of shelters and cabins, and appropriate PATC or U.S. Geological Survey Maps.

- The detailed data are designated for on-the-Trail use by hikers. They briefly describe the beginning and end of each Trail section, outline geographical features and mileages which would be useful in following it, and note the precise location of accommodations (shelters and cabins), water, and side trails.

The Trails

This GUIDE provides information on 106.6 miles (171.6 kilometers) of the Appalachian Trail and over 500 miles of side trails of various types. Of the total *AT* mileage, 95.0 is within the Park and 11.6 is outside (3.6 miles at the northern end and 8.0 miles at the southern end).

Types of Trails

In addition to the Appalachian Trail, several major types of side trails are described in this GUIDE.

- Blue-blazed side trails may be used for foot-travel only. Most are maintained by the Potomac Appalachian Trail Club (the PATC).
- Yellow-blazed trails are for use of both horses and foot-travelers. Most are maintained by Shenandoah Park crews with some assigned to horse-riding groups for maintenance. Most Park "fire" roads are yellow-blazed. Horses are limited to trails, including the fire roads, that are yellow-blazed.
- Nature trails, interpretive trails, and stroller trails are not paint-blazed.

Trail Markings

At key points along the Appalachian Trail and side trails the Park Service has erected concrete posts which provide trail information. The data are stamped on metal bands ringing the posts.

The Appalachian Trail itself is marked by white paint blazes, each about 2″ by 6″. A double blaze (two blazes, one placed above the other) is placed as a warning sign. It may indicate an obscure turn or a change in direction which otherwise might not be noticed.

Blue-blazed and yellow-blazed trails are marked similarly. A few trail sections may carry both yellow and either white or blue blazes, where a horse trail and a strictly foot trail overlap for a short distance.

Park Service stroller trails and nature trails, usually short in length, are marked with appropriate signs and are easily followed.

Trail Use

Those using the *AT* or side trails should, of course, be very careful not to damage property or to litter. Park regulations forbid the use of any motorized vehicle on trails. Fire and camping regulations are listed in detail. Cutting of any standing tree, dead or alive, is prohibited. Flowers should not be picked. All forms of wildlife are protected and firearms are prohibited.

Some of the side trails have their lower ends outside the Park on private land. Owners can and sometimes do close them to hikers—usually after some unfortunate event. It is, therefore, *extremely important that private property rights be respected.* If you are unsure about the current status of boundary access on private land, check with SNP.

Trail Maps

Three detailed maps of trails in the Shenandoah National Park are available in the Park or from the Potomac Appalachian Trail Club. It is recommended that they be used in conjunction with the GUIDE. The maps correspond to the three major sections of the Park: VI northern, VII central, and VIII southern. They are numbered, respectively, 9, 10, and 11.

The maps have been prepared by the Maps Committee of the Potomac Appalachian Trail Club and are based on U.S. Geological Survey quadrangles. They indicate the route of the *AT* (in contrasting color), side trails, cabins, highways, the Park boundary, Park facilities, overlooks on the Skyline Drive, and other major features. Relief is shown by contour lines and by separate elevation profiles for both the *AT* and the Drive. Insert maps of the major facilities are also included.

The maps, like the GUIDE, are periodically revised.

Appropriate U.S. Geological Survey quadrangle maps are noted at the beginning of each section. These quadrangles may be purchased from the USGS office at 1200 South Eads St., Arlington, Virginia 22202.

Picnic Shelters, Huts and Cabins

There are 5 picnic shelters, 7 huts and 6 locked cabins located near the Appalachian Trail or some side trail within the Park. The shelters (four of the five are called Byrds Nests) and huts are three-sided structures with picnic tables and fireplaces in front.

The picnic shelters are available for day use and emergency shelter only and *are not* available for overnight camping.

Appalachian Trail thru-hikers may camp in the huts, all of which are located along the *AT*. During the summer season a hut master is in attendance at each hut and a small fee is charged each camper for use of the facilities.

The cabins are locked structures and must be reserved in advance by contacting PATC Headquarters. Each cabin is provided with sufficient equipment so that the user need bring only personal gear, bedding (usually a sleeping bag), and food. A spring or other source of water is nearby. The toilet facilities are privies. Users should bring their own lanterns and fuel. There are 4 cabins located in the central section and 1 each in the northern and southern sections of the Park.

Other Facilities
(See chart opposite)

The visitor centers are strongly recommended (only the Big Meadows Center, however, is located close to the Appalachian Trail). They provide publications, displays, and audio-visual programs. Ranger-naturalists are on hand.

The waysides, lodges and restaurants are operated by a concessioner, ARA Virginia Sky-line Co. Inc. Reservations for the lodges may be made by writing this firm at P.O. Box 191, Luray, Virginia, 22835. Phone (703) 743-5108.

Park Regulations—General

1. Dogs are not permitted in the Park except on leash. They are prohibited on certain trails which are posted by appropriate signs.

2. No open wood or charcoal fires may be kindled except in fireplaces provided at trailside shelters and those provided in established picnic grounds and campgrounds.

3. No lighted cigarette, cigar, pipe heel, match or other burning material shall be thrown from any vehicle or saddle horse, or dropped into any grass, leaves, twigs, tree mold, or other combustible or inflammable material. Smoking within the Park may be prohibited or limited by the superintendent when, in his judgement, a current fire hazard makes such action expedient.

4. The use of fireworks or firecrackers in the Park is prohibited.

Camping Regulations

1. Permits are required for backcountry camping. See next section.

ACCOMMODATIONS IN SHENANDOAH NATIONAL PARK
(excluding shelters, huts and cabins)

Facility	Northern Section	Central Section	Southern Section
Picnic Areas	Dickey Ridge Elkwallow	Pinnacle Big Meadows Lewis Mountain South River	Loft Mountain Dundo (winter only)
Campgrounds	Mathews Arm (summer)	Big Meadows (closed Jan. & Feb.) Lewis Mountain (summer)	Loft Mountain Dundo (group camping, summer)
Waysides[1]	Elkwallow (mid-May—Oct. 31) Dickey Ridge (May thru Nov.)	Big Meadows (closed Jan. & Feb.) Big Meadows (open all year)	Loft Mountain (April thru Oct.)
Visitor Centers	—		—
Lodges (hotel-cottage)	—	Skyland (400) (April thru Oct.) Big Meadows (250) (mid-May thru Oct.) Lewis Mountain (24) (mid-May thru Oct.)	—
Restaurants[2]		Panorama (April thru early Nov.)	

[1] Provide refreshments and limited food supplies: Loft Mountain and Lewis Mountain have campers stores.
[2] In addition to seasonal food facilities at waysides and lodges. Located between northern and central sections.

2. At public campgrounds the regular fireplaces constructed for the convenience of visitors must be used. Firewood is sold at the waysides during the summer travel season.

3. No person, party or organization shall be permitted to camp in any public camping area in the Park for more than 14 days in any calendar year.

4. The installation of permanent camping facilities by visitors is prohibited. The digging or leveling of the ground in any camp site is prohibited.

5. Campers shall not leave their camps unattended for more than 24 hours without special permission of the superintendent, obtained in advance. Camping equipment left unattended in any public camping area for 24 hours or more is subject to removal by order of the superintendent, the expense of such removal to be paid by the person or persons leaving such equipment.

6. The superintendent may, with the approval of the Director of the National Park Service, establish hours during which quiet must be maintained at any camp, and prohibit the running of motors at or near a camp during such hours.

7. At all campsites, food or similar organic material must be either: (1) completely sealed in a vehicle or camping unit that is constructed of solid, nonpliable material; or (2) suspended at least ten (10) feet above the ground and four (4) feet horizontally from any post, tree trunk or branch. This restriction does not apply to food that is in the process of being transported, being eaten, or being prepared for eating.

Backcountry Camping Regulations

Definition of Terms

For purposes of clarification at Shenandoah National Park, "backcountry camping" is defined as any use of portable shelter or sleeping equipment in the backcountry. "Backcountry" is defined as those areas of the Park which are more than 250 yards from a paved road, and more than one-half mile from any Park facilities other than trails, unpaved roads and trail shelters.

A person or group of persons may camp overnight at any backcountry location within the Park, except:

BACKCOUNTRY CAMPING REGULATIONS

Permit Required

No person or group of persons traveling together may camp without a valid backcountry camping permit. The issuance of this permit may be denied when such action is necessary to protect Park resources or Park visitors, or to regulate levels of visitor use in legislatively-designated wilderness areas. Permits are available without charge at Park Headquarters, all Entrance Stations, and all Visitor Centers. Requests for permits by mail must be accompanied by the camper's name, address, number in party, and the location and date of each overnight camp.

Group Size

No person may camp in or with a group of more than nine (9) other persons.

Huts

The PATC operates and maintains 7 huts along the *AT* in the Park for rental to self-contained and self-propelled long distance Appalachian Trail hikers and to extended-visit backcountry campers with a 3-day or longer backcountry camping permit.

Bunk space in the huts is available up to the capacity of the hut but with priority being given to *AT* hikers on a first come-first served basis. Except in an emergency situation only one night's lodging is permitted per hut.

Hut guests are expected to pay a suggested donation of $1.00 per guest per night—either payable to the resident hutkeeper or placed in a locked depository on the honor system if no hutkeeper is in residence. (See Chap. 6: "Picnic Shelters, Huts and Cabins.")

Location of Camp

No person or group may backcountry camp:

(i) within 250 yards or in view from any paved Park road or the Park boundary;

(ii) within one-half mile or in view from any automobile campground, lodge, restaurant, visitor center, picnic area, ranger station, administrative or maintenance area, or other Park development or facility except a trail, an unpaved road or a trail shelter;

(iii) on or in view from any trail or unpaved road, or within sight of any sign which has been posted by Park authorities to

designate a no camping area;
  (iv) within view of another camping party or trail shelter;
  (v) within 25 feet of any stream.

Duration of Stay

No person shall backcountry camp more than two (2) consecutive nights at a single location. The term "location" shall mean that particular campsite and the surrounding area within a two hundred fifty (250) yard radius of that campsite.

Fires

No open wood or charcoal fires may be kindled in backcountry areas except in fireplaces provided at trailside shelters. The use of small gasoline, propane or solid fuel camping stoves is recommended.

Fires must not be left unattended.

Dogs

Dogs must be on a leash at all times. Dogs are prohibited on certain trails which are posted by appropriate signs.

Bears

At all campsites, food or similar organic material must be suspended at least 10 feet above the ground and 4 feet horizontally from any post, tree trunk or branch. This restriction does not apply to food that is in the process of being transported, being eaten, or being prepared for eating.

Sanitation

No disposing of refuse in other than refuse receptacles. Burnable trash may only be burned at fireplaces located at huts, shelters, or public campgrounds. Park regulations prohibit glass containers in the backcountry.

No bathing, or washing food, clothing, dishes, or other property at public water outlets, fixtures or pools, except at those designated for such purpose.

No polluting or contaminating park area waters—springs, streams, etc.

In developed areas, no disposal of human body waste, except at designated locations or in fixtures provided for that purpose.

In nondeveloped areas, no disposal of human body waste within 10 yds. of any stream, trail, unpaved road or Park facility. Fecal

matter must be placed in a hole and covered with at least 3" of soil.
Other
The cutting of green boughs for beds is prohibited.

The digging or leveling of the ground in any campsite without a ranger's permission is prohibited.

Any article likely to frighten horses shall not be hung near a road or trail used by horses.

Hunting or possession of fire-arms is prohibited. No camp may be established in the Park and used as a base for hunting outside the Park.

Saddle, pack, or draft animals shall not be kept in or near any camping area.

Clothing and Equipment

Hikers should keep in mind that temperatures are often much lower along the Blue Ridge crest than at low elevations, especially in winter. Snow accumulates sooner and lasts much longer in the Park than it does in the Washington area. In addition, when hiking along exposed ridges in windy weather, one must consider the chill factor as well as the actual temperature.

Long pants offer considerable protection from snakes, poison ivy, and nettles. In rainy weather water repellant jackets or ponchos are advisable and it is wise to have a set of dry clothes to change into.

Good shoes or boots are important if one is hiking very far. Special attention should be given to obtaining comfortable shoes with non-slip soles and heels.

The amount of equipment needed will, naturally, vary with the length of hike. But in general it is good advice to carry at least a compass, a first aid kit, a whistle and a small canteen (or a large canteen in hot weather).

Do not depend on springs for water during hot, dry weather. Carry enough water for your needs. Backcountry users are encouraged to treat all unprotected surface water by boiling it vigorously for at least one minute.

Poison Ivy and Snakes

Poison Ivy

Poison Ivy is found along the Trail. Poisoning is largely preventable if one knows how to identify the plants. They are usually vines but in full sunlight may grow as low shrubs. The leaves always consist of three leaflets. Only one three-part leaf leads off from each node on the stem.

The skin irritant of poison ivy is found in all parts of the plant including roots and fruit. But the danger of poisoning is greatest in spring and summer when sap is abundant.

While poisoning usually is caused by contact with some part of the plant, it may also be caused by contact with some intermediate object which has touched a plant, such as clothing, dogs and cats, etc.

The time between contamination and first symptoms varies greatly with individuals. They may appear in a few hours or even after 5 days or more. There is no absolute quick cure for all individuals. Prompt washing with a strong soap may help and certain lotions can reduce irritation.

Poisonous Snakes

Two types of poisonous snake inhabit the area covered by this GUIDE: the copperhead and the timber rattlesnake. *Copperheads* are rarely more than 3 ft. long; they have a coppery-to-dull brown head and a pale pinkish- or reddish-brown body marked with large cross bands of chestnut brown resembling dumbbells or hourglasses; the tail is tapered. The *timber rattlesnake* is usually 2.5 to 3.5 feet long; it may be yellow or tan with chevron-shaped cross bands of black or dull brown, but they are often so dull as to appear entirely black; the tail either is blunt or carries the characteristic rattles. Both snakes have heads that are rather flat on top and have wide jaws; immediately behind the jaw the neck is much smaller. The body tends to be fat and heavy. Neither is aggressive. They are dangerous only if cornered or surprised. Remember: snakes are protected from harm in the park.

Although both snakes are among the least venomous and cases of snakebite are relatively uncommon, they are serious enough to warrant care on the part of the hiker to avoid them. The most

DISTRESS SIGNAL—EMERGENCIES

important precaution is not to put your hands or feet in places you cannot see clearly. In particular, avoid piles of rock, wood, or brush. Do not sit on rock walls. For maximum protection wear high-topped boots and long pants. During cool spells and at night, watch the trail for snakes that may be too sluggish to get out of the way. Do not hike alone.

In case of snake bite, the most important thing is to get medical attention to the victim (or vice versa, if necessary) as soon and with as little excitement and exertion by the victim as possible. Antivenom (snakebite serum) is useful even if given hours after the bite. Because antivenom may have side effects, it is important to know definitely whether a bite is from a poisonous snake, and it is desirable to know which species is involved.

Distress Signal

An emergency call for distress consists of three short calls, audible or visible, repeated at regular intervals. A whistle is particularly good for audible signals. Visible signals may include: daytime, light flashed with a mirror; at night, a flashlight (use only in a genuine emergency).

Anyone recognizing such a signal should acknowledge it by a signal of two calls—if possible by the same method of signaling. Then, obviously, he should go to the distressed and determine the nature of the emergency. If more competent aid is needed, he should try to arrange for it.

Emergencies

Report emergencies to a ranger or to any uniformed personnel at Front Royal Entrance Station, Dickey Ridge Visitor Center, Piney River Ranger Station, Park Headquarters, Big Meadows, Swift Run Gap Entrance Station, Simmons Gap Ranger Station, or Rockfish Gap Entrance Station. Or call emergency number at 999-2227.

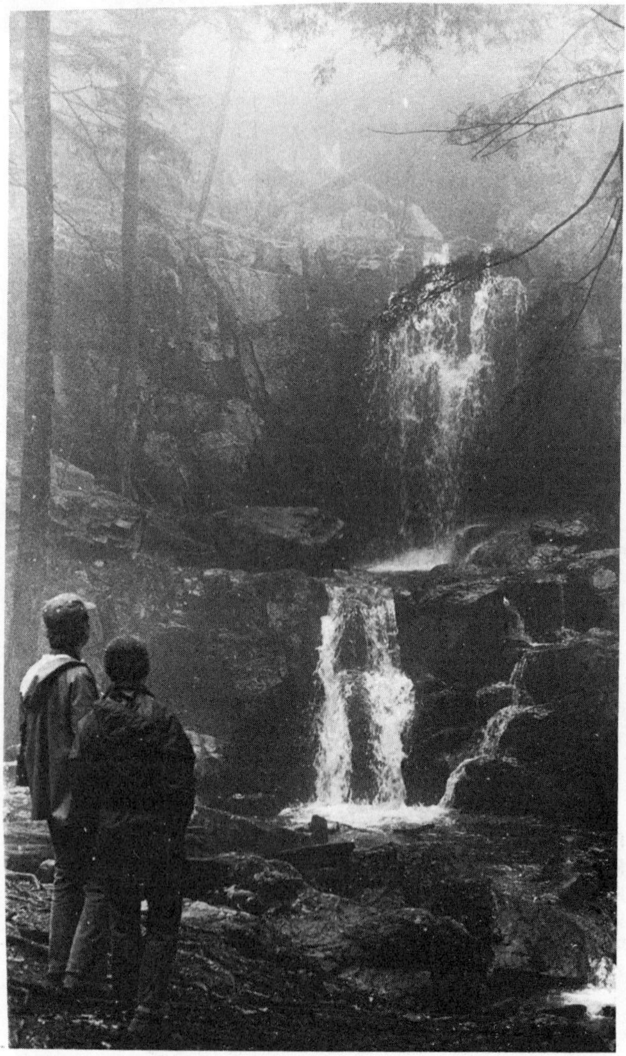

CHAPTER 2
THE APPALACHIAN TRAIL

The Appalachian Trail is a continuous, marked footpath extending from Mt. Katahdin, in the central Maine wilderness, some 2,000 miles south to Springer Mountain in Georgia. It is a skyline route along the crest of the ranges generally referred to as Appalachian; hence the name of the Trail.

Early History

The Appalachian Trail was originally proposed in 1921 by Benton MacKaye, forester and regional planner of Shirley Center, Massachusetts. From his early wanderings in the New England forests, he had conceived the vision of a trail which would be the backbone of mountain recreation in the East. He wrote up his plan in an article, "The Appalachian Trail, An Experiment in Regional Planning," in the October 1921 issue of the *Journal of the American Institute of Architects*.

There was some interest in the New York-New Jersey area; a section was constructed near Bear Mountain in the Palisades Interstate Park. But it was not until 1926, when Arthur Perkins of Hartford, Connecticut revived the endless footpath idea, that enthusiasm among outdoor groups initiated the inclusion of sections of trail already in use as portions of the Appalachian Trail.

The existing sections included the Appalachian Mountain Club's trails in New England, the Long Trail of the Green Mountain Club in Vermont, and the Dartmouth Outing Club's trail system between the Green Mountains of Vermont and the White Mountains of New Hampshire. With the Bear Mountain and Harriman sections of Palisades Interstate Park in New York, existing trails made up a total of about 350 miles out of the planned 2000 miles from Maine to Georgia.

In the south, trails in National Forests were developed. Some time later two National Parks, the Great Smoky Mountains and Shenandoah, each contributed some of the most used hiking trails. This was all on publicly owned lands.

The connecting trails, however, would have to be on private land. The trail pioneers worked out routes, mostly along mountain tops, for some of the best scenery in the East. Their enthusiasm persuaded land owners to become hosts to the Trail. Generally it was oral permission, quite adequate in the early 1930's. Owners really didn't expect too many folks to want to walk in their mountains.

New clubs were formed to build and maintain the Trail. The U.S. Forest Service and the National Park Service, state parks and forests translated their interest into real assistance.

The Trail Route

The Appalachian Trail traverses fourteen states. From Katahdin in Maine the route leads in a general southwesterly direction across Maine and New Hampshire and into Vermont, where it turns south on the Long Trail along the crest of the Green Mountains to the Massachusetts line. It then follows the highlands in western Massachusetts, has a rather circuitous course in western Connecticut, crosses the Hudson River at Bear Mountain Bridge, and follows close to the New York-New Jersey line to the base of the Kittatinny Range, which it follows to the Delaware Water Gap. West of the Water Gap it follows the crest of Blue Mountain to Swatara Gap where it turns northwest. After crossing several ridges and traversing the beautiful St. Anthony's Wilderness, it descends from Peters Mountain to cross the Susquehanna on the Clarks Ferry Bridge.

From the Susquehanna River south, the Trail follows Cove Mountain to Grier Point, crosses the Cumberland Valley, and then traverses South Mountain through Michaux State Forest in Pennsylvania to Pen Mar. It leads across Maryland to the Potomac River at Weverton, follows the towpath of the Chesapeake and Ohio Canal to cross the river on the footbridge cantilevered onto the B & O Railroad Bridge at Harpers Ferry. From the Potomac the Trail in general follows the crest of the Blue Ridge, continuing south through the Shenandoah National Park.

At Rockfish Gap the section maintained by the Potomac Appalachian Trail Club ends. Beyond, the route leads through the George Washington National Forest and, farther south, the Jefferson National Forest, forsaking the Blue Ridge just north of Roanoke, Va. to follow on south the long SW-NE ridges west of the

Blue Ridge. The Trail then straddles the North Carolina-Tennessee boundary as it passes through the Cherokee and Pisgah National Forests and the Great Smoky Mountains National Park. From here it cuts through the Nantahala Mountains in the Nantahala National Forest and in Georgia traverses the Chattahoochee National Forest to Springer Mountain.

The Appalachian Trail Conference

The Appalachian Trail Conference is the parent organization for the overall Trail. It coordinates efforts of trail clubs, national and state governments, and individuals in trail building, marking and maintenance. The Conference is headquartered in Harpers Ferry, W.Va. Office hours are 9-5 weekdays. Mailing address: P.O. Box 807, Harpers Ferry, W.Va. 25425. Phone (304) 535-6331.

The Trail route is divided into three regions with six representatives from each serving on the Board of Managers, the governing body of the Appalachian Trail Conference. Sessions of the Trail Conference are held every second or third year.

The membership consists of organizations which maintain the Trail or contribute to the Trail project, individuals who in either personal or an official capacity are responsible for the maintenance of sections of the Trail, and individual dues-paying members.

ATC annual membership is currently $18.00. Membership includes a subscription to the *Appalachian Trailway News,* published in January, March, May, August and November. (Subscriptions are $10.00 per year for non-members.) The Conference also publishes a monthly newsletter, bulletins, and guidebooks, which may be obtained from the Appalachian Trail Conference at the above address.

Guidebooks

Guidebooks issued by the Conference and/or available through it include:

Guide to the Appalachian Trail in Maine (issued by the Maine Appalachian Trail Club).

Guide to the Appalachian Trail in New Hampshire and Vermont.

GUIDEBOOKS—LEGISLATIVE DEVELOPMENTS

Guide to the Appalachian Trail in Massachusetts and Connecticut.

Guide to the Appalachian Trail in New York and New Jersey (issued by the New York-New Jersey Trail Conference).

Guide to the Appalachian Trail in Pennsylvania (issued by the Keystone Trails Association).

Appalachian Trail Guide: Maryland and Northern Virginia with Side Trails (issued by the Potomac Appalachian Trail Club).

Appalachian Trail Guide: Shenandoah National Park with Side Trails (issued by the Potomac Appalachian Trail Club).

Guide to the Appalachian Trail in Central and Southern Virginia.

Guide to the Appalachian Trail in Tennessee and North Carolina.

Guide to the Appalachian Trail in North Carolina and Georgia.

A complete list of publications, with current prices, is available from the Conference.

Legislative Developments

The first meeting of the Conference was held in March 1925. In the early years the primary responsibility of the group was to guide the construction and maintenance of the Trail. Since completion of the Trail in 1937, the Conference has been concerned with maintenance, preserving the continuity of the route, and providing information for those using the Trail.

In 1938 the Conference was instrumental in negotiating the signing of the Appalachian Trailway Agreement by the National Park Service, the U.S. Forest Service, and most of the states through which the Trail runs. It meant that on land under the jurisdiction of Federal agencies, no incompatible development would be permitted within a zone of one mile on either side of the Appalachian Trail. (The states subscribed to a ¼-mile zone because of smaller holdings.)

Events of the postwar years presaged the need for protecting the Trail and its environment. Representative Daniel Hoch, an ardent hiker from the Blue Mountain Eagle Climbing Club in Pennsylvania, introduced a bill in 1945 for the National System of Foot Trails as an amendment to the Highway Act. Because it had only a preliminary hearing, it was reintroduced in the next Congress, only to fail again.

But the emphasis was now on preservation of the Trail. It was clear that some kind of help from the Federal Government was essential if an unbroken Trail was to be maintained. In 1964 Senator Gaylord Nelson of Wisconsin introduced a bill to protect and promote the *AT*. Officers of the Conference worked with the legislators to draft the bill. Although it did not pass, it demonstrated the strong backing such legislation had from outdoor people generally.

Work continued behind the scenes. In 1968, a broader bill received both strong administration and broad bipartisan support in Congress. The work of years was culminated in its passage.

National Trails System Act

On October 2, 1968, President Johnson signed Public Law 90-543, the National Trails System Act. The Act established a national system of recreation and scenic trails and designated the Appalachian Trail and the Pacific Crest Trail as the first components of the system.

The Act stated that the Appalachian Trail should be administered primarily as a footpath by the Secretary of the Interior, in consultation with the Secretary of Agriculture. Continuation of traditional volunteer involvement was encouraged. The Secretary is required to establish an Advisory Council of not more than 35 persons to work with the Department on Trail matters.

The first Advisory Council met several times, but at the end of the five year term provided for in the Act it was not reappointed. By mid-1974 the clubs supported the need for a new Council with a far more effective role. In June 1975 the second National Scenic Trail Advisory Council was formally appointed. Out of their first meeting came a number of resolutions for getting the National Park Service into more active participation in securing the trail. In 1978 Congress reaffirmed its commitment to the Appalachian Trail by increasing authorized funding to $90 million for land acquisition, and an active NPS Trail protection program began. Several states carried on land acquisition programs under separate state legislation. Federal appropriations have been made each year for continued protection efforts. Through the involved process of designing the Trail corridor in consultation with affected landowners and organizations, the *AT* project is nearing completion of a permanently protected Trail route.

In 1981 the Appalachian Trail *Comprehensive Plan* was completed, describing the unique cooperative management system that would guide the project—a federal, state and private partnership. January 1984 marked a landmark in *AT* history. In an unprecedented action the National Park Service formally delegated management responsibility for NPS-acquired Trail lands to the Appalachian Trail Conference and its member clubs under unique authority found in the National Trails System Act.

Potomac Appalachian Trail Club

The Potomac Appalachian Trail Club, founded in November 1927, is one of the 32 organizations which maintains the Appalachian Trail under the Conference. It is also the third largest in number of members (over 2500) being surpassed only by the Appalachian Mountain Club in Boston and the Green Mountain Club in Vermont, both older organizations.

Altogether, the PATC is responsible for the maintenance of about 230 miles of the Appalachian Trail and approximately 500 miles of other trails. The *AT* is largely divided between the area reported in this GUIDE and the portion north of the Park (described in *Appalachian Trail Guide: Maryland and Northern Virginia with Side Trails*). In addition, PATC maintains side trails in George Washington National Forest and is currently developing an extended side trail known as the "Big Blue". (See Chapter 5: "Side Trails"). As noted earlier, PATC also maintains a network of shelters and cabins.

The Club issues a number of publications prepared by members. These include the maps and guides cited in Chapter 1 as well as two periodicals which are sent to members: a monthly newsletter, *Potomac Appalachian,* and an occasional special issue in magazine form. A complete list of publications, with prices, may be obtained from PATC Headquarters.

The Club has an active Mountaineering Section, which offers assistance and training in rock climbing techniques to beginners, as well as more difficult climbing opportunities for the advanced climber. Information on their weekly activities is contained in UP ROPE, a monthly publication of the Section, available from PATC Headquarters.

The Ski Touring Section conducts workshops for beginners, participates in work trips to improve ski trails in local areas and organizes ski trips to local and distant ski areas. These, as well as other activities, are described in UPSLOPE, the Section's monthly newsletter.

The Shenandoah Mountain Rescue Group is dedicated to wilderness search and rescue and to outdoor safety education. The group meets twice a month at PATC Headquarters and conducts frequent training workshops in the field.

PATC owns its own headquarters building which houses its many activities and provides an office to serve the public.

New Challenges

The ATC and the PATC have grown from Trail maintaining organizations to managers of extensive public lands. Planning for resource protection and public information and education will remain the challenge of the future.

Today, as more and more people turn toward the mountains to find respite from city life, there is a growing threat to the future of the Appalachian Trail. Despite the passage of the National Trails System Act, additional efforts are necessary to preserve enough acreage to protect the trail environment. Also, with the rapid pace of new commercial developments in the mountains of southern Pennsylvania, Maryland, and northern Virginia, the inevitable delays in procurement of land under the Trails Act may mean the loss of certain areas to the *AT* for good.

In the summer of 1969, the PATC made the first commitment for trail lands by purchasing 15 acres of land in northern Virginia containing 1/3 mile of the *AT* and a shelter. To finance future such acquisitions of endangered sections of trail lands, the PATC has established a Land Acquisition Fund and continues to solicit contributions from members and other persons who have an interest in the Trail and a desire to protect it for future generations of hikers.

To date over fifty additional acres have been purchased using

NEW CHALLENGES

this fund. The club members administering the money foresee a far greater role to be taken by the PATC in the future. No matter how much acquisition and protection is through federal and state auspices, it is the timely action by the club which could save an endangered piece of trail land or provide a connecting tract between assured trail land in a state program.

The Appalachian Trail Conference has established a similar fund for land acquisition.

An added dimension of the activities of the PATC is trying to answer requests for assistance in building and maintaining trails in other areas, including a Massanutten Trail System and a network of trails in the Allegheny Front Area of West Virginia.

In branching out, the Club is beginning to fulfill Benton MacKaye's dream of a network of foot trails with the Appalachian Trail as the backbone.

The Potomac Appalachian Trail Club expressly denies any liability for any accident or injury to persons using the Trail.

CHAPTER 3
THE SHENANDOAH NATIONAL PARK

The Shenandoah National Park extends for 80 miles along the Blue Ridge Mountains between Front Royal on the north and Waynesboro on the south. It contains over 300 square miles. There are 60 peaks ranging in elevation from 3000 to 4000 feet.

The Park is divided into three main sections by two U.S. highways: the north, extending from Front Royal south to Thornton Gap and U.S. Route 211; the central, from Thornton Gap to Swift Run Gap and U.S. Route 33; and the southern, from Swift Run Gap to Jarmans Gap.

The Skyline Drive extends the full length of the Park. It runs 105.4 miles from Front Royal to Rockfish Gap. Parking overlooks are provided at 75 points along the Drive. A single-entry fee is charged for those not carrying Golden Eagle or Golden Age passes.

History of The Park

Shenandoah National Park was established through a remarkable combination of efforts at the Federal, State, and local level. In 1923 the National Park Service recommended the establishment of a park in the Appalachian Range. The following year Congress passed a bill setting up a Southern Appalachian National Park Commission. A site in the Blue Ridge Mountains was recommended and a bill introduced in Congress providing for the acquisition of land. It was signed by President Coolidge in February 1925.

The next problem was the familiar one of financing. No Federal funds were available. A Shenandoah Park Association was formed to raise money. In the course of nine months, $1,249,000 was raised from private sources. The Virginia Assembly, at the request of then Governor Harry F. Byrd, voted an additional $1 million. Congress passed a bill in May 1926 to establish the Park when title to the lands had passed to the Federal Government.

Land purchases were begun by the State in 1926 and went on for eight years. Some land was not given up willingly. Altogether, 3870 private tracts were acquired. Approximately 400 families still living in the Park had to settle elsewhere. The Park was formally established with the deeding of the land—176,430 acres—to the Federal Government in December 1935. President Roosevelt dedicated the Park at Big Meadows on July 3, 1936.

The Civilian Conservation Corps moved in in 1933 and soon a thousand individuals were at work on fire protection and recreational developments. To provide other facilities, the Interior Department conceived the idea of awarding the entire Park to one concessioner; the first bid was received in March 1936.

The retreat on the Rapidan River which Herbert Hoover used while President of the United States was donated to the Federal Government by him at the close of his term in office. The property, known today as Camp Hoover, is now within the Shenandoah Park and is administered by the Park Service.

A Skyline Drive was visualized at the outset as one of the major attractions. Construction was started in July 1931. The central section was completed in September 1934. The northern section was opened in October 1936 and the southern section in 1939. Construction costs were paid out of Federal funds. They are reported to have averaged $47,000 per mile, or nearly $5 million for the total length.

Clearing of the original Appalachian Trail route in the Park was done by the Potomac Appalachian Trail Club in the late 1920's and early 1930's. The northern section was opened in 1929-30. Many sections subsequently had to be relocated with the construction of Skyline Drive and hence were built by the Park—more specifically the CCC—from 1933 to 1937.

The Park has not grown greatly in size since establishment—it presently contains 195,000 acres—for a number of legal and financial reasons. But the boundaries are subject to change as the Park exchanges property. Southeast of the Park boundaries in the central section a number of Virginia Wildlife Areas have been established.

Since 1965 the number of hikers and backcountry hikers has been increasing exponentially, or so it seems. Shelter areas, where camping was allowed on a first come, first served basis, had so deteriorated from overuse that the Park Service discontinued their use for camping and removed some of them entirely. More recently six shelters have been designated "huts" and these six may be used by backpackers with a valid backcountry camping permit for three or more nights (one night only per hut). To prevent overuse or improper use huts are monitored by volunteer hut-keepers supplied by the Potomac Appalachian Trail Club during the seasons of heavy use.

In 1976 a federal wilderness act established a number of wilderness areas in Shenandoah Park, covering about 80,000 of the total 195,000 acres of Park land. In these wilderness areas roads have been demoted to trails, a few trails have been eliminated, and the remaining ones may have less maintenance than formerly—with a narrower path, occasional blockage from downed trees, elimination of bridges over streams, etc.—but should be properly blazed.

For additional history on the Park a number of books are available. Those published by the PATC include *Shenandoah Heritage* and *Shenandoah Vestiges,* both by Carolyn and Jack Reeder, *Lost Trails and Forgotten People* by Tom Floyd and *The Dean Mountain Story* by Gloria Dean. Other books of interest are *Skyland, the Heart of Shenandoah National Park* by George Freeman Pollock, *Earth-Man Story* and *Herbert Hoover's Hide-away,* both by Darwin Lambert, and *Guide to Skyline Drive and Shenandoah National Park* by Henry Heatwole.

Other books on the Park include *Geology of the Shenandoah National Park* by Thomas M. Gathright II, *Trees of Shenandoah National Park* and *Ferns and Fern Allies of Shenandoah National Park,* both by Peter M. Mazzeo. All the above books are sold by the Shenandoah Natural History Association at the SNP visitor centers.

Natural History of the Park

The area presently composing the Park was once farmed and heavily lumbered. From the middle 1700's to the late 1800's the area was fairly prosperous. In the mid-1800's there was a flurry of interest in mining. But late in the 19th century economic decline began to set in; the demand for handicraft products of the hills dropped off and, early in the 20th century, blight killed most of the chestnut trees. Families began to move elsewhere and population dwindled.

With the decline of farming and lumbering, the forest began to take over. This process was further accelerated with the establishment of the Park. Today nearly all of the land is wooded.

Geology of the Shenandoah Park

Once upon a time (pre-Cambrian time), perhaps 800 million years ago, the area that is now the Shenandoah Park was a relatively level land with hills no higher than a thousand feet above the valleys. The underlying rock was granite or other igneous rock, with only a shallow soil on the hilltops and slopes, but with a deeper accumulation of eroded material in the low areas. Then came the only known major period of volcanic activity for this area. Lava welled up through cracks in the earth's crust and spread out rather evenly over the land, first filling the valleys but finally drowning the hilltops. There was not just a single flow but a series of at least seven for a total thickness of 1500 ft. (Eroded material which accumulated between the flows helps mark the divisions.) Finally, the volcanic action ceased and normal erosion again caused soil and gravel to accumulate.

Geologists today believe that mountain building has almost always been caused by collisions of continental plates. There is evidence that the Atlantic Ocean has opened and closed, perhaps several times, since the creation of the earth. One important era of mountain building occurred about 420 million years ago during a collision between North America and Europe. Although the mountains formed by this collision have been eroded away, traces of their existence still remain. The super-continent of Euro-America existed for a long time. During the period from about 325 to 300 million years ago there is evidence that the sea-level was high and that much of Euro-America was covered by shallow seas with some land along the present eastern coast of North America above sea level, while the present Appalachian region was part of an inland sea. Rains eroded these eastern highlands and the streams and rivers which originated in them dumped tremendous amounts of sand, then clay, then more sand into the shallow inland sea, covering deeply the older volcanic soil and the lava beds and igneous rock below. As the seas widened and deepened, sea animals (invertebrates only) flourished and their skeletons accumulated on the sea bottom as limey muds atop the earlier sands and clays. Pressure of the top layers caused the lower layers of sediment to harden the sand into sandstone, the clay into shale and the limey muds into limestone. Apparently, at some point during this geologic period, the land of the Blue Ridge rose above sea level whereas that farther west remained below sea level for many more years, receiving thick deposits of sand, clay and lime.

Then, about 250 million years ago, there was a tremendous continental collision as Africa moved in and rammed the continent of Euro-America. The destruction of ocean between Africa and Euro-America and the disappearing ocean floor created volcanic mountains on the Africa side. On the Euro-American side the edge of the continent was rumpled and uplifted, forming mountains. In some places the African plate was shoved over the North American plate. The tremendous pressure, coming from the southeast in our area, caused the earth's crust to fold, like a rug, into long parallel ridges. The mountain chain so formed extended from Poland and Germany (Harz Mtns.) west through Belgium, France and southern England, then on to Newfoundland and thence southwest to Birmingham, Ala. As the pressure continued the folds became higher and steeper and rocks which had been laid down in horizontal beds were tilted vertically in places.

In some places the deeply buried basaltic (lava) and granitic rocks were shoved westward over upturned layers of sandstone, shale and even limestone. The Blue Ridge Thrust Fault can be traced from Alabama to Roanoke and probably as far north as Pennsylvania. The present Blue Ridge mountains were then the lower western edge of a huge anticlinorium which formed a mountain range possibly 5 miles high, although erosion may have kept pace with the lifting of the land, in which case this early mountain range was never so high. Besides the folding of the earth's crust here, the same tremendous pressures caused much of the rock, both igneous and sedimentary, to be altered—the basalt into greenstone, the sandstone into quartzite, and the shales, at some localities, into slate.

The supercontinent, made up of Euro-America and Africa and called by geologists *Pangaea*, broke up around 190 million years ago when the Atlantic reopened between North America and Africa (leaving remnants of the African continent along a southeastern strip of N.A.). Separation of North America from Europe was not completed for another 100 million years.

By the beginning of Cretaceous time, 130 million years ago, the period of mountain building was over and erosion had leveled much of the land, leaving low hills here and there. River drainage was now to the east, into the Atlantic Ocean. Sometime in Early Cretaceous time the land was gently tilted, with the Appalachian region lifted as the coastal areas were lowered. This gave the formerly lazily flowing rivers renewed vigor, so they were able to cut through the hard rocks of the Blue Ridge. However, as time went on, the headwaters of many of the rivers and streams west of the present Blue Ridge were captured by the biggest rivers, the Potomac, the James and the Roanoke. The gaps the beheaded rivers had cut ceased to deepen and rose as the land rose. They make today's wind gaps. Thornton Gap may have orginally been cut by the Thornton River. Manassas Gap, just north of the Park, is one of the deepest of the wind gaps.

Looking at our mountains in the Shenandoah Park of today we can see reminders of their history. Most of the Blue Ridge crest in the Shenandoah National Park is capped by the hard, erosion-resistant greenstone. Although altered from the original basalt this rock still retains many of its original characteristics. One can find amygdules, filled gas bubbles, in almost every greenstone outcrop. In many places columnar jointing, characteristic of basalt, is still quite evident. It can be seen very strikingly at the southeastern viewpoint on Compton Mtn. (One must get down below the rocks to see this display.) It can also be seen on cliffs above the *AT* about 0.15m. north of Hawksbill Gap and again about 200 ft. south of Little Stony Man Parking Area. Evidence of the multiple layers of lava originally laid down can be seen along the *AT* below Franklin Cliffs and Crescent Rocks. In both places the *AT* follows a shelf "between layers" as shown by the vertical cliffs above and below the Trail. One of the ancient granite hills that was drowned by the lava flows can be seen along the walls of Whiteoak Canyon. The stepwise series of falls in this canyon also indicate the multiple lava flows.

In some places along the Blue Ridge crest in the Shenandoah

National Park the greenstone has been completely eroded away and it is the "base rock" that outcrops. One such place is at Marys Rock where the outcrop is the igneous rock, granodiorite. Radiogenic age measurements indicated that this rock is 1,100,000,000 years old! Some of the peaks on the eastern side of the main ridge consist primarily of granite. Old Rag Mtn. is one of these. Numerous greenstone dikes are present on Old Rag. Here the greenstone is eroding faster than the surrounding granite, leaving narrow passage ways, with vertical sides and surprisingly regular "steps" made by erosion of the columnar-structured dike material.

To the west of the main crest are the remnants of two lower paralleling ridges, both of sandstone—quartzite. These ridges took shape as the limestones west of them, the shale between them, and the conglomerate between the sandstone and greenstone of the main crest eroded much faster than they did. The remnants of these sandstone ridges show today as peaks on the side ridges that run from the Blue Ridge crest westward. On these side ridges the peak farthest from the main crest is composed of a type of sandstone—quartzite known as the Antietam formation. This sandstone is easily recognized as it is characterized by fine straight parallel tubes that cross the bedding at right angles; these tubes are the fossil burrows of sea worms—skolithos—filled with sand. (Because of its appearance this rock has been called pipe-rock.) Estimated age of the wormhole fossils is 500,000,000 years. Peaks underlain by the old Antietam sandstone include Rockytop (the highest and farthest out peak (2556') of the Rockytop ridge), Lewis Peak, Austin Mtn., Turk Mtn. and Brown Mtn. in the southern section of the park. Those in the central and northern sections are not as obvious to the hiker. In some places the greenstone and base rock were shoved west covering completely the sandstone and shale deposits and even some of the limestone. This is true at the very north end of the park and explains the location of Skyline Caverns, a limestone cave, located under the western slopes of the Blue Ridge.

Park Fauna

The favorite mammal of the Park is the white-tailed deer. This creature of the woods seems to sense that it is protected in the Park so shows little fear of humans. Since 1935 when this area was restocked with 15 deer, they have so multiplied that today there is a stable population of several thousand deer in the Park. They are most often seen in the early morning and at dusk.

The black bear has returned to the Park in good numbers, though it is not as plentiful here as in the Great Smokies. Unwary campers may wake to find their food stolen. Black bears weigh up to 400 or more pounds. Treat them with great caution. Once bears find food at a campground or at a trail shelter they will return again and again, and each time with less fear. So keep a clean camp. At established campgrounds store food and food refuse in the trunk of your hardtopped car (convertibles are not bear-proof). In the backcountry suspend your food between two trees well away from your tent or sleeping bag. Do not cook in your tent or take midnight snacks into your sleeping bag. So that bears may continue to be enjoyed as free wild creatures in the SNP do all you can to discourage their developing a dependence on man and his garbage.

Other mammals of the Park include the gray fox, raccoon, opposum and bobcat. Some persons have even claimed sightings of puma or mountain lion. Striped skunks, weasels, gray, flying, and red squirrels, chipmunks, woodchucks and a number of small rodents all make the Park their home.

Fishing is permitted in season and for trout only but a license is required; (a 5-day license may be purchased for use in the Park). Check Park regulations. The Staunton River and the Rapidan River are "fish-for-fun" streams with year round season. Here all fish caught (only artificial lures with one barbless hook may be used) must be returned to the water.

Among the birds breeding in the Park uplands are the pileated woodpecker, the wood thrush, veery, chestnut-sided warbler, blackburnian warbler, Canada warbler, scarlet tanager, rose-breasted grosbeak, dark-eyed junco, eastern wood peewee, white-breasted nuthatch, robin, rufous-sided towhee and red-eyed vireo. Turkey and black vultures, ruffed grouse, wild turkey and the common raven are frequently seen from the Skyline Drive and the *AT*. Red-tailed hawks are found here throughout the year, broad-winged hawks in spring, summer, and fall.

A Christmas bird count is conducted annually in the SNP. The count is sponsored by the Shenandoah Natural History Asso. in conjunction with the National Audubon Society.

Snakes are occasionally seen, black rat snakes probably being the most common. There are two poisonous snakes in the Park, the copperhead and the timber rattler. These pit vipers are generally much shorter than the black snakes but thicker. The rattlers vary considerably in color and banding but can be recognized by their triangularly-shaped heads and (usually) tell-tale rattles.

Of all the insects, the pesky gnat is the most annoying to hikers and campers. Mosquitoes are rarely encountered. An insect beauty often seen in the Park is the luna moth. In autumn one may discover a mountaintop covered with tiny red ladybugs, getting ready to hibernate. The Allegheny Mound ant lives in large colonies within huge, often two foot high, ant hills. The tent caterpillar and fall webworm often cover whole trees with their heavy webs, the black cherry being a particular favorite to the tent caterpillar.

The gypsy moth is becoming established in the Park and may cause areas of intense defoliation throughout the area. Campers should inspect their camping equipment before leaving the Park to be certain that the gypsy moth has not attached itself in some form.

Two arachnids are a nuisance to the hiker. One is the common tick, often a carrier of Rocky Mountain Spotted Fever; it is most often a problem in spring and early summer. Hikers should always check their bodies and clothes for ticks at a hike's end before these varmints have had a chance to bury their heads under the skin. Once they have taken hold, do not yank them out but use alcohol to encourage them to loosen their hold. A very tiny mite, the chigger or "red bug" of the deep south, can be an annoyance here. These tiny pests may form small red welts on legs or arms but their favorite place for locating on the human body seems to be along waistlines. The bite of a pinhead chigger can be as bad as that from a mosquito a hundred times its size.

Park Flora

If one looks at a botanical map of the United States, one will notice a long finger of the hemlock-hardwood forests typical of the Great Lakes Region and the northeastern USA extending down the

Appalachian mountains as far as Georgia. The boreal forests of Canada also extend southward, not as a long finger, but as isolated islands along the very highest peaks and ridges of the southern Appalachians. One of these "islands" is located in the Skyland-Big Meadows area of the Shenandoah National Park.

At low elevations in the Park we find flowers and trees typical of the South's Piedmont area. Above 2500 ft. we begin to find many plants more common to the northeast U.S. Finally, at elevations above 3500 ft. we may find Canadian Zone plants. How did such northern plants find their way to these scattered spots? Probably they are relics of the ice age when the country was colder than it is now. Balsam fir, red spruce, speckled alder, gray dogwood, round-leaved dogwood, quaking aspen, fly honeysuckle, and gray birch are native only in the Skyland to Big Meadows stretch of the Park. About six small stands of native white (or paper) birch exist in the Park. Other typically northern trees that are natives here include the American mountain-ash, black ash, and the mountain and striped maples. Small flowers of the Canadian Zone found in the Park include the "common" wood sorrel (Oxalis), which is not common here at all but can be found in the Limberlost area, and the three-toothed cinquefoil (Potentilla) which may be found along a few very high rock outcrops such as the Hawksbill summit and Bettys Rock. Bunchberry or dwarf cornel (Cornus) is known from the southern section of the Park—the only place in Virginia where it is found.

At the other extreme we find a few plants that are near the northern-most limit of their range. Trees in this category include the short-leaf pine, umbrella magnolia and the Carolina willow. The Catawba rhododendron is found only in the southern third of the Park and only in a few spots even there. Though beautiful it does not make the mass displays in the Park that it does just a short distance farther south.

The predominant trees of the Park are the oaks and hickories. The American chestnut was once the queen of the area but this important tree was destroyed by the chestnut blight before the establishment of the Park. The forests of the Park are by no means virgin, except in a few ravines. Man long ago axed or set fire to the trees for use as lumber or tanbark, or to clear the land for homesteads and farms. Virgin timber, chiefly hemlock, can be found in the deep gorges, especially in the Limberlost, Whiteoak Canyon and Cedar Run Canyon. In areas only recently going back to woods from farmlands one will find black locust, hawthorn, sumac, Virginia pine and white pine, trees typical of a "pioneer" forest.

Over 1200 species of flowering plants have been recorded as growing in the Park. It is not unusual to find the Park's first flower of spring blooming in low, wet areas as early as late February. This is the skunk cabbage *(Symplocarpus)*. Hepatica, red maple *(Acer)*, coltsfoot *(Tussilago)* and spice-bush *(Lindera)* soon join it, often blooming in early March after a week of warm weather. By early April the shadbush or service berry *(Amelanchier)* will be in bloom and bloodroot *(Sanguinaria)*, rue-anemone *(Anemonella)*, cut-leaved toothwort *(Centaria)*, and violets of many species line the trails at low elevations. Look for Dutchman's britches *(Dicentra)* and dogtooth violets *(Erythronium)* in low areas, golden ragwort *(Senecio)* along stream banks and trails, and bright yellow marsh marigold *(Caltha)* and the lovely foliage of the false hellebore *(Veratrum)* in swampy areas. As April progresses the same sequence of blooms will be found at higher and higher elevations.

In late April redbud *(Cercis)* and flowering dogwood *(Cornus)* decorate the woods at lower to mid elevations. Star chickweed *(Stellaria)*, may apple *(Podophyllum)*, wood betony *(Pedicularis)*, golden corydalis and a host of other flowers adorn the Park. Early May is blossoming time for the two species of pink azalea or pink honeysuckle, the pinxter-flower at lower to mid altitudes and the roseshell azalea at the mid to higher altitudes, *i.e.*, along the AT and Skyline Drive. These showy plants are particularly plentiful in the Central Section of the Park. White (or pink) trillium is plentiful in the Central Section of the Park. Wild geranium and sweet Cicily *(Osmorhiza)* with its lacy white flowers and aniselike odor are common along the AT; observant hikers may see Jack-in-the-pulpit *(Ariasaema)*, pink and yellow lady's slippers *(Cypripedium)* and showy orchises as well. In late May the Catawba rhododendron displays its showy purple-pink flowers along the Riprap Trail and near the Skyline Drive at Turk Gap.

June is the month for mountain laurel *(Kalmia)* to show off its beauty. Two interesting members of the lily family—fly-poison *(Amianthium)* and turkeybeard *(Xerophyllum)*—bloom at this time. The former is very common along the *AT* whereas the latter, which prefers sandy soil, is found growing along the sandstone ridges west of the main Blue Ridge crest in the Southern Section of the Park. On the roadbanks feathery wands of goatsbeard *(Aruncus)* and tall plumes of black cohosh *(Cimicifuga)* are much in evidence. In July the turkscap lily *(Lilium)* is quite common along the Drive. Many umbelliferae, including the huge cow-parsnip *(Heracleum)* will be found in bloom. By August, members of the compositae predominate—black-eyed Susans, sunflowers, coreopsis, Joe-Pye-weed, knapweed and goldenrods. Asters continue to bloom until late in the fall.

Ripening berries help color the September woods; beautiful clusters of vivid mountain-ash berries peek out between the rocks along the rocky crest of the Blue Ridge. The cardinal-flower *(Lobelia)* and great lobelia brighten stream banks. Brightest fall foliage often appears in early October when the dogwoods, sour gum, sumac and woodbine put on their leaf display. The peak of autumn brilliance is usually mid-October. By late in the month the entire Park turns to gold as the oaks and hickories blend their yellows, deep reds and browns. Last flower of the year, the witchhazel, will be found in bloom from late September to early December.

Winters in the Park are unpredictable. There may be periods of balmy springlike weather, followed by a week of severe cold, with Park temperatures hovering around zero. Some years there is much snow, other years almost none. One big ice storm can turn the ridges into fairyland; but such a storm can also do indescribable damage to the trees of the Park, especially those growing in exposed locations.

Among the plants of the Park one should mention a few that are immigrants from Europe and Asia that have made themselves very much at home here. Japanese honeysuckle *(Lonicera)* is so thick in some of the low elevation areas of the Park that it has made an almost impenetrable jungle. Dyers woad *(Isatis)* has a special liking for the Skyline Drive and grows profusely along the roadbanks. Viper's bugloss *(Echium)*, the common ox-eye daisy, chicory, mulleins, Queen Anne's lace, and bull thistle are thick along the roadsides during the summer months. Deep in the woods one may walk into thick patches of the shiny-leaved periwinkle (*Vinca*), often a sign of an old family cemetery site. Plants of daylilies (*Hemerocallis*) also persist near former homesites and the plants have continued to flourish though they seldom bloom in the deep shade. The princess tree (*Paulownia*), often mistaken for a catalpa, and the fast growing tree of heaven (*Ailanthus*) are also immigrants. Wineberry, a type of raspberry, is found at certain spots in the Southern Section.

Two very common plant pests should be mentioned. One of these is poison ivy, which is common in brushy areas and among exposed rocks. It is similar in appearance to woodbine (Virginia creeper) except that each leaf contains three leaflets rather than five. Another very annoying plant is the wood nettle (*Laportea*) which is densely covered with stinging hairs. Nettles are particularly troublesome on side trails of the Park which often get only one time a year maintenance. Best protection from nettles, ivy, greenbriers and berry bushes are long pants. The juice from the fleshy stems of jewelweed (*Impatiens*) may help to relieve the stinging sensation of nettle and the itching of poison ivy. It is often found growing near these pests.

HEIGHTS OF WATERFALLS IN SHENANDOAH NATIONAL PARK

(This chart is reproduced, with permission, from the Shenandoah National Park's PARK GUIDE, copyrighted in 1968.)

Waterfall	Height (feet)	District	Stream
Big Falls	93	North	Overall Run
Whiteoak #1	86	Central	Whiteoak Run
South River Falls	83	Central	South River
Lewis Falls	81	Central	Hawksbill Creek
Dark Hollow Falls	70	Central	Hogcamp Branch
Rose River Falls, Upper	67	Central	Rose River
Big Falls, Doyles R.	63	South	Doyles River
Whiteoak #2	62	Central	Whiteoak Run
Whiteoak #6	60	Central	Whiteoak Run
Whiteoak #5	49	Central	Whiteoak Run
Jones Run Falls	42	South	Jones Run
Whiteoak #4	41	Central	Whiteoak Run
Whiteoak #3	35	Central	Whiteoak Run
Twin Falls	29	North	Overall Run
Little Falls, Doyles R.	28	South	Doyles River
Rose River Falls, Lower	22	Central	Rose River

(*NOTE:* The waterfalls on Whiteoak Run are numbered from top to bottom.)

Measurements were made by Robert Momich and Gary Miller (Volunteers in the Parks) using a Wallace and Tiernan Altimeter accurate within 2 ft. One might consider an unrestricted drop of water a waterfall and the steeply slanting, downhill rush of water a cascade. Shenandoah Park falls of water are usually a combination; in particular, the tops and bottoms of the Park waterfalls are often indefinite and so the establishment of recording stations for the above measurements was necessarily arbitrary.

CHAPTER 4
APPALACHIAN TRAIL DATA

SECTION VI NORTHERN SHENANDOAH PARK
U.S. 522 TO THORNTON GAP
NORTH TO SOUTH

27.4 miles (44.1 kilometers)　　　　　　　(PATC Map No. 9)

Section VI of the Appalachian Trail in Virginia begins at U.S. 522 at a point 3.2m. southeast of its junction with Va. 55 in Front Royal. Except for the first three and a half miles the *AT* lies entirely within the Shenandoah Park. There are no longer open areas in the northern section of the park, so that good viewpoints are limited to occasional rock outcroppings. Trail description has been divided into two subsections, U.S. 522 to Gravel Springs Gap, and Gravel Springs Gap to Thornton Gap.

Maps:

PATC Map No. 9, USGS map of Shenandoah National Park, northern section, 1969, scale 1:62,500. Also USGS 7½′ quads: Front Royal, Bentonville, Chester Gap, Luray, Thornton Gap, and Washington, Va.

SUBSECTION:
U.S. 522 TO GRAVEL SPRINGS GAP

12.9 miles (20.8 kilometers)　　　　　　　(PATC Map No. 9)

General description:

From U.S. 522 just below Lake Front Royal, el. 940′, the *AT* leads south along the edge of National Zoological Park Conservation Center property. The Trail crosses Va. Sec. 602 in about 1½ miles and comes into Va. Sec. 601 1¼ miles farther, elevation about 1475 ft. From here the *AT* climbs steadily via graded trail, crossing into the SNP a short distance before reaching the crest of the Blue Ridge where it comes into the old road from Chester Gap to Compton Gap, former route of the *AT*. It follows the Compton Gap Rd. south to the Skyline Drive at Compton Gap, el. 2415′. From here it climbs over Compton Mtn. and over both

North and South Marshall Mtns. before reaching Gravel Springs Gap. The *AT* either crosses the Skyline Drive, or comes quite close to it, in several places, so that all parts of it are easily accessible. Spring water is available in several locations near the Trail.

Side trails:

The Dickey Ridge Trail, the Bluff Trail, the Lands Run Fire Road, Hickerson Hollow Trail, the Mt. Marshall Trail, Jordan River Trail, and the Browntown Trail offer good walking. In addition, there are two short but interesting trails, Big Devils Stairs Trail and The Peak Trail. For details on side trails see Chap. 5: "Side Trails, Northern Section." Also refer to the PATC publication: *Circuit Hikes in the Shenandoah National Park.*

Accommodations:

There are many motels and restaurants in Front Royal and a number of private campgrounds in the Front Royal area.

Located along the *AT,* 3.1m. from U.S. 522 (between Va. Sec. 601 and the Park boundary), there is the Tom Floyd Wayside, a primitive camping area with a few tent sites and a rain shelter. This wayside is for the use of the thru-hiker. Gravel Springs Hut is located at the south end of this subsection. Follow the *AT* south from Gravel Springs Gap, SDMP 17.7, for 0.2m., then go left on the Bluff Tr. for 0.2m. to reach the hut.

Mathews Arm Campground is a few miles south of Gravel Springs Gap at SDMP 22.2. It is generally open mid-April through October.

Detailed Trail data:

0.0 *AT* crosses U.S. 522 just below Lake Front Royal, el. 940', at a point 3.2m. SE of its junction with Va. 55 in Front Royal. The *AT* leads south, across a stile into a field, the property of the National Zoological Park Conservation and Research Center. The Trail follows bridges over stream and a swampy area, Sloan Creek Swamp, then climbs along edge of fields. From high on the hill one may see, with the help of field glasses, various zoo animals.

0.4 Enter woods. In early May there are showy orchises along the trail here.

0.9 Climb stile and immediately beyond reach summit of hill.

1.4 Cross Va. Sec. 602, a dirt road. (Trail leaves National Zoological Park property here and enters property of the Northern Virginia 4-H Educational Center. Trail is protected by easements across this property.) Just beyond road cross Moore Run.

1.6 Beyond a wet weather stream come into a field. Midway across the field there are good views of the fruit orchards in Harmony Hollow.

2.1 Cross a wet weather creek.

2.2 Cross through a narrow fence opening. (Trail leaves 4-H Educational Center land here and follows narrow easements on private property. STAY ON TRAIL.)

2.4 Here a side trail leads right 0.2m. through PATC property to a parking area on Va. Sec. 601. A tenth of a mile farther come into a farm road and follow it right. Pass white house on left of *AT*.

2.6 Come into Va. Sec. 601 at a sharp turn on the road. (From here it is 0.4m. down Rt. 601 to the PATC parking lot and 0.7m. to the main road through Harmony Hollow, Va. Sec. 604.) The *AT* follows up Rt. 601 just a few feet, then turns left onto a footpath, passing through a gap in a rock wall, then crossing a small creek, Barking Dog Spring. Trail now climbs by switchbacks toward the crest of the Blue Ridge.

3.1 Enter the Tom Floyd Wayside, a primitive camping area with tent sites and a rain shelter for the use of thru-hikers only. No open fires permitted. Ginger Spring is 800 ft. to the right of the *AT* here.

3.6 Enter the Shenandoah National Park. Just beyond the boundary the Possum's Rest Trail leads right 0.1m. to a viewpoint.

3.8 Come into horse trail, the former Compton Gap Rd., and follow it to the right (blazed both white and yellow). (To the left the horse trail leads 0.5m. down to Va. Sec. 610 at the Park boundary. Via 610 it is 1.8m. farther to U.S. 522 at Chester Gap. This, until 1974, was the route of the *AT*.) At this junction there's a do-it-yourself Backcountry Permit Booth. Backpackers who intend to camp in the Park should stop here and follow instructions for writing their own backcountry camping permit.

4.9 Springhouse Rd., yellow-blazed, leads right 0.7m. to intersect the Dickey Ridge Trail at a point on the latter 0.6m. north of its junction with the *AT*.

5.2 Reach trail junction marked by cement post. (To the right the Dickey Ridge Trail leads 9.2m. north to Front Royal town limits and entrance to the Skyline Drive, SDMP 0.0. Interesting Fort Windham Rocks are 0.2m. from the *AT* on this trail. To left of *AT*, a Park service road leads 0.4m. to Indian Run Maintenance Building, not available for camping. A spring is 250 ft. from the service road, on the left, about 0.1m. before reaching the building.

5.5 Cross to the right (south) of the Skyline Drive, SDMP 10.4, in Compton Gap, el. 2415'. Ascend Compton Mtn. by switchbacks. There is a patch of white clintonia (speckled wood lily) along the Trail here and a small clump of yellow lady's-slippers. (The latter bloom in mid-May, the former in early June.)

6.3 Signpost marks short blue-blazed trails leading right and left to viewpoints. Both are ungraded and offer only rough footing but are worthwhile. (Trail on left leads down 0.2m. to an interesting outcrop of columnar basalt. To see the columnar structure it is necessary to climb down below the rocks. Top of the outcrop affords good view east. Trail to right of *AT* leads over the top of Compton Mtn., el. 2909', and down 0.2m. to a rocky ledge offering excellent views to west and north.)

6.7 Pass Compton Springs. One is 50 ft. uphill on left; another is to right of *AT*, about 15 ft. away and downhill. *AT* descends fairly steeply for about a half-mile, then levels off. There is much mountain laurel (blooming in early June) and pink azalea (mid-May) between here and Jenkins Gap.

7.5 Cross yellow-blazed Jenkins Gap Trail in Jenkins Gap, el. 2398'. (To the left the Jenkins Gap Tr. leads across the Skyline Drive, SDMP 12.3, and continues 0.5m. to end on the Mt. Marshall Tr. To right this trail descends 1m. to end on Va. Sec. 634 at a point 2.2m. from Browntown.) Some parking is available at Jenkins Gap. Mt. Marshall Tr. can be reached by walking south along the Skyline Drive about 0.3m.

9.0 Trail passes along the foundations of an old building.

9.2 Cross to the left of Skyline Drive at Hogwallow Gap, SDMP 14.2, el. 2739'. Some parking available. Trail now ascends gently through the Hogwallow Flats area.

NORTH TO SOUTH

9.8 Pass Hogwallow Spring 30 ft. on left of Trail.

10.7 Reach summit of North Marshall, el. 3368'. (The name of this mountain grows out of the fact that these lands were formerly a part of the Blue Ridge holdings of John Marshall, the noted Chief Justice of the United States from 1801 to 1835. See "The Manor of Leeds" by Jean Stephenson in the April, 1934 PATC Bulletin.) Along the crest of the mountain, cliffs to the right of the Trail offer many good views to the west. As the Trail descends, just where it jogs sharply to the left, there is one outstanding viewpoint. At the next switchback some high cliffs on the left of the *AT* are worth scrambling up on. (These cliffs are quite visible from the Skyline Drive south of Mount Marshall.)

11.3 Cross to the right of the Skyline Drive, SDMP 15.9, el. 3087'. Some parking room here.

11.9 Reach summit of South Marshall, el. 3212'. Trail now descends gradually with ledges on right affording splendid views.

12.9 Reach Gravel Springs Gap at intersection of old Browntown-Harris Hollow Rd. with the Skyline Drive, SDMP 17.7, el. 2666'. Some parking available. (To the right the Browntown Trail, yellow-blazed, leads northwest down the mountain 3.4m. to Va. Sec. 631 at a point about 1m. south of Browntown. To the left the Harris Hollow Trail, also yellow-blazed, follows the access road toward Gravel Springs Hut, then turns left away from the road, soon comes into the Bluff Tr. and follows it briefly, then turns right and descends the hollow.)

SUBSECTION:
GRAVEL SPRINGS GAP TO THORNTON GAP

14.5 miles (23.3 kilometers) (PATC Map No. 9)

General description:

From Gravel Springs Gap, el. 2666', the *AT* climbs, reaching its highest elevation in the northern section of the Shenandoah Park on the Second Peak of Hogback, el. 3475'. It then descends over a thousand feet before reaching Elkwallow Gap, from which it climbs over several lesser high points including the summit of Pass Mtn. before descending to Thornton Gap, el. 2307'. Near the Range View Cabin and also on Pass Mountain the Trail passes through areas that were once quite open. Large old oak trees with wide-spreading low branches show that they grew to maturity in open fields. They are still to be seen, but now they must compete for light with the young but tall forest trees that surround them.

The *AT* is never very far from the Skyline Drive and crosses it several times. Many good one-day hikes can be made by utilizing short stretches of the *AT* plus connecting side trails. Water is available at the shelters and at other points along the Trail in this section.

Side trails:

At 3.8m. (PATC Map No. 9) the Big Blue-Tuscarora Trail connects with the *AT*. This trail offers a 220 mile route west of the *AT*, rejoining it northeast of Carlisle, Pa. From the junction in the SNP the Big Blue, concurrent with the Overall Run Trail, descends toward the northwest following along Overall Run. The Big Blue then bears to the right toward Thompson Hollow, eventually crossing U.S. 340 south of Bentonville. From there it crosses the Massanutten range and continues generally west to the Va.-W.Va. state line where it heads northeast, more or less paralleling the *AT*. It crosses the Potomac River at Hancock, Md. The Tuscarora section, that part of the Big Blue-Tuscarora north of the Potomac, trends northeastward to rejoin the *AT* near Carlisle, Pa. For more information see PATC publication: *Guide to the Big Blue Trail*.

The Gravel Springs-Thornton Gap area is rich with side trails, too many to enumerate here. See Chap. 5: "Side Trails, Northern Section;" also the PATC publication: *Circuit Hikes in the Shenandoah Park*.

Accommodations:

Two open-faced huts are available for the thru-hiker: Gravel Springs Hut, 0.2m. along the *AT* (then follow the Bluff Trail for 0.2m.) and Pass Mtn. Hut, 13.3m. (then follow spur trail 0.2m.). In addition to these there is one locked cabin, Range View, 5.1m. Reservations for the use of this cabin must be obtained in advance from PATC Headquarters. See Chap. 6: "Picnic Shelters, Huts, and Cabins."

Mathews Arm Campground, SDMP 22.2, offers extensive

NORTH TO SOUTH

camping facilities. Meals are available at Panorama Restaurant at Thornton Gap and lunches can be purchased at the Elkwallow Wayside, SDMP 24.0. None of these facilities is available during the cold months.

Detailed Trail data:

0.0 Intersection of old Browntown-Harris Hollow Rd. with the Skyline Drive, SDMP 17.7, el. 2666', *AT* crosses to left (east) side of the Drive and parallels the old Harris Hollow Rd. for several hundred feet. (This road, on the left of the *AT*, is utilized as an access road to the Gravel Springs Hut, 0.3m. The Harris Hollow Trail, yellow-blazed, follows the route of the old road down the mountain, except that it detours around the hut and spring. It intersects Va. Sec. 622 at a point about 5m. from Washington, Va.)

0.2 *AT* turns sharply to the right at concrete post where Bluff Trail comes in on left. (Bluff Tr. starts here, descends by switchbacks to Gravel Springs, 0.2m., where it crosses the old Browntown-Harris Hollow Rd. It continues on, slabbing the east sides of South and North Marshall Mtns., ending at the Mt. Marshall Fire Rd. (4.7m.). Gravel Springs Hut is 50 ft. south of the spring.) The *AT* now passes through an extended level area.

ALERT!!! AT may be relocated, starting here, to remain on the east side of Skyline Drive rejoining the present route at 4.7m.

1.3 Cross to the right side of Skyline Drive, SDMP 18.9.

1.5 Spur trail to left leads 100 ft. to Skyline Drive, SDMP 19.4, at junction of the Keyser Run Fire Rd. on east side of Drive. (Keyser Run Fire Rd. leads south along the east slopes of the Blue Ridge, passing the point known as "Four-Way" in 1.0m. See Chap. 5: "Side Trails;" also PATC publication: *Circuit Hikes in the Shenandoah Park.*)

1.8 *AT* reaches top of Little Hogback where there is a fine outlook from ledge 30 ft. to right of the Trail.

1.9 Spur trail, at signpost, leads straight ahead 50 ft. to Little Hogback Parking Overlook on the Skyline Drive, SDMP 19.7, as the *AT* veers right and descends, passing below the overlook. Trail then ascends steeply, by switchbacks, up the east face of First Peak of Hogback.

2.5 Reach crest; continue along ridge.

2.6 Pass a few feet to the left of the First Peak of Hogback, el. 3420'.

2.7 The Hogback Spur Trail leads to left, downhill, 0.2m. to a walled-in spring which is within sight of the Skyline Drive. *AT* now ascends.

2.8 Pass a hang glider launching area.

2.9 Pass radio towers on summit of the Second Peak of Hogback, el. 3474'. Trail follows tower road across its turnaround area, then goes to right of road and descends. Trail crosses to left of road in 0.1m.

3.1 *AT* comes into tower road just before it reaches the Drive. (Here a trail leads left 300 ft. to Drive.) Cross to left of Skyline Drive, SDMP 20.8. Ascend toward Third Peak of Hogback, el. 3440'. Near the top a side trail leads right 15 ft. to a spot offering a splendid view north over Browntown Valley and Dickey Ridge. Skyline Drive is directly below; there are enormous rocks here.

3.4 Cross to right of Skyline Drive, SDMP 21.1. Continue along crest of Hogback Mtn.

3.7 Side trail leads left 30 ft. to summit of Fourth Peak, el. 3440', with fine view south. From Fourth Peak, *AT* descends.

3.8 Junction with Big Blue-Overall Run Trail. (This is the southern terminus of the Big Blue-Tuscarora Trail which provides a 220m. route connected to the *AT* at each end. 5.6m. of the Big Blue Trail lies within the SNP. From the junction with the *AT* the Big Blue Trail (with the coincident Overall Run Trail), right, descends, passing at 0.7m. a trail leading left to Mathews Arm Campground. It passes near Overall Falls at 2.7m. At 4.8m. the Big Blue Tr. and Overall Run Tr. separate as the Big Blue bears right away from the run and reaches U.S. 340 at 6.9m. at a point on the highway 2.6m. south of Bentonville.)

4.1 Spur trail on right leads 50 ft. to summit of Sugarloaf. *AT* continues to descend.

4.4 Cross to left of Skyline Drive, SDMP 21.9. (0.2m. to right along the Drive is entrance road to Mathews Arm Campground. Fifty yds. left of the *AT*, on the Drive, is Rattlesnake Point Overlook, el. 3105', with views east over Piney Branch.) On *AT* pass Rattlesnake Point to right of the Trail.

NORTH TO SOUTH

4.7 Junction with Piney Branch Trail which leads left from *AT*. (See Chap. 5: "Side Trails.") Immediately beyond, *AT* comes into Range View Cabin service road and follows it left a few feet before turning left away from it. (This road comes in on right from Skyline Drive, SDMP 22.1, passing the Piney River Ranger Station. See large scale map of Elkwallow-Range View Cabin area on back of PATC Map No. 9.) ALERT: This is the southern end of the *AT* relocation being considered at this time.

5.0 Pass under power line. A trail, left, follows power line 0.1m. to Range View Cabin.

5.1 Post marks a second side trail leading 0.1m. to Range View Cabin. Spring is below cabin. (Cabin is a locked structure. Reservations are required for its use. See Chap. 6: "Picnic Shelters, Huts and Cabins.") Two hundred feet beyond, *AT* crosses access road to cabin. (A few feet down this road the Piney Ridge Trail takes off from the right of the road, just as the road bends left toward the cabin. See Chap. 5: "Side Trails;" also PATC publication: *Circuit Hikes in the Shenandoah Park*.) *AT* now descends gently toward Elkwallow Gap.

5.9 Cross to right of Skyline Drive, SDMP 23.9, el. 2480'. (200 yds. south on Drive is the Elkwallow Wayside where lunches may be obtained from mid-May through October; Elkwallow Picnic Area is beyond the wayside. There are no overnight accommodations.) *AT* now swings right, then circles the wayside and picnic area. 250 ft. beyond the Drive, cross Elkwallow Trail. (Left, trail leads 0.1m. to the wayside; right, trail leads 1.9m. to Mathews Arm Campground.)

6.2 A trail to the left leads 200 ft. to Elkwallow Picnic Grounds. *AT* turns sharply right here and descends.

6.4 To the left of the Trail is a spring.

6.5 Junction with Jeremys Run Trail which is straight ahead here. (Jeremys Run Tr. leads 6.5m. to Va. Sec. 611 at a point 3.5m. from Big Spring on U.S. 340. See Chap. 5: "Side Trails" for details of this trail and circuit hikes possible in this area; also see PATC publication: *Circuit Hikes in the Shenandoah Park*.) *AT* turns sharply left at this junction, crossing creek in 100 ft., and ascends.

6.7 Spring 5 yds. to right.

7.5 Reach crest of narrow ridge and follow along it.

8.6 Junction with blue-blazed Thornton Hollow Tr. (The Thornton Hollow Tr. crosses the Skyline Drive in 0.3m., then continues, descending along a branch of the Thornton River to the eastern Park boundary.)

9.8 A trail leads left 0.1m. to Neighbor Mtn. Parking Area on Skyline Drive, SDMP 26.8.

10.1 Intersection with yellow-blazed Neighbor Trail. (To the left the horse trail continues to Skyline Drive, SDMP 28.1, in 1.0m., passing near the Byrds Nest #4. To the right it leads 4.6m. to Jeremys Run, first following an almost level spur ridge to the peak of "The Neighbor," then descending sharply.) *AT* now tops the rise, then descends following the main ridge.

10.3 *AT* leaves the ridge crest and slabs the southwest side of the ridge.

11.0 Where the *AT* bends sharply right a blue-blazed trail leads left 0.5m. to Byrds Nest #4. (Piped-in water available at the picnic shelter, May through October.) There is a spring to the right of the Trail 100 ft. farther along the *AT*.

11.2 Spur trail on left leads 0.1m. to Beahms Gap Parking Overlook on Skyline Drive, SDMP 28.5.

11.4 Cross to left of Skyline Drive, SDMP 28.6. *AT* ascends gently from here.

11.5 Intersection with yellow-blazed Rocky Branch Trail.

12.1 Rocky area affords wintertime views to the right—views of Kemp Hollow, The Neighbor and Knob Mtn.

12.5 Reach summit of Pass Mtn., el. 3052'.

13.3 Pass Mtn. Trail leads left. Follow it 0.2m. to reach the Pass Mtn. Hut. Spring a few feet behind the hut. (See Chap. 6: "Picnic Shelters, Huts and Cabins.") (Pass Mtn. Trail leads east 3.0m. from *AT* to its terminus on U.S. 211. See Chap. 5: "Side Trails.)

14.1 *AT* comes into service road and follows it to right for 150 ft., then turns off the road to right.

14.4 Trail descends bank to service road within sight of the Drive. Follow road to the Drive and cross to the right side of the Drive.

14.5 Cross U.S. 211 at a point 0.15m. west of Skyline Drive in Thornton Gap, SDMP 31.5, el. 2307'.

SUMMARY OF DISTANCES ALONG THE *AT*
Section VI Northern

	Miles	Kilometers
U.S. 522	0.0	0.0
Indian Run Maintenance Bldg.	5.2+0.4	8.4+0.6
Compton Gap	5.5	8.9
Jenkins Gap	7.5	12.1
North Marshall Summit	10.7	17.2
Gravel Springs Gap	12.9	20.8
Gravel Springs Hut	13.0+0.2	20.9+0.3
2nd Peak of Hogback (tower)	15.8	25.4
Junction with Big Blue	16.7	26.9
Piney Branch Tr. junction	17.6	28.3
Range View Cabin	17.9+0.1	28.8+0.2
Piney Ridge Tr.	18.0	29.0
Skyline Drive, Elkwallow Gap	18.8	30.3
Jeremys Run Tr. junction	19.3	31.1
Neighbor Mtn. Tr. junction	23.0	37.0
Byrds Nest #4 (no camping)	23.9 +0.5	38.5+0.8
Skyline Drive, Beahms Gap	24.3	39.1
Pass Mtn.	25.4	40.9
Pass Mtn. Hut	26.2+0.2	42.2+0.3
U.S. 211 (Thornton Gap)	27.4	44.1

SUMMARY OF DISTANCES BY SKYLINE DRIVE TO POINTS ON *AT*
Section VI Northern

SDMP		From Thornton Gap S to N
0.0	Park Entrance, U.S. 340 at edge of Front Royal	31.5
10.4	Compton Gap, *AT* crossing	21.1
12.3	Jenkins Gap, *AT* is 0.1 m. to the west	19.2
14.2	*AT* crossing, Hogwallow Gap	17.3
15.9	*AT* crossing just south of North Marshall Mtn.	15.6
17.7	*AT* crossing, Gravel Springs Gap	13.8
18.9	*AT* crossing, 1.3 m. via Trail south of Gravel Springs Gap	12.6
19.4	Keyser Run Fire Rd. *AT* is 100 ft. north via spur trail	12.1
19.7	Little Hogback Parking Overlook, *AT* 50 ft. to north via spur trail	11.8
20.8	*AT* crossing, sag between Second and Third Peaks of Hogback	10.7
21.1	*AT* crossing, between Third and Fourth Peaks of Hogback	10.4
21.9	*AT* crossing at Rattlesnake Point. Range View Cabin is 0.7 m. south from here via the *AT*. Entrance to Mathews Arm Campground is 0.3 m. farther south along the Drive.	9.6
23.9	*AT* crossing, Elkwallow Gap. Wayside is 200 yds. south.	7.6
24.2	Elkwallow Picnic Grounds. Trail to the *AT* leads off from the second parking area for 200 ft.	7.3
26.8	Parking area for Neighbor Tr. Spur Tr. leads 0.1 m. west to *AT*.	4.7
28.5	Beahms Gap Overlook. *AT* is west of Drive, 0.1 m. via spur trail.	3.0
28.6	*AT* crossing, Beahms Gap	2.9
31.5	Thornton Gap. *AT* crosses U.S. 211 0.15 m.	0.0

NORTH TO SOUTH

SECTION VII CENTRAL SHENANDOAH PARK
THORNTON GAP TO SWIFT RUN GAP
NORTH TO SOUTH

34.3 miles (55.2 kilometers) (PATC Map No. 10)

U.S. 211 crosses the Blue Ridge and intersects the Skyline Drive in Thornton Gap, SDMP 31.5, at a point 9 miles east of Luray, 7 miles west of Sperryville, and 83 miles from Washington, D.C. The southern end of this section is at Swift Run Gap, SDMP 65.7, where U.S. 33 crosses the mountain. From Swift Run Gap it is 7 miles west to Elkton, 8 miles east to Stanardsville, and 110 miles to Washington, D.C.

The Blue Ridge crest is higher in this section of the Park than in the northern and southern sections. The highest peak in the Park, Hawksbill, just south of Skyland, has an elevation of 4050 ft. The *AT* reaches its highest point in the Park, 3812 ft., on Hazeltop Mtn. which is 4.0m. south of Big Meadows Campground. The Skyline Drive itself reaches its highest altitude, 3680 ft., right at the northern entrance to Skyland.

The central part of the Shenandoah Park is the section most widely used by the motoring public, by campers, and by hikers. The *AT* is heavily used, as are the chief side trails. Favorite short hikes include the Stony Man and Story of the Forest Nature Trails, the Little Stony Man Trail and *AT* loop trip, the Dark Hollow Falls Trail and the Limberlost Trail. Longer favorites are the Whiteoak Canyon Trail, the trails up Old Rag Mtn., the trails up Hawksbill, and the stretch of the *AT* from Thornton Gap (Panorama) to Marys Rock. There are also special trails for horseback riding, with stables at Skyland.

There are two large campgrounds located in the area, one at Big Meadows (closed Jan. & Feb.) and another at Lewis Mountain. Skyland, Big Meadows, and Lewis Mountain have lodging facilities available for tourists—both lodge and cabins; only at Big Meadows are these open most of the year (closed Jan. & Feb.). For complete information on tourist facilities and for reservations write to the ARA Virginia Sky-Line Co., Inc., Box 727, Luray,

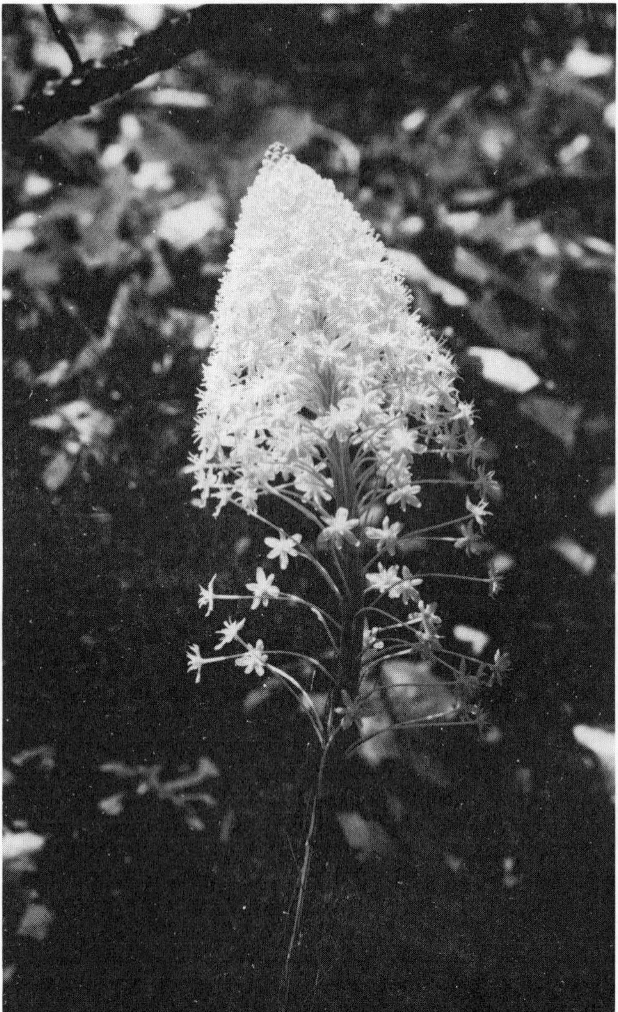

Va. 22835. Phone (703) 743-5108.

The Skyland resort antedates the Park, having been developed by George F. Pollock, with its beginnings in the 1880's. Camp Hoover, developed when Herbert Hoover was President, is on the eastern slopes of the Blue Ridge near Big Meadows. It is now managed by the Park Service, but is still reserved for use by presidential guests. For more information about the history of this area read "Skyland Before 1900" by Jean Stephenson in the July, 1935 PATC Bulletin and the book, *Skyland,* by George Freeman Pollock.

For convenience Section VII is divided into 3 subsections: Thornton Gap to Skyland, Skyland to Fishers Gap, and Fishers Gap to Swift Run Gap.

Maps:

PATC Map No. 10. Also available are the USGS map of the Shenandoah Park, Central Section, scale 1:62,500 and the USGS 7½' quads (scale 1:24,000) of Thornton Gap, Old Rag, Big Meadows, Fletcher, Elkton East, and Swift Run Gap. (The following quads cover areas of the central section of the Park not traversed by the *AT:* Washington, Va., Luray, Stanley, Madison, and Stanardsville.)

SUBSECTION:
THORNTON GAP TO SKYLAND
NORTH TO SOUTH

9.4 miles (15.1 kilometers)　　　　　　　(PATC Map No. 10)

General description:

From U.S. 211, about 0.1m. west of the Skyline Drive at Thornton Gap, SDMP 31.5, el. 2307', the *AT* swings through the woods, passing to the west of Panorama Restaurant. A spur trail leads to the upper parking area there. The Trail climbs steadily, reaching the ridge crest just beyond the peak of Marys Rock, 3514'. A side trail, to the right, leads to the northern tip of Marys Rock which affords one of the most outstanding panoramic views in the entire Park. The *AT* then follows the ridge crest, climbs over The Pinnacle, el. 3730', passes below the Jewel Hollow Overlook, and then goes through the Pinnacles Picnic Grounds. From here on, the *AT* generally stays a little below the ridge crest on the western side. As the western slopes are generally quite steep in this area there are many good views westward. The *AT* passes below the main cliffs of Little Stony Man along a very scenic shelf of rock. It enters the Skyland area through a lovely grove of white pine, crosses one of the Skyland paved roads and passes just below the long Dining Hall building. Here the section ends.

There are no dependable sources of water on the *AT* along this stretch of trail except the piped water, available "in season" at Byrds Nest #3, at the Pinnacles Picnic Grounds, and at Stony Man Mountain Parking Overlook. The springs at Meadow Springs and Shavers Hollow are each 0.3m. downhill from the *AT*. (See PATC Map No. 10).

Side trails:

The Park is wide on the east side of the Drive in this area and there are many trails. One group of trails is centered around "Hazel Country", that section near the Hazel River and Hazel Mountain. These interconnect with trails centered around Nicholson (Free State) Hollow and Corbin Cabin. The Skyland area includes a wide variety of trails. See Chap. 5: "Side Trails", Central section, for detailed descriptions of these trails.

Accommodatioins:

In season, Panorama, at the northern end of the section, offers meals but no lodging facilities. Skyland has an excellent restaurant, a lodge, and cottages. A stable is maintained here and there is a network of horse trails as well as hiking trails in this area. The nearest public campground is at Big Meadows, SDMP 51.2, about 9 miles south of Skyland. One section of the campground is kept open during the winter except during Jan. & Feb. The lodge and wayside are also closed Jan. & Feb.; Byrd Visitor Center is open throughout the year.

There are no huts available for camping in this subsection. An open-faced shelter, Byrds Nest #3 (3.0m.), can be used for picnicking. A locked structure, Corbin Cabin, reached via the Corbin Cabin Cut-Off Trail, is 1.4m. east of the Skyline Drive, SDMP 37.9. For its use reservations must be obtained in advance from PATC Headquarters. See Chap. 6: "Picnic Shelters, Huts and Cabins."

NORTH TO SOUTH 51

Detailed Trail data:

0.0 This section of the *AT* begins at the Trail's intersection with U.S. 211, about 0.1m. west of the Skyline Drive, SDMP 31.5, el. 2307'. Proceed through the woods passing west of the Panorama Restaurant. (A spur trail here leads left to the parking area at Panorama.) The *AT* ascends along the northern and then eastern slopes of the mountain.

1.7 Spur trail leads right 0.1m. to the northern tip of Marys Rock. The view from this point is unsurpassed anywhere in the Park. (Highest point, 3514 ft., is reached by climbing to the top of the huge rock outcrop, dangerous in wet or windy weather. The rock is granodiorite and geologists have determined its age to be over a billion years!) Beyond the junction, the *AT* follows the ridge crest south, with occasional views westward, and descends gradually.

2.4 In a sag the Buck Hollow Trail intersects the *AT*. (Buck Hollow Trail leads left, downhill, passing Meadow Springs on its left in 0.3m. It continues downhill crossing the Skyline Drive, SDMP 33.5, in 0.7m. and continuing down to reach U.S. 211 in 3.7m. at a point on U.S. 211 3.4m. west of Sperryville.) The *AT* continues along the ridge crest which is narrow here. There is an excellent view to the west from a rock outcrop 0.1m. farther along the Trail.

2.7 Reach another good viewpoint. Here Trail switches back to the left, then descends toward sag at base of The Pinnacle.

3.0 *AT* comes into service road and follows it right 180 ft. to Byrds Nest #3. (To left, service road leads 0.3m. to Skyline Drive, SDMP 33.9. Piped water available at the shelter during the warmer months. See Chap. 6: "Picnic Shelters, Huts and Cabins.") Beyond shelter *AT* ascends gradually.

3.7 Obscure spur trail, right, leads 100 ft. to fine view north.

3.8 Fifty feet to right of *AT* are jagged rocks forming the North Peak of The Pinnacle. Beyond, the *AT* leads for a short distance along the level ridge crest, affording splendid views of the sheer western slopes of this ridge.

4.0 Pass to left of highest point of The Pinnacle, el. 3730'. Descend through heavy growth of mountain laurel (blossoming in early June) with occasional views of Stony Man Mtn. ahead.

4.7 Cross blue-blazed Leading Ridge Trail. (To left, trail leads 0.1m. to the Drive. To right it climbs over Leading Ridge, then descends steeply toward the Shenandoah Valley, and comes into Va. Sec. 669 outside the Park boundary, at a point about 2 m. from U.S. 211 using the shortest route. See PATC Map No. 10.) *AT* now passes through some tall white pine, descending gently.

4.8 Side trail, left, leads 100 ft. to scenic Jewell Hollow Parking Overlook, SDMP 36.4, el. 3335'. *AT* passes below the Overlook.

5.0 A second trail, left, leads back 75 ft. to the Jewell Hollow Overlook. *AT* ascends gradually along the crest of a narrow ridge. There are fine views westward across Jewell Hollow.

5.1 *AT* comes up to, then parallels to the right, the entrance road to Pinnacles Picnic Grounds, SDMP 36.7. At fork in the path the *AT* follows the unpaved right fork which leads around the picnic grounds. Follow white blazes! Trail route is through tall laurel.

5.3 Trail passes toilets and drinking fountain. There are large Appalachian Trail signs at adjacent parking area; bear right here and also 200 ft. beyond, where paved picnic area path bends to the left. Enter woods, ascend slightly, then descend.

5.7 An impressive old white pine grows to left of the *AT* here. A tenth of a mile farther the *AT* passes under power line. Trail then ascends over knob at head of Nicholson Hollow.

6.1 Where the *AT* switchbacks sharply to the right, descending, there is an excellent viewpoint. The *AT* here is close to, but above, the Skyline Drive and presents an unobstructed view of Nicholson (Free State) Hollow and Old Rag Mountain beyond. (The mountaineers who once lived in Nicholson Hollow were reputed to be so mean they were a "law unto themselves" and the local sheriffs were afraid to enter the hollow, hence the name "Free State." See George F. Pollock's book, *Skyland*.)

6.2 Shaver Hollow spring is 0.3m. downhill to the right. (Left of the *AT*, a trail leads 150 ft. to Skyline Drive at the Shaver Hollow Parking Area, SDMP 37.9. Across the Drive here the Corbin Cabin Cut-Off Trail leads 1.5m. to Corbin Cabin and the Nicholson Hollow Trail. See Chap. 6: "Picnic Shelters, Huts and Cabins.") From the trail intersection the *AT* continues with several

NORTH TO SOUTH

gentle dips and climbs.

6.8 Cross Crusher Ridge Tr., blue-blazed, which here follows an old woods road known as Sours Lane. (To the right, the trail leads along Crusher Ridge, then down into Shaver Hollow near Va. Sec. 669. To the left, the trail ends on the Nicholson Hollow Trail just a few feet from the Skyline Drive.)

7.0 Junction with the blue-blazed Nicholson Hollow Trail. (The Nicholson Hollow Trail leads 0.1m. to the Drive, SDMP 38.4, and diagonally across it. It then drops down into Nicholson Hollow and follows the Hughes River for another 5.8m. to reach Va. Sec. 600 west of Nethers.)

7.3 A side trail, left, leads 200 ft. to south end of the Stony Man Mtn. Overlook in Hughes River Gap, SDMP 38.6, el. 3097'. Drinking water and toilets here. Continuing around the head of Nicholson Hollow, the *AT* parallels the Drive. Trail emerges from woods with fine view west of Page Valley, the Massanutten Range, New Market Gap and Luray, and a near view south of Little Stony Man cliffs and the Stony Man Mtn. "profile." The *AT* ascends, paralleling the Skyline Drive.

7.7 Spur trail, left, leads 150 ft. to Little Stony Man Parking Area on the Skyline Drive, SDMP 39.1. Ascend Stony Man Mtn. gradually, by long switchbacks, first left, then right.

8.0 At trail junction marked by a concrete signpost, take right fork. (Left fork is the Little Stony Man Trail which affords an alternate route over Stony Man Mtn., el. 4011', rejoining the Appalachian Trail at Skyland. See map of Skyland area on back of PATC Map No. 10. The Little Stony Man Trail involves more climbing and is 0.2m. longer. Combined with the *AT* it makes an excellent short circuit hike. Via the Little Stony Man Tr. it is uphill 0.2m. to Little Stony Man where cliffs offer fine views west, 0.8m. to Stony Man Nature Tr., 1.1 to Stony Man cliffs and 1.5m. to Dining Hall area of Skyland. *AT* crosses Skyland just below the Dining Hall.)

8.1 Follow ledge below Little Stony Man cliffs. Excellent views here. (Little Stony Man Tr. is directly above the *AT* here, atop the cliffs.) The route of the *AT* around Little Stony Man and Stony Man Mtn. is a slight relocation of George Freeman Pollock's original Passamaquoddy Trail in 1932. (Passamaquoddy is a Maine Indian word signifying "abounding in pollock".) This bit of *AT* is exceptionally beautiful as it follows the base of rocky cliffs and passes by huge hemlock trees.

9.0 Pass Skyland power line and housed Furnace Spring 25 ft. to left of Trail. Enter fine hemlock grove, then in 200 ft. turn left on the former Skyland Road. (The yellow-blazed Furnace Spring Tr. leads left from the *AT* 0.5 mile to join the Stony Man Horse Tr. at the Stony Man Nature Tr. Parking Area just off Skyline Drive at the northern entrance to Skyland. To the right of the *AT*, the Old Skyland Road Trail descends 3m. to the "foot of the mountain". Road is gated at Park boundary where it becomes Va. Sec. 672 at a point about 8m. from Luray.)

9.1 Turn left off road at signpost. Ascend through woods.

9.2 Cross paved Skyland Road and continue through woods. (Road leads left to northern entrance of Skyland and the Nature Trail Parking Area. To right it leads down to the cabin area of Skyland.)

9.3 Come into paved path and follow it left, uphill, toward the Skyland Dining Hall. At a sharp bend to the right, a side trail leads straight ahead. (This trail leads to service road, in the vendor's dormitory area of Skyland. Road can be followed uphill toward north entrance of Drive, to where the Stony Man Nature Trail begins.)

9.4 This section of the *AT* ends just below the Dining Hall where the *AT* forks to the right leaving the paved path. There is a wooden signboard here.

Skyland is located between SDMP 41.7 and 42.5 about 23m. north of U.S. 33 at Swift Run Gap and 10m. south of U.S. 211 at Thornton Gap via the Drive.

SUBSECTION:
SKYLAND TO FISHERS GAP
NORTH TO SOUTH

6.3 miles (10.1 kilometers) (PATC Map No. 10)

This stretch of the Appalachian Trail starts at Skyland, just

NORTH TO SOUTH

below the Skyland Dining Hall. The Blue Ridge in this area was at one time covered by a series of lava flows. (See Chap. 3: "Geology of the Shenandoah Park".) Today this lava, in its present form of greenstone, is the rock seen in the many rock outcrops along the Skyline Drive and Appalachian Trail in this section. On the west side of the ridge, where the slope is very steep, the old layers of lava show as a series of vertical cliffs, one above another, thus affording a very rugged and photogenic section of Trail.

The summit of Hawksbill Mtn., el. 4050', is the highest point in the Park. The *AT* slabs along the northwestern slopes of this mountain but side trails lead to the summit.

Two typically northern evergreens, red spruce and balsam fir, are found in this area. The spruce is native to Hawksbill, the balsam to Crescent Rock, and both are found in the Limberlost area east of Skyland and on Stony Man Mtn. just north of Skyland. Going north on the *AT* these trees are not found again until one reaches Vermont. They are found farther south but at much higher elevations such as on Mt. Rogers, el. 5729' (and White Top nearby) in southwestern Virginia.

Side trails:

As in the preceding subsection the Park is wide here, especially to the east of the Skyline Drive. The lovely Whiteoak Canyon-Cedar Run Circuit Hike is in this area. The scenic rock-sculptured top of Old Rag Mountain beckons the hiker here. Several routes lead to the top of Hawksbill Mountain. For details of these and other side trails see Chap. 5: "Side Trails", Central Section.

Accommodations:

Public accommodations are available at Skyland from mid-April through November. The lodge and cottages can accommodate 350 persons. A stable is maintained here and there is a network of horseback trails in the area. The Big Meadows Developed Area just south of Fishers Gap offers the Byrd Visitor Center, picnic grounds, a lodge and cabins with lodging and meals for 200 persons, a wayside, stables (wagon rides only), and a tremendous camping area with standard facilities for campers—both tent and trailer—store, laundry, showers, etc. Big Meadows is the only campground in the Park open most of the year (closed Jan. &

Feb.); the visitor's center remains open during the winter. For information and lodging reservations write to the ARA Virginia Sky-Line Co., Inc., Box 727, Luray, Va. 22835.

Camping for *AT* thru-hikers is available at the Rock Spring Hut, 4.4m. (spur trail 0.2m.) (See Chap. 6: "Picnic Shelters, Huts and Cabins.") Byrds Nest #2, an open-faced shelter atop Hawksbill Mtn., is available for picnicking only. It can be reached from the *AT* at Hawksbill Gap, 3.1m., via the Hawksbill Tr., 0.9 m. or, at 4.1m. via the Nakedtop Tr., 0.9m. Considerably east of the Drive are two additional picnic shelters, Byrds Nest #1 on the western ridge of Old Rag Mtn., and the Old Rag Shelter, 0.4m. up the Saddle Trail from the junction of three Park fire roads, the Old Rag Fire Rd., the Weakley Hollow Fire Rd. and the Berry Hollow Fire Rd. See PATC Map No. 10.

One locked cabin, Rock Spring, 4.4m. (spur trail to cabin 0.2m.) is also available. Reservations for its use must be obtained in advance from PATC Headquarters. (See Chap. 6: "Picnic Shelters, Huts and Cabins.")

Detailed Trail data:

0.0 Signpost on path 75 ft. below the Skyland Dining Hall marks start of this section. The *AT* follows an unpaved path south through woods. (To reach the *AT* at start of the section follow paved path leading downhill (west) from the Skyland Dining Hall for 75 ft. Turn left onto the *AT* at signpost.)

0.2 *AT* bears left, then crosses paved road; there is a small trail marker visible in the distance. (The Millers Head Trail starts from the road about 200 ft. to the right of the *AT* crossing. This trail leads 0.8m. over Bushytop to Millers Head with beautiful views.) The *AT* continues along a power line, then through the woods.

0.5 Cross paved road leading to stables a short distance to the right of the *AT*. At trail intersection just beyond, a horse trail leads left to Whiteoak Canyon and on to Big Meadows, while *AT* bends right. Follow *AT* blazes and Park signs. The Trail proceeds along a fence. It then descends slightly toward the west edge of an escarpment.

0.8 Trail leads along cliffs on west edge of ridge under Pollock Knob, el. 3560′ (named for George Freeman Pollock, founder of Skyland). There are occasional views to the right from the Trail.

NORTH TO SOUTH

1.3 Here, where the *AT* begins descent by switchbacks, there is a spectacular view of Hawksbill Mtn. and Ida Valley. Beyond, the *AT* parallels the Drive, passing through a thicket of laurel.

1.7 Spur trail, left, leads uphill 300 ft. to Timber Hollow Parking Overlook on the Skyline Drive, SDMP 43.3.

1.8 Pass a piped spring 4 ft. left of the *AT*. Trail climbs over a small ridge, then descends gently, slabbing the steep western slopes of the Blue Ridge. Here the Trail passes some picturesque contorted trees. A big oak on the right extends a "sitting limb".

2.6 Cement post marks spur trail leading uphill for 0.1m. to a junction a few feet north of the parking area, with short (0.3m.) trail leading north from the Crescent Rock Parking Overlook, SDMP 44.4, to Bettys Rock. (The views from Bettys Rock are lovely.) The *AT* next passes under the cliffs of Crescent Rock. Excellent views of Nakedtop and Hawksbill Mtn. from the Trail along here.

3.1 Reach Hawksbill Gap. A trail leads right, down the mountain, to a spring in 450 ft. To left, a trail leads uphill 300 ft. to Hawksbill Gap Parking Area on the Drive, SDMP 45.6, el.3361'. On the east side of the Drive here is the start of the Cedar Run Trail. (From the Hawksbill Gap Parking Area, the Hawksbill Tr. leads steeply up for 0.8m. to Byrds Nest #2 and the summit just beyond. From the summit, el. 4050', the Hawksbill Trail descends southward to the Upper Hawksbill Parking Area on the Drive, SDMP 46.7. The Nakedtop Trail also starts at the shelter and descends the west ridge of Hawksbill, ending on the *AT* in 0.9m. See Chap. 6: "Picnic Shelters, Huts and Cabins." Hawksbill Mtn., 4050', is the first summit near the *AT* to reach this much elevation south of Killington, Vt. Its exposed top affords a magnificent panoramic view. Among the hardwoods on its upper slopes are a scattering of conifers—balsam fir and red spruce—both rare in Virginia. North of the Stony Man to Hawksbill area they are not found again growing as natives along the *AT* until Vermont. Farther south they are found again along the Trail in the Mt. Rogers area of SW Virginia and down into North Carolina and Tennessee at elevations above 5000 ft.) From Hawksbill Gap the *AT* ascends, then slabs along the steep northern face of Hawksbill Mtn., passing under cliffs in a wild, rugged setting. There are splendid views, looking backward, of Crescent Rocks, Stony Man and Old Rag Mountain; also northward views of Ida Valley and Luray. Note the balsam fir along the Trail here.

4.1 Intersection with the Nakedtop Trail in a sag between Hawksbill and Nakedtop. (The Nakedtop Trail leads left 0.9m. to the summit of Hawksbill.)

4.4 Here the *AT* comes out of deep woods into an old orchard now rapidly being overgrown with black locust, sumac, and pines. A road enters the Trail from the left. It comes 0.2m. from the Skyline Drive, SDMP 47.8, and serves as a Park service road to Rock Spring Cabin. Twenty ft. farther along the *AT* a signpost marks the graded spur trail leading right 0.2m. down to Rock Spring Cabin, a locked structure, and to Rock Spring Hut. (For use of the cabin reservations must be obtained in advance from PATC Headquarters. See Chap. 6: "Picnic Shelters, Huts and Cabins.") A spring is 50 yds. north of the cabin.

5.0 Spur trail, left, marked by post, leads 150 ft. uphill to the Skyline Drive at Spitler Knoll Parking Overlook, SDMP 48.1, nearest parking spot for Rock Spring Cabin. Beyond the overlook the *AT* continues, again slabbing along the western slopes of the main Blue Ridge.

5.8 Pass a wet weather spring 15 ft. to the right of the *AT*. One hundred ft. farther, at cement post, an obscure trail leads left, uphill, 0.3m. to the north end of Franklin Cliffs Overlook.

6.1 Pass a second trail, marked by post, leading left 0.1m. to the south end of Franklin Cliffs Overlook, SDMP 49.0, el. 3135'.

6.3 Intersect the Red Gate Fire Road in Fishers Gap. (To the right, the road, gated at the Drive and again at the Park boundary, leads down the mountain 4.8m. to Va. Sec. 611 about 4m. east of Stanley. Although hikers can use this road it is not recommended, as Park personnel and concessioners use this road for hauling supplies and for commuting to Big Meadows. To the left the road leads 350 ft. to the northern end of the Fishers Gap Parking Overlook, SDMP 49.3, el. 3061'. East of the Drive here is the northern end of the Dark Hollow Falls-Rose River Loop Trail. Also from here the Rose River Fire Road, gated at the Drive, leads down the east side of the mountain, crossing Hog Camp Creek just below Dark Hollow Falls. In pre-Shenandoah Park days this road

NORTH TO SOUTH

was known as the Gordonsville Turnpike. See Chap. 5: "Side Trails", Central Section. Also PATC Map No. 10 and PATC publication: *Circuit Hikes in the Shenandoah National Park.*)

SUBSECTION:
FISHERS GAP TO SWIFT RUN GAP
NORTH TO SOUTH

18.6 miles (30.0 kilometers)　　　　　(PATC Map No. 10)

General description:

From Fishers Gap, el. 3061', the *AT* skirts the Big Meadows Developed Area, then continues on to Milam Gap where it crosses the Skyline Drive. It climbs to the summit of Hazeltop where the *AT* reaches its highest elevation in the Shenandoah Park, 3816', then descends to Bootens Gap. The Trail now climbs two low mountains, Bush and Bearfence; the latter is very scenic. The *AT* skirts the Lewis Mtn. Developed Area, climbs over Baldface Mtn., drops down to skirt around the South River Picnic Grounds, then follows an old road over a spur of Saddleback Mountain and finally descends steeply to Swift Run Gap, el. 2367'.

Side trails:

In the Big Meadows Area there are many trails and a number of circuit hikes that are popular; the Dark Hollow Falls-Rose River Loop circuit is probably the favorite one. The Rapidan Fire Rd. and several trails lead eastward from the Skyline Drive and *AT* to Camp Hoover, located within the Park on the Rapidan River. On Laurel Prong near Camp Hoover one can find growing the rosebay rhododendron, (R. maximum).

Farther south is the short, but very scenic, South River Falls Trail. An excellent circuit hike can be made from Pocosin Cabin by using the Pocosin Fire Rd., the Pocosin (Horse) Tr., the South River Fire Rd., the South River Falls Trail and the *AT*. (See Chap. 5: "Side Trails", Central Section, and the South River inset on the back of PATC Map No. 10.)

Many fire foot trails, fire roads, and other old roads beckon the hiker. Some are well marked and easy to follow, but others may be

APPALACHIAN TRAIL DATA

Accommodations:

Both picnic and camping (tent and trailer) facilities are available at Big Meadows (closed Jan. & Feb.) and Lewis Mtn. Cabins are also available at both places. For use of the latter, reservations can be made with the ARA Virginia Sky-Line Co., Inc, Box 727, Luray, Va. 22835. Big Meadows also has a lodge, a wayside and the Byrd Visitor Center. Lewis Mtn. has a camp store.

The open-faced Bearfence Mtn. Hut, 9.5m., is available for thru-hikers. One locked structure, Pocosin Cabin, 12.3m., is near the Trail here. A second cabin, the Jones Mtn. Cabin, is located too far to the east for easy accessibility from the *AT*. Best approach to this cabin is from the Piedmont. See Chap. 6: "Picnic Shelters, Huts and Cabins."

Detailed Trail data:

0.0 Intersection with the Red Gate Fire Road 350 ft. west of the Skyline Drive, just north of the Fishers Gap Overlook, SDMP 49.3, el. 3061'. (To right of the *AT*, a fire road leads 4.8m. down the mountain to Va. Sec. 611 at a point about 4m. from Stanley. This road is not ideal for hiking as it is used by Park personnel and concessioners for commuting to Big Meadows and for hauling supplies. Across the Drive here is the northern end of the Rose River-Dark Hollow Falls Loop Trail. Also from here the Rose River Fire Road leads 6.5m. down the mountain, crossing Hog Camp Creek just below Dark Hollow Falls in 1.0m. See Chap. 5: "Side Trails", Central Section, also PATC Map No. 10 and PATC publication: *Circuit Hikes in the Shenandoah National Park.*)

0.1 Pass post marking spur trail, left, which leads 100 ft. to Fishers Gap Parking Overlook.

0.2 Pass to right of split rock. Ascend gradually. Pass through beautiful hemlock grove. Continue to ascend.

1.0 David Spring is 50 ft. to right of the *AT* here. A trail comes in from the left. (See Big Meadows inset on back of PATC Map No. 10.) The *AT* skirts the north edge of the Big Meadows Campground. (Several short unmarked trails lead left to the camp-

NORTH TO SOUTH

ground.) Openings along the *AT* give fine views to the north and west—of Hawksbill Mtn. in the foreground, Stony Man Mtn. farther away, and, in the distance, Knob Mtn. and The Neighbor. Across the Page Valley, Signal Knob can be seen at the north end of the Massanutten range.

1.3 Cross over a small rocky knob, the Monkey Head. There are views here also. Beyond, the *AT* skirts the western edge of the ridge.

1.5 A trail goes left uphill about 0.1m. to the Amphitheatre Parking Area of Big Meadows. *AT* now passes below the open-air amphitheatre.

1.6 Cement post marks trail intersection. The *AT* is straight ahead. The trail to the right leads 1.2m. to Lewis Falls. Trail to left, the Lodge trail, leads to the Amphitheatre Parking Area. One can follow the exit road to the Campground entrance and from there follow signs to reach the Story of the Forest Nature Trail. Follow it "in reverse" about 0.9m, then a short spur trail to reach the Dark Hollow Falls Parking Area. The Lewis Falls Tr. and *AT* together offer a 3.1m. circuit hike. (See back of PATC Map No. 10.)

1.9 Pass under sheer cliffs on Blackrock.

2.1 Trail to left of *AT* leads 0.1m. to Blackrock viewpoint and another 0.2m. to Big Meadows Lodge. The *AT* continues along the west slope of the ridge, descending, with occasional views to the west from rocks to the right of the Trail.

2.5 Cross service road. (To left this road leads about 0.3m. to the Skyline Drive, SDMP 51.4, at a point 0.1m. south of the Big Meadows Wayside. Lunches are available at the wayside most of the year. Here too is located the Harry F. Byrd Sr. Visitor Center. To right of the *AT* the service road leads down to a sewage disposal area. To reach Lewis Falls follow the road downhill for about 150 ft. (Note small pumphouse to right of road here.) Turn left off the road onto a footpath that leads 0.5m. downhill to Lewis Falls and on to Big Meadows.) Beyond the service road intersection the *AT* passes the outlet of housed-in Lewis Spring. The Trail continues through woods, descending gradually.

2.8 Cross Tanners Ridge Horse Trail. Continue straight ahead and cross the horse trail again in about 0.1m. Cross open field with cemetery to the right. Here are splendid views; ahead is Hazeltop Mtn.

3.1 Cross Tanners Ridge Fire Road. (The road, gated at the Drive and at the Park boundary, leads right for 1.4m. to the Park boundary where it becomes Va. Sec. 682. To left it leads 0.1m. to the Drive, SDMP 51.6.)

3.3 Pass spring 50 ft. to left of the *AT*. Beyond, pass through fields still fairly open.

4.2 Cross Skyline Drive, SDMP 52.8, just south of Milam Gap, el. 3257'. *AT* bears east through a field. Cement post marks the Mill Prong Trail which leads left from the *AT*. (This blue-blazed trail, 1.0m., leads to the Mill Prong Horse Trail.) Beyond the junction the *AT* ascends along the north ridge of Hazeltop.

4.6 Bear right along ridge crest. From rock to left of Trail is wintertime view of Doubletop and Fork Mtns. (Former Pres. Herbert Hoover's Camp is in the Rapidan Valley between these peaks.) The *AT* ascends very gradually along the ridge crest. Here may be found a fine stand of stiff gentians among the white and purple asters in the autumn.

5.7 Reach the north end of Hazeltop.

6.1 Cross the wooded summit of Hazeltop, el. 3812', highest point on the *AT* in the SNP.

6.6 Junction with blue-blazed Laurel Prong Trail. (Laurel Prong Tr. leads left from the *AT* down 2.8m. to Camp Hoover. This is one of the few trails in the Park that passes through areas with rosebay rhododendron (or great laurel) which blooms in late June or early July. Other wild flowers found here include the false lily-of-the-valley, trillium, and wild iris. About 1m. from the *AT* in Laurel Gap, the Cat Knob Tr. leads east 0.5m. to end on the Jones Mtn. Tr.)

7.0 In Bootens Gap, el. 3243', cross the Conway River Fire Road, gated. (Skyline Drive, SDMP 55.1, is 150 ft. to right, with parking space for two cars. To left, the road leads down the Conway River, one fork of the road becoming Va. Sec. 615 and continuing to Graves Mill; the other fork, which continues down the Conway River, becomes Va. Sec. 667 and comes into Va. 230 about 3m. north of Stanardsville.) The *AT* descends gradually for 0.2m., then continues with little change in elevation, paralleling

NORTH TO SOUTH 63

the Skyline Drive.

7.7 Ascend gradually, following along the western slope of Bush Mtn.

7.9 *AT* approaches within 150 ft. of the Drive. Ascent continues for about 0.2m., then Trail is level for about 0.2m. before again ascending along the ridge of Bearfence Mtn.

8.4 Trail intersection. (To right, blue-blazed trail leads 0.1m. to the Skyline Drive at the Bearfence Mtn. Parking Area, SDMP 56.4. Naturalist-led hikes start here in the summer. To left, an unimproved trail (blazed) leads to spectacular jagged rocks of Bearfence Mtn. Views from the rocks are excellent. This is a rough trail requiring the use of hands in some places. In 0.3m. it connects with the graded loop trail over Bearfence Mtn. The two trails, with the *AT*, make a rough figure eight.)

8.6 Bearfence Mtn. Loop Trail (graded) leaves *AT* on left. (Views along this trail are rewarding. The loop trail is only 150 ft. longer than the stretch of *AT* between the junctions.)

8.8 The Bearfence Loop Trail comes in from the left. The *AT* now descends steeply with a series of zigzags, with a splendid view to the east from a rock ledge near the top.

9.4 In gap, cross the Slaughter Trail. (The trail is gated just below the *AT*. Down the road (trail) 0.1m. the access road to Bearfence Hut leads right for 0.2m. The Slaughter Trail, yellow-blazed, continues to the Conway River Fire Rd. at the Park boundary. To the right of the *AT* the road leads a few feet to the Skyline Drive, SDMP 56.8. On west side of the Drive, the road continues as the Meadow School Fire Road and descends to Va. Sec. 759.)

9.5 Spur trail, left, leads downhill 0.1m. to Bearfence Mtn. Hut. Spring is 50 ft. south of the hut. (See Chap. 6: "Picnic Shelters, Huts and Cabins.") The *AT* now ascends gradually the north slope of Lewis Mtn. As Trail levels off at about 3400 ft., several paths lead right, first to the Lewis Mtn. Picnic Grounds (water available "in season") and then to the Lewis Mtn. Campground. There is a camp store on the campground road, open June thru October.

10.4 Here a post marks a trail, right, leading 300 ft. to the campground. (Water fountain "in season" directly across camp road.)

10.5 Pass trail intersection. (To right a trail leads to the campground. To left the Lewis Mtn. East Tr., blue-blazed, leads along the ridge crest for less than a mile, then dead-ends. There are plans to continue this trail to connect with Pocosin Hollow Tr., also to build a connecting link with the Slaughter Tr. Across the Skyline Drive from the entrance to Lewis Mtn. Campground the Lewis Mtn. West Tr., blue-blazed, leads down to Va. Sec. 625 at a point about 8m. from Elkton, but is not currently maintained. Be on the alert for a change of route.) The *AT* now descends steadily.

11.1 Left of the *AT* an old road descends toward Pocosin Hollow. To the right of the Trail, Skyline Drive is only a few feet away. *AT* soon bears away from the Drive.

12.0 Pass spring to the right of the Trail.

12.2 Cross Pocosin Fire Rd. (To right, fire road leads 0.1m. to Skyline Drive, SDMP 59.5. To left of the *AT*, the Pocosin Fire Road leads downhill passing Pocosin Cabin in 0.1m. About 0.8m. farther along the fire road, the Pocosin Horse Trail leads right from the road for 1.3m. to join the South River Fire Road, making an excellent loop trail possible (or a complete circuit by returning to Pocosin Fire Road via the *AT*). On down the road another 0.3m. or so the Pocosin Hollow Trail, blue-blazed, goes left and descends the mountain. See Chap. 5 "Side Trails", Central Section, and PATC Map No. 10.) Beyond the fire road intersection, the *AT* ascends gradually.

12.3 Graded spur trail leads left, downhill, 250 ft. to Pocosin Cabin and to the spring just south of the cabin. (Pocosin Cabin is a locked structure; reservations for its use must be obtained in advance from PATC Headquarters. See Chap. 6: "Picnic Shelters, Huts and Cabins." From the cabin there is a fine view east over the Conway River Valley. Three mountains can be seen across the valley. The local mountaineers called these, from right to left: Panther, Bear Stand, and Sawney Macks; these names are not recognized on current maps. "Pocosin" is said to be of Indian derivation, meaning a "dismal" or swamp.)

12.5 *AT* ascends steeply by switchbacks for 0.1m. It next passes through a relatively flat area known as Kites Deadening, now completely wooded. (A deadening was an area where the early settlers, instead of felling the trees to clear the land for a field, saved time and effort by just ringing the trees—removing the lower bark—to kill the trees without the task of cutting them down. They would then plant their crops amid the "deadened" trees.)

13.5 Reach crest of Baldface Mtn., el. 3600'.

13.8 Rocks to right of the Trail offer views to the west.

14.2 Cross old road which leads left past an old quarry. (To the right road leads 0.1m. past the site of a former CCC camp to the Skyline Drive, SDMP 61.8.)

15.1 Cross South River Fire Road. (To left the yellow-blazed road leads down toward South River Falls. In 0.8m. from the *AT* a road, blue-blazed, leads right from the fire road down to the South River at a point 0.1m. below the falls. The South River Falls Tr. utilizes the lower portion of this road. Follow a footpath for 0.1m. up the river to the base of the South River Falls. The South River Fire Rd. continues eastward. In another 1.2 m. the Pocosin Horse Trail leads left from it for 1.3m. to its junction with the Pocosin Fire Rd. Beyond this junction the South River Fire Rd. descends, becoming Va. Sec. 642 outside the Park. To the right of the *AT*, the fire road leads 0.3m. to the Skyline Drive, SDMP 62.7, el. 2960'. Across the drive here the Dry Run Falls Fire Rd. leads 2.6m. down the west slope of Dean Mtn. to Va. Sec. 625.) From the fire road intersection, the *AT* ascends, then skirts the east slope of the knob on which the South River Picnic Area is located.

15.6 Cross graded trail, the South River Falls Trail. (To left this trail leads 1.5m. downhill to the South River Falls. To the right it leads 0.1m. to the eastern edge of the South River Picnic Grounds. Water is available here "in season".)

15.9 In pine thicket old road comes in on right from the Drive, SDMP 63.1. *AT* turns left onto this road and follows it.

16.1 *AT* takes right fork of road. (Left fork is the blue-blazed Saddleback Tr. It leads past the South River Maintenance Bldg. where there is a spring, 0.3m., and then bears south and west to end on the *AT*, 1.4m.)

16.5 At bend in Trail an old road comes in from the left. The *AT* ascends.

16.7 Still following the old road, reach top of rise, just west of the westernmost peak, el. 3296', of Saddleback Mtn. There is much trillium along the trail here in early May.

17.2 Junction with the Saddleback Mtn. Tr. which comes in from the left.

17.9 *AT* turns left off of the old road it has been following.

18.3 Trail passes under power line.

18.6 Reach Skyline Drive, just where the entrance road from U.S. 33 comes into the Drive in Swift Run Gap, SDMP 65.5, el. 2367′. (Swift Run Gap is 7 miles east of Elkton and 8 miles west of Stanardsville via U.S. 33.)

NORTH TO SOUTH

SUMMARY OF DISTANCES ALONG THE *AT*
Section VII Central

	Miles	Kilometers
Thornton Gap and U.S. 211	0.0	0.0
Marys Rock Summit	1.7 + 0.1	2.7 + 0.2
Buck Hollow Trail	2.4	3.9
Byrds Nest #3	3.0	4.8
Pinnacles Picnic Grounds	5.3	8.5
Nicholson Hollow Trail	7.0	11.3
Stony Man Parking Overlook	7.3	11.8
Little Stony Man Parking Area	7.7	12.4
Skyland (Dining Hall)	9.4	15.1
Whiteoak Canyon Trail	9.9 + 0.1	15.9 + 0.2
Hawksbill Gap	12.5	20.1
Byrds Nest #2 and summit of Hawksbill	12.5 + 0.8	20.1 + 1.3
Rock Spring Cabin	13.8 + 0.2	22.2 + 0.3
Rock Spring Hut	13.8 + 0.2	22.2 + 0.3
Fishers Gap	15.7	25.2
Big Meadows—Amphitheatre area	17.3	27.8
Lewis Spring Service Rd.	18.2	29.2
Skyline Drive crossing, Milam Gap	19.9	31.9
Hazeltop Mtn. Summit	21.8	35.0
Bearfence Mtn. Loop Trail	24.3	39.0
Bearfence Mtn. Hut	25.2 + 0.2	40.5 + 0.3
Lewis Mtn. Campground	26.2	42.2
Pocosin Cabin	27.9 + 0.1	44.9 + 0.2
South River Falls Trail	31.3	50.3
Swift Run Gap and U.S. 33	34.3	55.2

SUMMARY OF DISTANCES BY SKYLINE DRIVE TO POINTS ON *AT*
Section VII Central

SDMP		Mileage from Thornton Gap
31.5	U.S. 211 at Thornton Gap	0.0
33.5	Buck Hollow Trail crossing, 0.7 m. to *AT*	2.0
33.9	Service Road to Byrds Nest #3, 0.3 m. to *AT*	2.4
36.4	Jewell Hollow Overlook	4.9
36.7	Pinnacles Picnic Grounds	5.2
37.9	Shaver Hollow Parking Area	6.4
38.4	Nicholson Hollow Trail crossing, 0.1m. to *AT*.	6.9
38.6	Stony Man Mtn. Overlook	7.1
39.1	Little Stony Man Parking Area	7.6
41.7	Skyland, North Entrance, 0.3 m. to *AT*	10.2
42.5	Skyland, South Entrance, 0.1 m. to *AT*	11.0
43.3	Timber Hollow Overlook	11.8
44.4	Crescent Rock Overlook	12.9
45.6	Hawksbill Gap	14.1
48.1	Spitler Knoll Parking Overlook (parking for Rock Spring Cabin)	16.6
49.0	Franklin Cliffs Overlook	17.5
49.3	Fishers Gap	17.8
51.2	Big Meadows Developed Area, 1.0 m. to *AT* via Campground Rd.	19.7
51.6	Tanners Ridge Fire Rd., 0.1 m. to *AT*	20.1
52.8	Milam Gap, *AT* crossing	21.3
55.1	Bootens Gap	23.6
56.4	Bearfence Mtn. Parking Area, 0.1 m. to *AT*	24.9
56.8	Slaughter Trail	25.3
57.5	Lewis Mtn. Campground, 0.1 m. to *AT*	26.0
59.5	Pocosin Fire Rd., 0.1 m. to *AT*	28.0
62.7	South River Fire Rd., 0.2 m. to *AT*	31.2
62.8	South River Picnic Grounds, 0.3 m. to *AT*	31.3
63.1	Service Road to South River Maintenance Bldg. 0.1 m. to *AT*	31.6
65.5	Swift Run Gap	34.0

NORTH TO SOUTH

SECTION VIII SOUTHERN SHENANDOAH PARK
SWIFT RUN GAP TO ROCKFISH GAP
NORTH TO SOUTH

Distance 44.9 miles (72.3 kilometers)   (PATC Map No. 11)

This section of the Appalachian Trail commences where U.S. 33 (Spotswood Trail) crosses the Blue Ridge at Swift Run Gap, SDMP 65.5, el. 2367'. Swift Run Gap is 7 miles east of Elkton and 8 miles west of Stanardsville (110 miles from Washington, D.C.). Rockfish Gap is 4 miles east of Waynesboro via U.S. 250 and 22 miles west of Charlottesville (about 140 miles from Washington, D.C.).

The southern section of the Shenandoah Park is the wildest and least developed section. Much of it has wilderness status. The *AT* itself follows the main crest of the Blue Ridge, so is rarely far from the Skyline Drive and crosses it frequently. There are many interesting side trails and fire roads in the section that can be used in conjunction with the *AT* for interesting hiking trips. The *AT* leaves the Shenandoah Park at Jarman Gap. South of Jarman Gap the Trail passes through a corridor of land acquired by the U.S. National Park Service for that purpose, except for a short stretch on Calf Mtn. south of Jarman Gap. The *AT* follows the Skyline Drive to cross over U.S. Interstate 64 and U.S. 250.

One large campground, the Loft Mountain Campground, is in this section of the Park. In addition to a picnic area and campsites, there are shower and laundry facilities, and a camp store. The campground is closed during the winter. Dundo Campground is open from April through October for organized youth group use only; the remainder of the year Dundo is open as a picnic area. Facilities are limited.

The Calf Mtn. Shelter has been constructed recently on the western slope of Calf Mtn. It is for the use of thru-hikers. A locked cabin, Doyles River Cabin, may be rented by hikers. Reservations for its use must be made at PATC Headquarters. See Chap. 6: "Picnic Shelters, Huts and Cabins."

Section VIII is divided for convenience into four subsections: Swift Run Gap to Simmons Gap, Simmons to Browns Gap, Browns to Jarman Gap, and Jarman to Rockfish Gap.

Maps:
PATC Map No. 11. Also available are the USGS map of Shenandoah National Park, Southern Section, scale 1:62,500, and the USGS 7½' quads: Swift Run Gap, McGaheysville, Browns Cove, Crimora and Waynesboro East. (Other 7½' quads covering areas of the southern section not traversed by the *AT* include Grottoes, Elkton East, and Crozet.)

SUBSECTION:
SWIFT RUN GAP TO SIMMONS GAP
NORTH TO SOUTH

9.6 miles (15.4 kilometers) (PATC Map No. 11)

General description:
From Swift Run Gap, el. 2367', the *AT* climbs over 1200 ft. to near the summit of Hightop Mtn., el. 3587'. This is the highest elevation of the *AT* in the southern section of the Park. The Trail then loses even more elevation than it had gained as it descends to Powell Gap. Still following the main crest of the Blue Ridge it climbs over a shoulder of Flattop Mtn. before reaching Simmons Gap.

Side trails:
Because the SNP is very narrow through most of this subsection there are few side trails and those that do exist lead out of the Park.

Accommodations:
There is one open-faced hut, Hightop Hut, 3.4m. (follow spur trail 0.1m.) along this section. See Chap. 6: "Picnic Shelters, Huts and Cabins."

There are no public accommodations along this section. Closest public lodgings, open only during the warmer months, are at Lewis Mtn., SDMP 57.5, in the central section of the Park. There is neither gasoline nor food available at Swift Run Gap.

Detailed Trail data:
0.0 The cement post on east side of Skyline Drive, directly opposite the place where the entrance road from U.S. 33 reaches

the Drive, is the starting point for this section. *AT* follows pedestrian footway along edge of bridge. Beyond the bridge, cross to right side of the Skyline Drive and climb bank. Trail shortly comes into old road which it follows for a few feet.

0.1 Trail turns sharply left from the old road and climbs. It soon levels off and follows an old farm road through what remains of an apple orchard, then descends gently.

1.3 Trail crosses to left of Skyline Drive in grassy sag, SDMP 66.7, el. 2637'. From sag Trail ascends steeply, by switchbacks, up the north slope of Hightop Mtn.

2.7 As *AT* nears summit there are two excellent viewpoints from ledges right of the Trail, one about 100 ft. farther along the Trail than the other. In another 100 ft. a spur trail, left, leads 350 ft. to site of former Park Service Lookout Tower at the summit of Hightop Mtn., el. 3587'. No view from the summit. *AT* now descends.

2.9 There is a protected spring at the foot of a large boulder just to the left of the *AT*. Trail continues to descend.

3.4 Spur trail leads right 0.1m. to Hightop Hut. (Spring is 400 ft. downhill from hut on graded trail.)

3.5 Cross dirt road. (Service road leads right to Hightop Hut. To left it leads to the Smith Roach Gap Fire Rd. at a point about 0.8m. from the Drive.) *AT* descends steadily.

4.6 Trail crosses Smith Roach Gap Fire Road, then turns right and parallels it to the Skyline Drive.

4.7 Cross to right of Skyline Drive in open Smith Roach Gap, SDMP 68.6, el. 2622'. Trail continues with little change in elevation around the east and south sides of Roundtop Mtn., affording wintertime views of Powell Gap and Flattop Mtn. Continue along ridge crest.

5.8 Summit of Little Roundtop Mtn. is 50 yds. to the right here. View of Powell Gap is to be had, just as Trail starts to descend steeply the west slope of the mountain.

6.3 Reach Powell Gap, SDMP 69.9, el. 2294', and cross to left of Drive. The *AT* now ascends a shoulder of Flattop Mtn.

6.6 Turn sharply left here, where old road, which *AT* has been following, continues straight ahead. Continue to ascend.

6.8 Excellent views of the Roach River Valley (Powell Gap and

Bacon Hollow) from rock ledges just to the left of the Trail. Continue to ascend very gently.

8.0 Reach summit of the shoulder of Flattop Mtn. and start gradual descent.

8.1 The *AT* comes close to the edge of the SNP here. There is an open field about 50 ft. to left of the Trail. From the field, but not from the *AT*, there are views, especially of Flattop Mtn., el. 3325'. Trail continues to descend.

8.7 Trail bends right to parallel an old road on its left and descends steeply.

9.1 *Alert: A relocation of the AT around the Simmons Gap Ranger Station is proposed for the future.* At present the Trail comes into the old road and follows it right for about 0.2m. (The road leads down to the Simmons Gap Ranger Station, formerly the Simmons Gap Episcopal Mission.)

9.3 Turn slightly right, away from the road. Come into Simmons Gap Rd. and follow it 40 ft. to the Drive.

9.6 Reach Simmons Gap, SDMP 73.2, el. 2253', at the intersection of the Simmons Gap Fire Rd. and Skyline Drive. (The Simmons Gap Rd. is gated on both sides of the Drive and at the Park boundaries. Outside the Park, on both east and west sides of the Drive, the road becomes Va. Sec. 628. A short distance south on the road is the ranger's residence and beyond it are the Park Service maintenance facilities. Water available here.) *AT* crosses to right (west) of Skyline Drive.

SUBSECTION:
SIMMONS GAP TO BROWNS GAP
NORTH TO SOUTH

12.2 miles (19.6 kilometers)　　　　　　(PATC Map No. 11)

General description:

This portion of the Trail starts at Simmons Gap, SDMP 73.2, el. 2253'. There are two 600 ft. climbs and one 800 ft. one, from Ivy Creek to the summit of Loft Mtn., but little other climbing. Between the peak of Loft Mtn. and Big Flat Mtn., site of the Loft

Mtn. Campground, the *AT* passes through considerable open area, a pleasant change from wooded territory. On Big Flat Mtn. the *AT* skirts the east, south, and then western edges of the Loft Mtn. Campground, then descends very gently toward Browns Gap, SDMP 82.9, el. 2599'.

The Shenandoah Park is much wider in this subsection than in the preceding one. Most of this section of the Park west of the *AT* is designated as a Wilderness Area. A roughly triangular area between the ridges of Rockytop, Brown Mtn. and Loft Mtn. and drained by tributaries of Big Run comprises the largest watershed in the Park, 11 square miles.

Side trails:

The greater width of Park here gives space for a wide variety of trails. The Big Run Loop Trail and the Doyles River Trail are both loop trails, connected at each of their ends with either the *AT* or Skyline Drive. There are, in addition, other blue-blazed trails, a number of horse trails, and three gated Park fire roads—Simmons Gap Rd., Browns Gap Rd., and Madison Run Fire Rd. For details of these see Chap. 5: "Side Trails," Southern Section.

Accommodations:

The Loft Mtn. Developed Area includes a wayside, camp store, campground with shower and laundry facilities, picnic grounds and two nature trails. Campground and other facilities are generally open April through October. (Store open in mid-May through October.)

One open-faced hut, the Pinefield Hut, 2.1m., is available for the thru-hiker. (The former Ivy Creek Shelter is now a PATC maintenance cabin not available for camping use.)

One locked cabin is available, the Doyles River Cabin, one quarter mile from the *AT* (10.0m.) down the Doyles River Trail. Reservations for the use of this cabin must be obtained in advance from PATC Headquarters. See Chap. 6: "Picnic Shelters, Huts and Cabins."

Detailed Trail data:

0.0 West side of the Skyline Drive, at junction with the Simmons Gap Fire Rd., SDMP 73.2, el. 2253'. (A short distance to the south on the fire road is the ranger's residence and beyond it are the Park Service maintenance facilities. Water available here. The Simmons Gap Rd. is gated on both sides of the Drive and at the Park boundaries. Outside the Park, on both east and west sides of the Drive, the road becomes Va. Sec. 628.) Trail ascends the northwestern face of Weaver Mtn.

1.1 Reach top of Weaver Mtn., then descend gently through sparse, scraggly woods, primarily black locust.

1.9 Cross to left of Skyline Drive at Pinefield Gap, SDMP 75.2. Continue through level area.

2.1 Cross access road to Pinefield Hut. Spring is located along this road, 20 yds. left of the *AT*. Hut is 150 yds. farther down the road. A second spring is 250 ft. behind the hut. (See Chap. 6: "Picnic Shelters, Huts and Cabins.") Trail now ascends.

2.3 Here *AT* comes within 100 ft. of the Skyline Drive.

2.7 At a spot where the *AT* turns sharply left, an unmarked trail leads right approximately 200 ft. to Skyline Drive. (From here one can follow the Drive north a few feet to reach the start of the blue-blazed Onemile Run Tr. The Twomile Run Parking Overlook is 0.1m. farther north, SDMP 76.2, and the start of the blue-blazed Rocky Mount Trail another 0.2m.) *AT* continutes to ascend.

3.1 Reach unnamed summit, el. 3050', then descend gently.

3.7 Reach north end of the Ivy Creek Overlook, SDMP 77.5. *Alert: The next 0.2m. of the AT may be relocated to eliminate the two Skyline Drive crossings. AT* passes along the overlook, parallels the Drive a few feet farther, then crosses to the right (west) of the Skyline Drive.

3.9 Cross to the left of the Skyline Drive, SDMP 77.7, and ascend unnamed peak, el. 3080', then descend.

4.4 Trail reaches excellent viewpoint, with Skyline Drive immediately below the Trail. (View covers an area from Trayfoot Mtn. on the left to Rockytop on the right.) *AT* continues to descend.

5.1 Cross Ivy Creek in a very lovely miniature canyon at an elevation of about 2550'. Trail now starts the ascent of Loft Mtn., the longest climb in this portion of the *AT,* climbing along the east bank of Ivy Creek for 0.2m., then bearing left away from it.

5.8 A spur trail leads right 0.1m. to the Ivy Creek Maintenance

NORTH TO SOUTH

Bldg. (no camping permitted) and a spring.

6.1 *AT* passes to right of the peak of Loft Mtn., about 3320', and follows crest of the ridge. For the next mile or so, as far as Big Flat Mtn., the *AT* passes through Patterson Field, an area that was once a large, 240 acre pasture. Now grass has been replaced by blackberry vines and other shrubby growth. Black locust now covers much of the land, but in the midst of the young woods stand several old oak trees with very large low-spreading branches, showing that these oaks gained their maturity while the land was still open pasture.

6.7 Panoramic (270°) view from the Trail. A short distance farther the Deadening Nature Trail (see Loft Mtn. inset, back of PATC Map No. 11), a Park Service trail, enters from the right and follows along the *AT*. (This interpretive trail starts from the Skyline Drive at the entrance to the Loft Mtn. Campground, SDMP 79.5, climbs to the *AT*, follows it south about 0.1m., then descends to its starting point.)

6.8 Deadening Nature Trail leaves *AT* here. *AT* begins descent toward sag between Loft and Big Flat Mtns.

7.4 *AT* crosses old road in sag. (To right, road leads to the paved Loft Mtn. Campground road. To left, road soon dead-ends.)

7.9 A spur trail leads right, uphill, to the Loft Mtn. Camp Store which is open "in season," generally mid-May through October. (Store carries a complete line of groceries. Adjoining laundromat is equipped with coin-operated washers, dryers and showers.) Trail climbs gently toward Big Flat Mtn., el. 3387'.

8.1 The *AT* circles clockwise around the Loft Mtn. Campground. Excellent views can be had, first to the east, then south and finally to the west, as the *AT* swings around the camping area located on summit of Big Flat Mtn. The Trail is almost level here. Cement posts at 8.5m. and 9.0m. mark side trails leading to the Loft Mtn. Campgrounds.

9.2 Cement post marks junction where a trail leads right 0.3m. to the Loft Mtn. Amphitheatre.

9.7 Here there is an excellent panoramic view: from left to right: Rockytop, Brown Mtn., Rocky Mtn., Rocky Mount, and, to right (east) of the Drive, Loft Mtn. *AT* continues to descend.

10.0 *AT* intersects the Doyles River Trail. (Skyline Drive,

SDMP 81.1, is 200 ft. to right. To reach northern end of Big Run Loop Trail at the Big Run Parking Overlook, go south on Drive for 250 ft. Big Run Loop Tr. leads west and south 4.2m. to its southern terminus on the *AT,* 11.6m.) (The Doyles River Trail leads down on the left of the *AT,* passing below the Doyles River Cabin and spring in 0.3m. Reservations for the use of this cabin must be obtained in advance from PATC Headquarters. See Chap. 6: ''Picnic Shelters, Huts and Cabins'' and Chap. 5: ''Side Trails.''.) From the Doyles River Tr. intersection the *AT* closely parallels the Skyline Drive and is relatively level.

10.9 Trail passes through the Doyles River Parking Overlook, SDMP 81.9.

11.1 Trail follows along ledges affording wintertime views south.

11.3 *AT* crosses to the right of the Skyline Drive, SDMP 82.2, with fine view of Cedar Mtn. and Trayfoot Mtn. from the Drive.

11.6 Junction with Big Run Loop Trail. (Big Run Loop Trail, 4.2m. long, runs from here to Big Run Parking Overlook, SDMP 81.1, near the Doyles River Trail.) Beyond junction, *AT* gradually descends.

12.2 Junction with the Madison Run Fire Road at a point 100 ft. to the right of the Skyline Drive, SDMP 82.9, el. 2599′, in Browns Gap. Junction is marked with cement post. (Madison Run Rd. leads west down Dundo Hollow to the Park boundary, 5.7m. and joins Va. Sec. 663 and 659 at a point 1.8m. from Grottoes on U.S. 340. East of the Drive the Browns Gap Fire Rd. leads beyond the Park boundary and becomes Va. Sec. 629.) Browns Gap was used several times by Gen. Stonewall Jackson during the Civil War's Valley Campaign.

SUBSECTION:
BROWNS GAP TO JARMAN GAP
NORTH TO SOUTH

15.1 miles (24.3 kilometers)   (PATC Map No. 11)

General description:

After crossing the Skyline Drive in Browns Gap, SDMP 82.9, el. 2599′, the *AT* passes along the east side of the Dundo Area

NORTH TO SOUTH

(used as an organized youth group campground April through October and as picnic grounds November through March). It then recrosses the Drive and climbs to Blackrock, a mammoth rock pile and one of the most interesting spots in the entire Shenandoah Park. The Trail then descends to Blackrock Gap, losing 750 ft. of elevation. From the gap it follows the crest of the Blue Ridge with a succession of short climbs and shorter dips, gradually rereaching an altitude of over 3000'. The final five miles of this section is primarily downhill all the way to Jarman Gap, el. 2173'.

This southern area of the Park, like the preceding section, Simmons Gap to Browns Gap, is quite wild and most of it is designated a Wilderness Area. Rhododendron, which is quite scarce in the Park, is found along the Riprap Trail and along the *AT* in the same general area. Mountain laurel (kalmia) is very plentiful in this area, especially along the Moormans River Fire Rd. east of the Drive from Blackrock Gap.

Side trails:

There are a number of very worthwhile side trails. Some lead to places of special scenic interest such as Riprap Ravine, Calvary Rocks, Trayfoot Mtn. and the falls on both Jones Run and Doyles River. The old Moormans River Fire Road, which was at one time the route of the *AT,* leads down the north fork of the Moormans River from Blackrock Gap and up the south fork to Jarman Gap. For more information refer to Chap. 5: "Side Trails," Southern Section; also the separate PATC publication: *Circuit Hikes in the Shenandoah National Park.*

Accommodations:

The Dundo Group Campground, SDMP 83.7, is reserved for organized youth groups from April through October. Reservations may be made with Park Headquarters (703) 999-2243. There is no store here and no shower or laundry facilities. The remainder of the year the Dundo area is operated as picnic grounds.

One open-faced hut, Blackrock Hut, 3.0m. (follow spur trail 0.2m.) is available for use by thru-hikers. (See Chap. 6: "Picnic Shelters, Huts and Cabins.")

Detailed Trail data:

0.0 Cement post marks junction of the *AT* and the Madison Run

Fire Road at a point 100 ft. to the west of the Skyline Drive, SDMP 82.9, el. 2599'. (Madison Run Rd. leads west down Dundo Hollow to Park boundary where it joins Va. Sec. 663 and 659 at a point 1.8m. from U.S. 340 at Grottoes. East of the Drive the Browns Gap Fire Rd. leads down into Browns Cove, crossing the Doyles River Trail in 1.7m. Both roads are gated at the Drive and Park boundaries.) The *AT* crosses diagonally to the left side of the Skyline Drive, then ascends gently.

0.4 The Trail skirts the east side of the Dundo Area, SDMP 83.7, for the next 0.2m. Several unmarked paths lead up to Dundo. Water is obtained there from April through October.

0.6 *AT* turns sharply left. A trail to right leads to Dundo.

1.2 Intersection with the Doyles River Trail. (To right, the Doyles River Tr. leads uphill 100 ft. to the Jones Run Parking Area; to the left, it descends Jones Run, then ascends Doyles River, intersecting the Browns Gap Road about halfway up, passing below the Doyles River Cabin, and recrossing the *AT* to reach the Skyline Drive, SDMP 81.1. Hiking distance along the Doyles River Trail, 4.6m.) The *AT* now passes through remnants of an old apple orchard.

1.4 Cross to right side of Skyline Drive, SDMP 84.3, and ascend very gently.

2.1 Here the *AT* and Trayfoot Mtn. Tr. come within a few feet of each other, then parallel but do not cross. (Trayfoot Mtn. Tr. leads back 250 yds. to the Skyline Drive, SDMP 84.7. This former fire road is the shortest approach to Blackrock from the Drive.) After about 0.1m. the *AT* bears right, away from the road, and circles the north, west, and south sides of Blackrock, el. 3092'. Blackrock is a tremendous mass of lichen-covered blocks of rock, piled haphazardly one upon another. The area is reminiscent of New Hampshire's White Mountain terrain above tree-line. The view from the rocks is excellent.

2.4 The blue-blazed Blackrock Spur Trail leads right from the *AT* at its highest elevation at Blackrock and follows the ridge leading to Trayfoot Mtn. (It comes into the Trayfoot Mtn. Tr. where that road (trail) reaches the ridge, about 0.2m. from the *AT*.)

2.5 *AT* crosses the Trayfoot Mtn. Tr. From here Trail descends

NORTH TO SOUTH

steadily toward Blackrock Gap, following along the east side of a narrow ridge. (An old road parallels the trail on the west side of the ridge, just out of sight of the trail.)

3.0 Spur trail, left, leads steeply down 0.2m. to Blackrock Hut. (Hut is located in a deep ravine. Spring is 10 yds. in front of hut. See Chap. 6: "Picnic Shelters, Huts and Cabins.") One hundred feet beyond spur trail, the *AT* crosses to west of the old road, parallels it for 0.2m., then comes into it and follows it on down to its intersection with the Skyline Drive.

3.5 Cross to the left of the Skyline Drive, SDMP 87.2, and continue along the east side of the Drive for a quarter mile.

3.7 Cross the Moormans River Fire Rd., yellow-blazed, in Blackrock Gap, SDMP 87.4, el. 2321'. (Moormans River Fire Rd. follows the north fork of the river down to the Charlottesville Reservoir where it meets Va. Sec. 614. From there the fire road climbs along the south fork of the river, reaching the Skyline Drive at Jarman Gap, hiking distance 9.4m. This fire road was at one time the route of the *AT*.) (On the west side of the Blackrock Gap, the Paine Run Tr., yellow-blazed, descends 3.7m. to the Park boundary at a point approximately 2m. from U.S. 340.) From the road intersection the *AT* climbs over a small knob, descends to a sag at 4.8m., with the Skyline Drive 50 ft. to the right. Trail now climbs over a second small knob.

5.5 Trail crosses to right of Skyline Drive, SDMP 88.9, in a sag, then climbs.

6.2 At summit of a knob, el. 2988', reach junction with blue-blazed Riprap Trail. (Riprap Tr. leads west to Calvary Rocks, 1.0m. and on down Cold Spring Hollow and Riprap Hollow to its lower end on the Crimora Fire Rd., 4.5m. The lower end of the Wildcat Ridge Tr., also blue-blazed, is on the Riprap Tr. about 0.9m. from its lower end. The Wildcat Ridge Trail intersects the *AT* in 2.6m. The Riprap Tr. and Wildcat Ridge Tr., along with the 3.1m. stretch of *AT*, make an excellent circuit hike of about 9.3m.) From junction, *AT* descends rather steeply.

6.6 A graded trail, left, leads 300 ft. down to Riprap Parking Area on the Skyline Drive, SDMP 90.0. Trail continues to descend steeply for another 0.1m., then more gradually. For the next two miles Trail alternately climbs and dips gently. There is occasional rhododendron (Catawba) here. It is found in only a few other places in the SNP.

9.3 Intersection with Wildcat Ridge. (To left Wildcat Ridge Trail leads 0.1m. to Skyline Drive at the Wildcat Ridge Parking Area, SDMP 92.1. To right, it follows the Wildcat Ridge west, then drops down into Riprap Hollow ending on the Riprap Tr. From junction with Wildcat Ridge Tr., *AT* ascends gently.

9.6 *AT* crosses to left of Skyline Drive, SDMP 92.4, and continues to ascend, reaching a summit, el. 3080', in 0.5m. Beyond summit there are wintertime views of peaks in the George Washington National Forest, Pedlar District, south of Rockfish Gap. Trail descends to a slight sag, reclimbs to about the same elevation, then descends fairly steeply toward Turk Gap.

11.6 A cement post near the Skyline Drive marks the start of the Turk Branch Tr., yellow-blazed, left of the *AT*. (Turk Branch Tr. leads down the mountain 2.4m. to the South Fork of the Moormans River Fire Rd.) *AT* now crosses to the right side of the Skyline Drive at Turk Gap, SDMP 94.1, el. 2610'. (Turk Gap Tr., yellow-blazed, leads down the west slope of the Blue Ridge for 1.6m. to the Park boundary near the old Crimora mines.)

11.8 The Turk Mtn. Tr., blue-blazed, leaves the *AT*, right, and follows along a side ridge which shortly divides into two ridges, one Turk Mtn., the other Sawmill Ridge. The hiker will find the 1.1 m. side trip to the top of Turk Mtn. via the blue-blazed Turk Mtn. Trail well worth his time. See Chap. 5: "Side Trails." 250 ft. beyond the trail junction the *AT* reaches crest and starts long gentle descent.

13.2 Cross to left of Skyline Drive, SDMP 95.3, in a deep sag at the north edge of Sawmill Run Parking Overlook. Trail now climbs. Looking backwards while ascending, there are views of Turk Mtn., Sawmill Ridge and the city of Waynesboro.

13.8 Reach summit of unnamed hill, el. 2453'. As Trail starts to descend there are views to the east of Bucks Elbow Mtn.

14.2 Cross grass-covered pipeline diagonally to the right. Continue to descend.

14.6 Reach South Fork of the Moormans River, a small creek here, and follow up the creek along its west bank to its source.

14.9 Cross Moormans River Fire Road. (Road leads right 0.1m.

NORTH TO SOUTH

to Skyline Drive at Jarman Gap, SDMP 96.8, el. 2173'. To left it follows down the South Fork of the Moormans River to the Charlottesville Reservoir, then ascends the North Fork of the Moormans River.) 200 ft. farther, pass spring on left of *AT*, then climb.

15.1 Reach Bucks Elbow Mtn. Fire Road, 100 yds. east of the Skyline Drive, SDMP 96.8, and end of this section of *AT*. (To right, road leads to Skyline Drive at its intersection with the Moormans River Fire Rd. in Jarman Gap. To left it leads out of the Park along the ridge of Bucks Elbow Mtn. to a radio tower. A branch of the road leads down the Lickinghole Hollow and becomes Va. Sec. 611.) (West of the Drive the former Jarman Gap Fire Rd. has been totally abandoned and is covered with scrubby growth.)

SUBSECTION:
JARMAN GAP TO ROCKFISH GAP
NORTH TO SOUTH

8.0 miles (12.9 kilometers)　　　　　　　(PATC Map No. 11)

General description:

The route of the *AT* from Jarman Gap to Rockfish Gap is within a corridor of land recently purchased by the National Park Service except for a short stretch on Calf Mtn. south of Jarman Gap. From Jarman Gap the *AT* climbs Calf Mtn., descends to Beagle Gap, where it crosses the Skyline Drive, climbs over Bear Den Mtn., drops to McCormick Gap, where it recrosses the Drive, climbs up Scott Mtn., then slabs along the west side of the ridge as it gradually drops toward Rockfish Gap. Descending steeply to the Skyline Drive just before reaching the Gap, it follows the Skyline Drive bridges over Interstate 64 and U.S. 250, where the section ends, as does the Drive, at milepost 105.4. For continuation of the *AT* south see PATC Map No. 12.

Much of the Trail's route is bare of trees, so views are excellent, but caution is needed in following the Trail in rain, snow, or fog. Rock outcrops on the summits in this section consist of green shale, rather than greenstone, the basaltic rock so predominant along the ridge crest in the SNP.

APPALACHIAN TRAIL DATA

Side trails:
   None other than old roads.

Accommodations:
   Gasoline, restaurant, and lodging facilities are available at Rockfish Gap and in Waynesboro 4 miles northwest via U.S. 250. The Calf Mtn. Shelter, completed in 1984 by the PATC, is available for use by *AT* backpackers.

Detailed Trail data:
   Start of this section is on the Bucks Elbow Mtn. Fire Road, about 0.1m. east of the Skyline Drive in Jarman Gap, SDMP 96.8, el. 2175′. (Bucks Elbow Mtn. Fire Rd. is the more southerly of the two roads that intersect at the Skyline Drive. The other is the Moormans River Fire Rd.)

   0.0 From Bucks Elbow Mtn. Fire Rd., ascend southward.

   0.5 Pass under power lines.

   0.7 Cross abandoned road.

   1.1 Side trail leads right to a spring, 0.2m., and Calf Mtn. Shelter (completed during summer of 1984) 0.3m.

   1.2 Trail comes into the open and follows pasture road through grass and staghorn sumac.

   1.5 Reach cairn marking summit of Calf Mtn., el. 2974′. Continue along the ridge.

   2.2 *AT* passes to left of second peak of Calf Mtn., el. 2910′. Trail now descends.

   2.5 Cross Skyline Drive in Beagle Gap, SDMP 99.5, el. 2532′. Trail now ascends open slopes of Bear Den Mtn.

   3.1 Reach summit, el. 2885′. (A police radio installation here.) Continue past a second summit, el. 2810′.

   4.3 Cross Skyline Drive in McCormick Gap, SDMP 102.1, el. 2434′. From the Gap, climb stile and follow a dirt road a few feet, then turn right from the road and ascend steeply through brush and locust trees.

   4.5 Trail ceases to climb and begins to slab along the west side of the ridge, just below the ridge crest.

   5.6 Come into old trail and follow it south.

   6.1 Come into another old trail and continue south.

   6.3 Pass through gate. Shortly beyond this point pass a trail leading west, then another gate.

6.8 Pass through a third gate.

7.2 Trail to right leads 0.2m. to the Southern Entrance Station of Skyline Drive.

7.8 Reach Skyline Drive and follow the Drive south.

8.0 End of section at south end of Skyline Drive, on bridge over U.S. 250, in Rockfish Gap, SDMP 105.4, el. 1902'. (For description of *AT* south of Rockfish Gap see *Guide to the Appalachian Trail in Central and Southwestern Virginia* and PATC Map No. 12.)

SUMMARY OF DISTANCES ALONG THE *AT*
Section VIII Southern

	Miles	**Kilometers**
Swift Run Gap	0.0	0.0
Hightop Hut	3.4+0.1	5.5+0.2
Smith Roach Gap, Skyline Drive crossing	4.7	7.6
Powell Gap, Skyline Drive crossing	6.3	10.1
Simmons Gap, Skyline Drive crossing	9.6	15.4
Pinefield Hut	11.7+0.1	18.7+0.2
Ivy Creek Overlook, S. Drive	13.3	21.3
Ivy Creek Maintenance Building	15.4+0.1	24.7+0.2
Loft Mtn. Camp Store	17.5	28.1
Doyles River Trail (near north end of Big Run Loop Trail)	19.6	31.5
Doyles River Cabin	19.6+0.3	31.5+0.4
Big Run Loop Tr.	19.6	31.5
Big Run Loop Trail, south end	21.2	34.0
Browns Gap, Skyline Drive crossing	21.8	35.0
Doyles River Trail south end	23.0	36.9

Blackrock	24.2	38.9
Blackrock Hut	24.8+0.2	39.8+0.3
Blackrock Gap—Moorman's River Fire Road	25.5	41.0
Riprap Trail	28.0	45.0
Wildcat Ridge Trail	31.1	50.1
Turk Gap, Skyline Drive crossing	33.4	53.7
Skyline Drive crossing just north of Sawmill Ridge Overlook	35.0	56.3
Jarman Gap, *AT* 0.1m. east of Skyline Drive	36.9	59.3
Calf Mtn. Shelter	38.0+0.3	61.8+0.5
Beagle Gap, Skyline Drive crossing	39.4	63.4
McCormick Gap, Skyline Drive crossing	41.2	66.3
Rockfish Gap, end of Section VIII	44.9	72.3

SUMMARY OF DISTANCES BY SKYLINE DRIVE TO POINTS ON *AT*
Section VIII Southern

	SDMP	from Swift Run N to S	from Rockfish Gap S to N
Swift Run Gap	65.5	0.0	39.9
Smith Roach Gap	68.6	3.1	36.8
Powell Gap	69.9	4.4	35.5
Simmons Gap	73.2	7.7	32.2
Pinefield Gap	75.2	9.7	30.2
Ivy Creek Overlook	77.5	12.0	27.9
Loft Mtn. Developed Area (1.3m. to *AT* thru campground)	79.5	14.0	25.9
Doyles River Trail and Doyles River Cabin Parking (200 ft. to *AT*)	81.1	15.6	24.3
Doyles River Parking Overlook	81.9	16.4	23.5
Browns Gap	82.9	17.4	22.5
Doyles River Trail (south end 100 ft. to *AT*)	84.1	18.6	21.3
Trayfoot Mtn. Tr., closest auto approach, 0.1m. to *AT*)	84.7	19.2	20.7
Blackrock Gap	87.4	21.9	18.0
Riprap Trail Parking Area 300 ft. to *AT*	90.0	24.5	15.4
Wildcat Ridge Trail Parking Area, 0.1m. to *AT*	92.1	26.6	13.3
Turk Gap	94.1	28.6	11.3
Sawmill Run Parking Overlook	95.3	29.8	10.1
Jarman Gap, 0.1m. to *AT*	96.8	31.3	8.6
Beagle Gap	99.5	34.0	5.9
McCormick Gap	102.1	36.6	3.3
Rockfish Gap	105.4	39.9	0.0

SECTION VIII SOUTHERN SHENANDOAH PARK
ROCKFISH GAP TO SWIFT RUN GAP
SOUTH TO NORTH

44.9 miles (72.3 kilometers)　　　　　　　　(PATC Map No. 11)

Section VIII of the Appalachian Trail begins in Rockfish Gap where U. S. 250 (and Interstate 64) meet the Skyline Drive at its southern end (and the Blue Ridge Parkway at its northern end). Rockfish Gap is four miles east of Waynesboro via U. S. 250 and 22 miles west of Charlottesville (and about 140 miles from Washington, D.C.). The highway junction is 105.4m. from the northern end of the Skyline Drive in Front Royal. Distance covered by the *AT* from Rockfish Gap to U. S. 522 just north of the Park is 106.6 miles (171.6 kilometers). Section VIII ends at Swift Run Gap where U. S. 33 crosses the Blue Ridge and intersects the Drive, SDMP 65.5. Swift Run Gap is 7m. east of Elkton, 8 miles west of Stanardsville and about 111 miles from Washington, D.C.

The National Park Service has purchased a corridor of land through which the 8.0 mile stretch of Appalachian Trail from Rockfish Gap to Jarman Gap passes except for a short distance over the northernmost summit of Calf Mtn. There are open areas on both Bear Den Mtn. and Calf Mtn. along the Trail route.

From Jarman Gap to Swift Run Gap the Trail follows the ridge crest, crossing the Skyline Drive frequently. The southern section of the Park is the wildest and the least developed. Much of it lies in an area officially designated *Wilderness*. There are many interesting side trails and fire roads in this section that can be used either alone or in conjunction with the *AT* for interesting hiking trips.

Loft Mountain Campground facilities include showers, coin laundry and camp store, as well as campsites and a picnic area. It is closed in winter. Dundo, from April through October, is open only for camping of organized youth groups and reservations are needed. Make reservations at Park Headquarters (703) 999-2229. In the winter this area is open only for picnicking. Doyles River Cabin, a locked structure, can be rented by hikers; reservations must be made at PATC Headquarters. See Chap. 6: "Picnic Shelters, Huts and Cabins."

Section VIII has been divided for convenience into four subsections: Rockfish Gap to Jarman Gap, Jarman to Browns Gap, Browns to Simmons Gap, and Simmons to Swift Run Gap.

Maps:
PATC Map No. 11. Also available are the USGS map of Shenandoah National Park, Southern Section 1969, scale 1:62,500 and the USGS 7½' quads: Waynesboro East, Crimora, Browns Cove, McGaheysville, and Swift Run Gap. (Other 7½' quads, covering areas on the southern section of the Park not traversed by the *AT*, include Crozet, Grottoes and Elkton East.)

SUBSECTION:
ROCKFISH GAP TO JARMAN GAP
SOUTH TO NORTH

8.0 miles (12.9 kilometers)　　　　　　　(PATC Map No. 11)

General description:
Except for a short distance over the northern summit of Calf Mtn. utilized by the *AT* with the owner's permission, the Appalachian Trail from Rockfish Gap to Jarman Gap is located entirely within a corridor of land recently purchased by the National Park Service. Much of the route is bare of trees so views are excellent, but caution is needed in following the Trail in rain, snow or fog. Rock outcrops on the summits in this section consist of a green shale, rather than greenstone, the basaltic rock so predominant along the ridge crest in the Shenandoah Park itself.

This section of Trail starts at the south end of the Skyline Drive Overpass over U. S. 250 and follows along the east side of the Drive, passing over Interstate 64 and continuing along the Drive for another tenth mile where it turns right, away from the road, and ascends steeply at first. It then slabs the western side of the ridge, staying well below the ridge crest but far above Skyline Drive. A short (0.2m.) blue-blazed trail leads to the Park Entrance Station where a self-registration station for backcountry camping is located.

The *AT* crosses the Skyline Drive in McCormick Gap. It then climbs over Bear Den Mtn. (good views), drops into Beagle Gap where it recrosses the Drive, climbs over Calf Mtn. (more good

Side trails:
  None other than old roads

Accommodations:
  Gasoline, lodging and restaurant facilities are available at Rockfish Gap and in Waynesboro 4 miles northwest via U. S. 250.
  A shelter for long distance hikers is located 0.3m. off the *AT* near the summit of Calf Mtn.

Detailed Trail data:
  0.0 Skyline Drive at south end of overpass over U.S. 250 in Rockfish Gap, SDMP 105.4, el. 1902′. Trail follows the footway along the right (east) side of the Drive.
  0.1 Cross over Interstate 64, utilizing the Skyline Drive overpass. Continue along the right side of the Drive.
  0.2 At cement post and *AT* trail marker, turn right away from the Drive. Ascend steeply.
  0.8 A trail leads left 0.2m. down to the Southern Entrance Station of Shenandoah National Park. Backpackers can obtain camping permits here.
  1.2 Pass through gate.
  1.7 Pass through second gate. In a few feet pass a trail leading west; then pass through a third gate.
  1.9 At trail junction avoid the right fork.
  2.4 At another trail junction avoid the right fork.
  3.5 Trail starts to descend.
  3.7 Cross Skyline Drive in McCormick Gap, SDMP 102.1, el. 2434′. Ascend through pine thicket, then across open land, along the ridge of Bear Den Mtn.
  4.9 Reach bare summit of Bear Den Mtn., el. 2885′. (Police radio installation here.) Trail now descends northeastward.
  5.5 Cross Skyline Drive in Beagle Gap, SDMP 99.5, el. 2532′. Trail now ascends Calf Mtn.
  5.8 Pass slightly to the right of the first peak of Calf Mtn., el. 2910′.
  6.4 Reach the open summit of Calf Mtn., el. 2974′. Descend through staghorn sumac and grass.
  6.9 A blue-blazed trail leads to spring (0.2m.) and the Calf Mtn. Shelter (0.3m.).

SOUTH TO NORTH

7.3 Cross abandoned road.
7.5 Pass under two power lines.
8.0 Reach Bucks Elbow Mtn. Fire Rd. at a point on the road 0.1m. east of the Skyline Drive at Jarman Gap, SDMP 96.8, el. 2175'.

SUBSECTION:
JARMAN GAP TO BROWNS GAP
SOUTH TO NORTH

15.1 miles (24.3 kilometers)   (PATC Map No. 11)

General description:
  This section starts at the intersection of the *AT* with the Bucks Elbow Mtn. Fire Road at a point about 100 yds. east of the Skyline Drive in Jarman Gap, SDMP 96.7. The Trail first descends along the South Fork of the Moormans River from its source for a short way, then climbs to the crest of the main ridge of the Blue Ridge, which it continues to follow for the most part throughout this section. It crosses the Skyline Drive at a number of points. Much of this section of the Park is in a wilderness area. There are a number of side trails, some of which, like the Riprap and Wildcat Ridge Trails, can be used along with the *AT* for interesting circuit hikes. Blackrock, a tumbled mass of large lichen-covered blocks of stone, is interesting in itself and also affords splendid views. The *AT* skirts the east side of Dundo shortly before reaching Browns Gap.

Accommodations:
  There is one developed area, Dundo, SDMP 83.7, used from April through October as an organized youth group campground for which reservations should be made at SNP Headquarters. There is a camping fee of $10.00 per group site (maximum of 20 persons per site). The remainder of the year Dundo is open only for picnicking. There are no shower or laundry facilities here and no store. Water is available from April through October.
  The first open-faced hut that is reached within the SNP and is available for the use of thru-hikers is Blackrock Hut, 12.1m. (plus

0.2m. along spur trail). It is the only one along this subsection of the *AT*. See Chap. 6: "Picnic Shelters, Huts and Cabins."

Side trails:

This is one of the wildest areas of the Park. There are a number of very worthwhile side trails. Some lead to places of special scenic interest such as Riprap Ravine, Calvary Rocks, Trayfoot Mtn., and the falls on both Jones Run and Doyles River. The old Moormans River Road, which was at one time the route of the *AT*, leads from Jarman Gap down the south fork of the Moormans River and up the north fork to Blackrock Gap. Refer to Chap. 5: "Side Trails," Southern Section; also the separate PATC publication: *Circuit Hikes in the Shenandoah National Park.*

Detailed Trail data:

To reach the *AT* at Jarman Gap, follow the Bucks Elbow Mtn. Fire Road east from the Skyline Drive, SDMP 96.9, el. 2173', for 0.1m. (Bucks Elbow Mtn. Fire Rd. and the Moormans River Fire Road intersect right at the east side of the Drive, the Bucks Elbow Mtn. Fire Rd. being the more southerly one.)

0.0 Junction of *AT* with Bucks Elbow Mtn. Fire Rd. Trail descends.

0.2 Pass spring on right of the *AT*. 100 yds. farther, cross the Moormans River Fire Rd. Continue descent along the west bank of the South Fork of the Moormans River at its upper end.

0.5 Here the *AT* leaves the creek and ascends unnamed hill. Partway up it crosses diagonally to the right a grass-covered pipeline area.

1.3 Reach summit of the hill, el. 2453'. Looking backwards, toward the east, is a view of Bucks Elbow Mtn. Then, as Trail begins to descend, there are forward views of Turk Mtn., Sawmill Ridge and the city of Waynesboro.

1.9 *AT* crosses to the left of the Skyline Drive, SDMP 95.3, in a sag at the north edge of Sawmill Run Parking Overlook.

3.3 Trail reaches summit of knob, 2650'; 250 ft. farther along the *AT* the Turk Mtn. Trail, blue-blazed, leads left 0.9m. to the summit of Turk Mtn. (This is a very worthwhile side trip for *AT* hikers.)

3.5 Reach Turk Gap, el. 2625', SDMP 94.1. (Here the

SOUTH TO NORTH

yellow-blazed Turk Gap Tr. leads west, down the mountain. This former road is permanently blocked at the western Park boundary.) *AT* crosses to the east side of the Skyline Drive here. A cement post marks the junction of the *AT* with the Turk Branch Trail, also yellow-blazed. (This trail leads right from the *AT* for 2.4m. to end on the South Fork of the Moormans River Fire Rd.) Trail ascends 400 ft., dips gently, then ascends to a second summit with about the same elevation as the first. There are backward views in winter of peaks in the George Washington National Forest, Pedlar District, south of Rockfish Gap. Trail now descends.

5.5 *AT* crosses to the west side of the Skyline Drive, SDMP 92.4.

5.8 Junction of *AT* and Wildcat Ridge Trail, blue-blazed. (Wildcat Ridge Tr. leads east 0.1m. to Skyline Drive, SDMP 92.1, and west 2.6m. to its terminus on the Riprap Tr., also blue-blazed. One can follow the Riprap Tr. north and east to rejoin the *AT*. The Wildcat Ridge–Riprap Trail loop, with both ends on the *AT*, is 6.2m.) *AT* continues along west side of ridge crest, passing through one of the few areas in the SNP having any rhododendron.

8.3 Here Trail ascends steeply for half a mile around slope of Riprap Hollow.

8.5 A graded trail to right leads 300 ft. down to Riprap Parking Area on the Skyline Drive, SDMP 90.0.

8.9 Reach summit of knob, el. 2988'. Riprap Trail comes in from the left. *AT* now descends.

9.6 In a sag, cross to the right of Skyline Drive, SDMP 88.9. *AT* now climbs over a small knob.

10.3 Trail comes into a sag with Skyline Drive 150 ft. to left. *AT* now climbs a second knob, then descends steadily.

11.4 Cross the Moormans River Fire Rd. in Blackrock Gap, SDMP 87.4, el. 2329'. From here Trail continues along east side of Drive for a quarter mile.

11.6 *AT* crosses to left (west) of Drive, SDMP 87.2. It now ascends along an old road for 0.2m., then angles off slightly to the left of the road and parallels it.

12.1 Trail crosses to the east of the old road. One hundred feet beyond, a graded trail leads right, steeply down, for 0.2m. to the Blackrock Hut. (Hut is located in a very deep ravine. Spring is 10 yds. in front of the shelter.) *AT* continues to ascend along east side of ridge. (The old road parallels it on Trail's left, just out of sight along the ridge crest.)

12.6 Junction with the blue-blazed Trayfoot Mtn. Tr. Three hundred feet farther, the *AT* starts circling around Blackrock, el. 3092′, a curious mass of dark lichen-covered blocks heaped upon each other. It is reminiscent of terrain above tree-line on Mt. Washington. Views are excellent here.

12.7 A graded trail leads left from the *AT* along the ridge leading to Trayfoot Mtn. (It joins the Trayfoot Mtn. Tr. where the latter reaches the ridge, about 0.2m. from the *AT*.)

12.9 Here the *AT* and the Trayfoot Mtn. Tr. come within a few feet of each other but do not cross. They are parallel for about 0.1m. Then the *AT* bears off to the left. (The blue-blazed trail leads out 750 ft. to the Skyline Drive, SDMP 84.7. This is the shortest approach to Blackrock from the Drive. There is parking space for several cars a few hundred feet up this road from the Drive.)

13.7 Cross to right side of Skyline Drive, SDMP 84.3. From here Trail passes through remnants of an old apple orchard.

13.9 Junction with the Doyles River Trail. (To left of *AT*, uphill, trail leads to the Jones Run Parking Area, SDMP 84.1; to the right the Doyles River Tr. descends Jones Run, then ascends Doyles River, passing below the Doyles River Cabin and recrossing the *AT* to reach the Skyline Drive, SDMP 81.1. Hiking distance along Doyles River Trail, 4.7m.) From junction *AT* continues with little change in elevation.

14.4 *AT* turns sharply to the right, while a trail straight ahead leads to Dundo Developed Area (in summer used for organized youth group camping, in winter a picnic ground), SDMP 83.7. *AT* skirts the east side of the developed area. Several unmarked trails lead left to this area. (Water available at Dundo April through October.) Beyond Dundo, Trail descends gently.

15.1 Trail reaches Browns Gap, where the Skyline Drive intersects the old Browns Gap Rd. Here *AT* crosses Drive, SDMP 82.9, el. 2599′. (The Doyles River Trail is 1.4m. east, downhill, via the old Browns Gap Rd.; this road continues outside the Park eventually becoming Va. Sec. 629 about a mile before reaching Va. Sec. 810 at Browns Cove. From Browns Cove it is 11m. to Crozet and 12.5m. to U. S. 250 via Va. Sec. 810 and 18m. north to Stanardsville and U. S. 33, also via Va. Sec. 810. The Madison Run Rd., west of the Drive, leads down Dundo Hollow to the Park boundary at junction of Va. Sec. 663 and 659, 1.8m. from Grottoes. Both the Browns Gap Rd. and the Madison Run Rd. are gated at the Skyline Drive and at the Park boundaries.)

SUBSECTION:
BROWNS GAP TO SIMMONS GAP
SOUTH TO NORTH

12.2 miles (19.6 kilometers)　　　　　　(PATC Map No. 11)

General description:

This part of the Trail starts at its junction with Madison Run Road about 100 ft. west of the Skyline Drive, SDMP 82.9, in Browns Gap. (On the east side of the Drive this road is called the Browns Gap Road.) The *AT* at Browns Gap is 23.1m. by Trail from Rockfish Gap and 21.8m. from Swift Run Gap.

The elevation of the *AT* at Browns Gap is 2599'. The trail reaches elevations of 3300' and above in the area of Big Flat Mtn. (where the Loft Mtn. Campground is located) and Loft. Mtn., drops to 2550' where it crosses Ivy Creek, gains 500 ft., then loses it again to reach Pinefield Gap, climbs over Weaver Mtn., then descends to Simmons Gap at 2253'. For a mile south of the peak of Loft Mtn. the Trail passes through considerable open area; otherwise it is heavily wooded. The *AT* crosses the Drive several times and comes within a few hundred feet of it in a few other places.

A roughly triangular area between the ridges of Rockytop, Brown Mtn. and Loft Mtn. and drained by tributaries of Big Run comprises the largest watershed in the Park, about eleven square miles.

Accommodations:

The Loft Mtn. Developed Area includes a wayside, campground, picnic grounds, and camp store with shower and laundry facilities—also a nature trail. Campground and other facilities are generally open May through October. (Exception: store open mid-May-October.)

Along the *AT* in this subsection one open-faced shelter, Pinefield Hut (10.1m.), is available for use by thru-hikers.

One locked cabin is available, the Doyles River Cabin, 0.4 mile from the *AT*, (2.2m.). Reservations for the use of this cabin must be obtained in advance from PATC Headquarters. See Chap. 6: "Picnic Shelters, Huts and Cabins."

Side trails:

This region has several side trails which provide an opportunity for making interesting circuit hikes, the Doyles River Trail and the Big Run Loop Trail being the chief ones. See Chap. 5: "Side Trails:" Southern Section.

Detailed Trail data:

0.0 Browns Gap. (Gen. Stonewall Jackson used this gap several times during the Valley Campaign of the Civil War.) Start of this section of *AT* is at junction with the Madison Run Rd. (the western portion of the old Browns Gap Rd.) about 100 ft. to the left (west) of the Skyline Drive in Browns Gap and is marked by a cement post, SDMP 82.9, el. 2599'. Trail ascends gaining 250 ft. altitude, then levels off.

0.6 From the *AT* graded Big Run Loop Trail, blue-blazed, leads off to the left for 4.2m. to reach its northern trailhead at the Big Run Parking Overlook, SDMP 81.1.

0.9 *AT* crosses to the right of the Skyline Drive, SDMP 82.2, with fine view of Cedar Mtn. and Trayfoot Mtn.

1.1 Trail follows along ledges affording wintertime views south.

1.3 Trail passes through Doyles River Parking Overlook, SDMP 81.9.

2.2 *AT* intersects the Doyles River Trail. (Skyline Drive is 200 ft. to left, SDMP 81.1. Follow Drive south for 250 ft. to reach northern end of Big Run Loop Tr. at the Big Run Parking Overlook. Doyles River Trail leads down on the right of the *AT*, passing below the Doyles River Cabin in 0.3m. See Chap. 6:

SOUTH TO NORTH

"Picnic Shelters, Huts and Cabins.") *AT* now ascends Big Flat Mtn., el. 3389'.

2.5 There is an excellent panoramic view here of, from left to right: Rockytop, Brown Mtn., Rocky Mountain, Rocky Mount, and, to the right (east) of the Drive, Loft Mtn.

3.0 Cement post marks junction where a side trail leads left toward the Loft Mtn. Amphitheatre, 0.3m. *AT* now skirts the southern and eastern edges of the Loft Mtn. Campground for about a mile. There are a number of good views along this stretch; at first, views are to the west, then south, and finally due east. Cement posts at 3.2m and 3.7m. mark side trails leading left to the campground.

4.3 From the *AT* a trail leads left, uphill, to the Loft Mtn. Camp Store which is open mid-May through October. (Store carries a complete line of groceries. Laundromat, with coin-operated washers, dryers, and showers, adjoins store.) For the next mile or so, as far as the summit of Loft Mtn., the Trail passes through Patterson Field, an area that was once a large, 240 acre pasture. Now the grass has been replaced by berry vines, other shrubby growth and black locust trees. But in the midst of the young woods stand several old oak trees with very large lowspreading branches indicating that these oaks gained their maturity while the land was still pasture.

4.8 Trail crosses old road. (To left, road leads to paved road to Loft Mtn. Campground. To right, road soon dead-ends.)

5.4 Reach crest of Loft Mtn. ridge. Here a trail enters the *AT* from the left. (The Deadening Nature Tr., which starts from the Skyline Drive at the entrance to the Loft Mtn. Campground, SDMP 79.5, enters the *AT* at this point, follows it north about 0.1m., then descends to its starting point. See inset, back of PATC Map No. 11.) Along the *AT*, about 150 ft. beyond the junction, is an excellent 270° panoramic view.

6.1 Trail passes slightly to left of the peak of Loft Mtn., el. about 3320', then starts descending toward Ivy Creek.

6.4 From the *AT* a trail leads left 200 yds. to Ivy Creek Maintenance Bldg. and spring. The *AT* continues to descend, following the right bank of Ivy Creek.

7.1 Trail crosses Ivy Creek, very picturesque here, at an elevation of about 2550' It then ascends.

7.8 Trail reaches an excellent viewpoint showing an area from Trayfoot Mtn. on the left to Rockytop on the right. Skyline Drive is immediately below the Trail here. *AT* continues to ascend for 0.2m., then descends. *Alert: AT may be relocated here to eliminate the Skyline Drive crossings just ahead.*

8.3 *AT* crosses to the left of the Drive, SDMP 77.7, then in 0.1m. recrosses it.

8.5 Trail reaches the south end of the Ivy Creek Overlook, SDMP 77.5. It passes along the Overlook, then ascends gently for a half mile.

9.1 *AT* reaches summit of hill, el. 3080', then descends through patches of white pine, interspersed with areas of locust and young oak.

9.5 At a spot where the *AT* turns sharply to the right, an unmarked trail leads left approximately 200 ft. to the Skyline Drive. (From here one can follow the Drive north a few feet to reach the Onemile Run Trail, or continue 0.1m. farther to reach the Twomile Run Parking Overlook, and another 0.2m. to reach the start of the Rocky Mount Trail, SDMP 76.1.)

9.9 *AT*, still descending, again comes within a hundred feet of the Drive.

10.1 *AT* crosses access road to Pinefield Hut. Twenty yards to the right of the *AT* along this road is a spring. (Hut is 0.1m. on down the road. There is another spring about 250 ft. behind the shelter.)

10.3 *AT* crosses to left of Skyline Drive at Pinefield Gap, SDMP 75.2. Trail now ascends, winding through sparse, scraggly woods, primarily black locust.

11.1 Reach top of Weaver Mtn. Trail descends along the northwestern side of the ridge.

12.2 *AT* reaches Simmons Gap at the junction of the Simmons Gap Fire Rd. and Skyline Drive, SDMP 73.2, el. 2253' (A short distance to the south on the fire road is the Ranger's residence and beyond it are the Park Service maintenance facilities. Water available here. The Simmons Gap Rd. is gated on both sides of the Drive and at the Park boundaries. Outside the Park, on both east and west sides of the Drive, the road becomes Va. Sec. 628.)

SOUTH TO NORTH

SUBSECTION:
SIMMONS GAP TO SWIFT RUN GAP
SOUTH TO NORTH

9.6 miles (15.4 kilometers) (PATC Map No. 11)

General description:

This part of the *AT* starts at Simmons Gap at the junction of Simmons Gap Fire Road and the Skyline Drive, SDMP 73.2. The Simmons Gap Road becomes Va. Sec. 628 outside the Park on both east and west sides. The road is gated on both sides of the Drive and at the Park boundaries. (To the west Rt. 628 leads 10m. past Beldor on to U. S. 33. To the east Rt. 628 leads 5.8m. to Va. Sec. 810.)

From Simmons Gap the *AT* climbs a ridge on the east side of the Skyline Drive, then descends to Powell Gap where it crosses the Drive. It then climbs, skirting the south and east sides of Roundtop Mtn. and crosses again to the east of the Drive in Smith Roach Gap. From here it ascends steadily to the top of Hightop Mtn. Open ledges to the west of the summit afford excellent views south and west. The Trail now descends the north slope of Hightop by switchbacks. It crosses the Drive in a sag and continues on through scraggly woods to Swift Run Gap where U. S. 33 (Spotswood Trail) crosses the Blue Ridge.

Swift Run Gap, SDMP 65.5, el. 2367', is 39.8m. from Rockfish Gap and 34.0m. from Thornton Gap via the Skyline Drive; it is 6 miles from Elkton and about 110 miles from Washington, D.C.

Accommodations:

There are no public accommodations along this section. The nearest public lodgings are at Lewis Mtn., SDMP 57.5, but these are closed during the winter. There is no gas or food available at Swift Run Gap.

There is one open-faced hut, Hightop Hut, 6.1m., along this section that is available for camping by thru-hikers. See Chap. 6: "Picnic Shelters, Huts and Cabins."

Side trails:

Because the Shenandoah Park is very narrow in this area, there are few side trails, and these lead out of the Park.

Detailed Trail data:

0.0 *Alert: Watch for a relocation of the AT here to bypass the Ranger Station.* Begin intersection of Simmons Gap Fire Road and Skyline Drive, SDMP 73.2, el. 2253'. *AT* follows Simmons Gap Rd. east of the Drive for about 40 ft., then turns left onto path.

0.3 *AT* turns slightly left to follow old road. (To the right the road leads down to the Simmons Gap Ranger Station, formerly the Simmons Gap Episcopal Mission.) Two-tenths of a mile farther, the Trail turns slightly left off the old road but parallels it.

0.9 *AT* turns sharply left while the old road continues straight ahead. Trail continues to ascend.

1.5 Near top of rise there is open field about 50 ft. to right of the Trail and beyond a wire fence. There are views, especially of Flattop Mtn., 3325', from the field but not from the *AT*.

1.6 Reach summit of a shoulder of Flattop Mtn. Trail continues along northern ridge crest.

2.8 Excellent views of the Roach River Valley (Bacon and Powell Gap Hollows) from rock ledges just to the side of the Trail. *AT* descends gradually.

3.0 Turn sharply right onto well-worn trail, a former road, leaving the old road bed, now overgrown, in 0.1m. Continue descent.

3.3 Reach Powell Gap, SDMP 69.9, el. 2294', and cross to left of Drive. Trail crosses grass and angles along edge of woods. It then ascends the west slope of Little Roundtop Mtn.

3.8 Summit of Little Roundtop Mtn. is 50 yds. to left of the *AT* here. Trail continues along the ridge crest, then swings around the south and east sides of Roundtop Mtn., affording wintertime views of Powell Gap and Flattop Mtn. Trail now continues with little change in elevation.

4.9 Cross to right of Skyline Drive in open Smith Roach Gap, SDMP 68.6, el. 2622'. From the Drive the *AT* parallels the Smith Roach Gap Fire Road, a few feet to the right of this road, for about

300 ft. Then the *AT* crosses the road and ascends steadily through woods.

6.1 Cross the Hightop Hut service road. (On left of the *AT*, the service road leads to Hightop Hut; to the right it leads to the Smith Roach Gap Fire Rd. at a point 0.8m. from the Skyline Drive.)

6.2 From the *AT* a trail leads left 0.1m. to Hightop Hut. (Spring is 400 ft. downhill from hut on graded trail.)

6.7 There is a piped, covered spring at the foot of a large boulder just to the right of the *AT*. Trail continues to ascend.

6.8 From the *AT* a trail leads to the right 350 ft. to site of former Park Service Lookout Tower at the summit of Hightop Mtn., el. 3587'. There is no view from the summit now. One hundred feet farther along the *AT* there is an excellent view from ledges to the left of the Trail. Shortly farther along the Trail there is a second good viewpoint. Beyond, the Trail descends sharply, veering first to the east, then switchbacking down the north slope of the mountain.

8.3 Trail crosses to left (west) of Skyline Drive in grassy sag, SDMP 66.7, el. 2637'. *AT* continues along former farm road, ascending slightly, passing through the remains of an old apple orchard, then descending.

9.5 Trail turns sharply right on an old road which comes in from the left. It follows this road for a few feet only, then climbs to its right. Just beyond, the Trail drops steeply down to the highway bridge which carries the Skyline Drive over U. S. 33. *AT* follows pedestrian footway along edge of bridge.

9.6 Reach cement signpost marking the *AT*. It is located on the east side of the Drive, about 300 ft. north of the bridge and directly opposite the place where the entrance road from U. S. 33 reaches the Skyline Drive in Swift Run Gap, SDMP 65.5, el. 2376'.

SUMMARY OF DISTANCES ALONG THE *AT*
Section VIII Southern

	Miles	Kilometers
Rockfish Gap	0.0	0.0
McCormick Gap, Skyline Drive crossing	3.7	6.0
Beagle Gap, Skyline Drive crossing	5.5	8.9
Calf Mtn. Shelter	6.9 + 0.3	11.1 + 0.5
Jarman Gap	8.0	12.9
Sawmill Ridge Overlook Skyline Drive crossing	9.9	15.9
Turk Gap, Skyline Drive crossing	11.5	18.5
Trail junction	13.8	22.2
Riprap Trail junction	16.9	27.2
Wildcat Ridge Blackrock Gap, Moormans River Fire Rd.	19.4	31.2
Blackrock Hut	20.1 + 0.2	32.4 + 0.3
Blackrock	20.7	33.3
Doyles River Trail, south end	21.9	35.3
Browns Gap, Skyline Drive crossing	23.1	37.2
Big Run Loop Trail, south end	23.7	38.2
Doyles River Trail, north end (near north end, Big Run Loop Tr.)	25.3	40.7
Doyles River Cabin	25.3 + 0.3	40.7 + 0.4
Loft Mtn. Camp Store	27.4	44.1
Ivy Creek Overlook, Skyline Drive	31.6	50.9
Pinefield Hut	33.2 + 0.1	53.4 + 0.2
Simmons Gap, Skyline Drive crossing	35.3	56.8
Powell Gap, Skyline Drive crossing	38.6	62.1

Smith Roach Gap, Skyline Drive crossing	40.2	64.7
Hightop Hut	41.5 + 0.1	66.7 + 0.2
Swift Run Gap, end of Section VIII	44.9	72.2

For summary of distances by Skyline Drive to points on the *AT* see end of Section VIII, North to South.

SECTION VII CENTRAL SHENANDOAH PARK
SWIFT RUN GAP TO THORNTON GAP
SOUTH TO NORTH

34.3 miles (55.2 kilometers) (PATC Map No. 10)

The section starts at Swift Run Gap, SDMP 65.6, where U.S. 33 crosses the mountain. Swift Run Gap is 7m. east of Elkton, 8m. west of Stanardsville (108m. from Washington, D.C.). The northern end of Section VII is at Thornton Gap, SDMP 31.5, where U.S. 211 crosses the Blue Ridge. Thornton Gap (Panorama) is 9m. east of Luray and 7m. West of Sperryville (83m. from Washington, D.C.).

The Blue Ridge crest is higher in this section of the Park than in either the southern or northern section. The *AT* reaches its highest point in the Park on Hazeltop, el 3816', about 4m. south of Big Meadows Campground. The Skyline Drive itself reaches its maximum elevation, 3680', right at the northern entrance to Skyland. The highest peak in the Park, Hawksbill, has an elevation of 4050'.

The central part of the Shenandoah Park is the part most widely used by the motoring public, by campers, and by hikers. The *AT* is heavily used, as are the chief side trails. Favorite short hikes include the Stony Man Trail—*AT* loop, the Dark Hollow Falls Trail and the Limberlost Trail. Longer favorites are the Whiteoak Canyon Trail, the trails up Old Rag Mtn., the trails over Hawksbill, and the stretch of *AT* from Thornton Gap to Marys Rock. There are also special trails for horseback riding, with stables at

Skyland and at Big Meadows. (Wagon rides but no horseback riding at Big Meadows.)

Two large campgrounds, Lewis Mountain and Big Meadows (the latter open all year except Jan. & Feb.), are located in the area. Skyland, Big Meadows, and Lewis Mountain also offer lodging for 350, 200 and 25 persons, respectively. For complete information on tourist facilities at these places and for reservations write to the ARA Virginia Sky-line Co., Inc., Box 727, Luray, Va. 22835.

The Skyland resort antedates the Shenandoah Park, having been developed by George Freeman Pollock, with its beginning in the 1880's. Camp Hoover, developed when Herbert Hoover was President of the USA (1929-33), is on the eastern slopes of the Blue Ridge near Big Meadows. It is now managed by the Park Service but is still reserved for use by presidential guests. For more information about the history of this area read "Skyland Before 1900" by Jean Stephenson in the July, 1935 PATC Bulletin and the books, *Skyland,* by George Freeman Pollock (Washington, Judd and Detwiler, 1960) and *Herbert Hoover's Hideaway* by Darwin Lambert (Shenandoah Natural History Assoc. Inc., Luray, Va. 1971).

For convenience Section VII is divided into 3 subsections: Swift Run Gap to Fishers Gap, Fishers Gap to Skyland, and Skyland to Thornton Gap.

Maps:

PATC Map No. 10; also available are the USGS map of the Shenandoah National Park, Central Section, 1969, scale 1:62,500, and USGS 7½' quads, scale 1:24,000 for: Thornton Gap, Old Rag, Big Meadows, Fletcher, Elkton East, and Swift Run Gap. (USGS quads that cover parts of the central section not traversed by the *AT* include those of Luray, Washington, Va., Stanley, Madison, and Stanardsville.)

APPALACHIAN TRAIL DATA

SUBSECTION:
SWIFT RUN GAP TO FISHERS GAP
SOUTH TO NORTH

18.6 miles (30.0 kilometers) (PATC Map No. 10)

General description:

From the intersection of the Skyline Drive and the entrance road from U.S. 33 in Swift Run Gap, el. 2367', the *AT* climbs, soon coming into an old road which it follows over a spur of Saddleback Mountain. The Trail skirts the South River Picnic Grounds, then starts a long gradual ascent over Baldface Mountain, el. 3600'. It loses 500 ft. of altitude to reach the gap beyond Pocosin Cabin. The *AT* skirts the east side of the Lewis Mountain Campground, passes a very scenic area on Bearfence Mountain, then, beyond Bush Mountain, descends to Bootens Gap. North of Bootens Gap the *AT* reaches its highest elevation in the Park, 3816', on Hazeltop. At Milam Gap the *AT* crosses to the west of the Drive. It then skirts the west and north edges of the Big Meadows Campground before reaching Fishers Gap, el. 3061'.

Side trails:

The South River Falls Trail is short, but steep and very scenic. An excellent circuit hike can be made using this trail, the South River Fire Road, Pocosin (Horse) Trail, Pocosin Fire Road, and return via the *AT*.

In the Big Meadows Area there are many trails and a number of popular circuit hikes, the Dark Hollow Falls-Rose River Loop-*AT* circuit is probably the favorite one. Trails and a fire road lead down from the Drive and the *AT* to Camp Hoover located in the Park on the Rapidan River. The Camp Hoover area is one of the few places in the SNP where one can find Rosebay rhododendron (R. maximum) growing. Many blue-blazed and yellow-blazed trails, fire roads and other old roads and trails beckon the hiker. Unblazed trails and roads may be overgrown or may "give out" deep in the woods so they should be traveled only by the experienced woodsman/woodswoman.

Accommodations:

The Lewis Mountain Developed Area has picnic grounds, camp store and a campground; a few cabins are available. The Area is closed from November until mid-April. The Big Meadows Area includes a large campground, picnic grounds, both lodge and cabins, stables (wagon rides only), a wayside, and the Byrd Visitor Center. The visitor center is open throughout the year; cabins and campground are closed in Jan. & Feb. Reservations for lodging can be made with the ARA Virginia Sky-Line Co., Inc., Box 727, Luray, Va. 22835.

The Bearfence Mtn. Hut, 9.3m., is available for use by *AT* thru-hikers. In addition, one locked structure, Pocosin Cabin, 6.6m., is found on this stretch of Trail. A second cabin, the Jones Mountain Cabin, is located on the eastern slopes of the Blue Ridge, about 4m. "as the crow flies" from the *AT* on Bush Mtn. For the use of these cabins, reservations must be obtained in advance from PATC Headquarters. (See Chap. 6: "Picnic Shelters, Huts and Cabins.")

Detailed Trail data:

0.0 A signpost on the eastern side of the Skyline Drive in Swift Run Gap, SDMP 65.5, el. 2367', at a point where the entrance road from U.S. 33 joins the Drive, marks the start of this section of the *AT*. From here Trail ascends through the woods.

0.3 *AT* passes under power line.

0.7 Trail turns right onto old road which it follows over Saddleback Mountain, passing west of the summit, for a distance of about 2 miles.

1.4 Saddleback Mtn. Tr., blue-blazed, leads right from *AT* for 1.1m. to the South River Maintenance Bldg. (spring nearby) and on another 0.3m to end on the *AT*.

1.9 Still following the old road, the *AT* reaches the top of the rise just west of the westernmost peak of Saddleback Mtn., el. 3296'. One will find trillium blooming here in profusion in early May. Trail now descends.

2.1 At sharp left bend in the *AT* an old road comes in from the right.

2.5 At junction of old roads, the *AT* follows the left fork. The right fork is the Saddleback Trail. (There is a spring on this trail in 0.3m.)

2.7 *AT* turns right off the old road and passes through a pine woods. (Road bears left and leads 0.1m. to Skyline Drive, SDMP 63.1.) *AT* now skirts the east side of the South River Picnic Grounds.

3.0 Cross the graded South River Falls Trail. (To left trail leads 0.1m. to picnic grounds. Water available here "in season". To right of the *AT* the trail leads steeply downhill for 1.5m. to lovely South River Falls.)

3.5 Cross South River Fire Road. (To right road leads down toward South River Falls. About a mile from the *AT* a road leads right from the fire road down to the South River at a point 0.1m. below the falls. The South River Falls Trail utilizes the lower part of this road. A foot trail leads up to the falls. The South River Fire Rd. itself swings northeast at the road intersection and in another mile the Pocosin (Horse) Trail enters it from the left. From here the road descends, becoming Va. Sec. 642 outside the Park. To left of the *AT* the fire road leads 0.2m. to the Skyline Drive, SDMP 62.7, el. 2960'. Across the Drive here the Dry Run Falls Fire Rd. leads 2.6m. down the west slope of Deans Mountain to Va. Sec. 625.) From the South River Fire Rd. intersection the *AT* begins a long gentle ascent of Baldface Mountain.

4.4 Cross old road which leads, right, past an old quarry. (To left road leads past the site of a former CCC camp 0.1m. to the Drive, SDMP 61.8.)

4.8 Rocks to left of the Trail offer views to the west.

5.1 Reach summit of Baldface Mtn., el. 3600', and descend gently.

5.9 *AT* here passes through a relatively flat area known as Kites Deadening, now completely wooded. (A deadening was an area where the early settlers, instead of felling the trees for a field, saved time and effort by just ringing the trees, removing the lower bark, to kill the trees without the task of removing them. They would then plant their crops amid the "deadened" trees.)

6.0 Trail descends steeply, by switchbacks, for 0.1m.

6.3 Spur trail leads right, downhill, 250 ft. to Pocosin Cabin and to spring south of the cabin. (Pocosin Cabin, el. 3120', is a locked structure. Reservations for its use must be obtained in advance from PATC Headquarters. See Chap. 6: "Picnic Shelters, Huts and Cabins." From the cabin there is a fine view east over the Conway River Valley. Three mountains can be seen across the valley. The local mountaineers called these, from right to left: Panther, Bear Stand and Sawney Macks; these names are not shown on today's maps. The word "Pocosin" is said to be of Indian derivation meaning a "dismal" or swamp.) Beyond spur trail *AT* descends gently.

6.4 Cross Pocosin Fire Road. (To left fire road leads 0.1m. to Skyline Drive, SDMP 59.5. To right, the fire road leads downhill passing Pocosin Cabin in 0.1m. About 0.8m. farther along the fire road, the Pocosin Horse Trail leads right from the road approximately 1.3m. south to intersect the South River Fire Rd., making an excellent loop trail possible. Another 0.3m. down the fire road the Pocosin Hollow Tr. leads left and descends the mountain. See Chap. 5: "Side Trails"; also PATC Map No. 10.)

7.5 Where *AT* is close (30 ft.) to the Drive, an old road leads right from the *AT* descending toward Pocosin Hollow. *AT* soon ascends.

8.1 Pass trail intersection. (To left a trail leads to Lewis Mountain Campground. To the right the Lewis Mtn. East Tr., blue-blazed, leads along the ridge crest of Lewis Mtn., then disappears. (There are plans to extend this trail to the Park boundary, also to build a trail connecting it with the Slaughter Tr. and Pocosin Hollow Tr.)

8.2 A post marks a trail, left, leading 300 ft. to Lewis Mtn. Campground. (Water fountain "in season" directly across camp road here. A camp store is located on road. Across the Skyline Drive from the entrance to the Lewis Mtn. Campground, SDMP 57.5, the Lewis Mtn. West Tr., blue-blazed, leads 3m. down to Va. Sec. 625 at a point about 8m. from Elkton. *Alert! The lower half of this trail may be rerouted to end on Meadow School Rd.)* *AT* now descends gently. Several paths, unmarked, lead left to camping area and then the picnic area of Lewis Mtn. Water available "in season".

9.1 Spur trail, right, leads downhill 0.2m. to Bearfence Mtn. Hut. Spring 50 ft. to right of hut. (See Chapter. 6: "Picnic

SOUTH TO NORTH

Shelters, Huts and Cabins.'')

9.2 In gap cross the Slaughter Tr., yellow-blazed. (It is gated just to the right of the Trail. About 0.1m. beyond the gate an access road leads right 0.2m. to Bearfence Mtn. Hut. The Slaughter Tr. continues 3.8m. to join the Conway River Fire Rd. at the Park boundary. Left of the *AT* road leads to the Drive, SDMP 56.8. On west side of Drive, the old road continues as the Meadow School Fire Rd. and descends to Va. Sec. 759.) *AT* now ascends steeply, by switchbacks, the southwest slope of Bearfence Mtn.

9.8 Junction with Bearfence Loop Trail which leads right. (Views on this short trail are very rewarding. Loop Tr. is only 150 ft. longer than the stretch of *AT* between the junctions.)

10.0 Loop Trail reenters *AT* from the right.

10.2 Cross blazed trail. (To left, trail leads 0.1m. to the Bearfence Mtn. Parking Area on the Skyline Drive, SDMP 56.4. Here hikes led by a SNP naturalist start during the summer. To the right of the *AT* an unimproved trail leads to spectacular jagged rocks of Bearfence Mtn.; they offer excellent views. This rough trail requires the use of hands in some places. It connects with the loop trail over Bearfence Mtn., the two trails making a rough figure eight with the *AT*.) Beyond the intersection the *AT* remains rather level for 0.3m., then descends gradually along the western slope of Bush Mtn.

10.7 *AT* approaches within 150 ft. of the Drive. Trail continues to descend for another 0.2m., then levels off and finally climbs again gently for 0.2m.

11.6 In Bootens Gap, el. 3243′, cross old road, the Conway River Fire Road. (Skyline Drive, SDMP 55.1, is 150 ft. to left, with parking space for two cars. To right, the fire road leads down the Conway River, becoming Va. Sec. 667 outside the Park. Rt. 667 comes into Va. 230 3m. north of Stanardsville.) *AT* now starts ascent of Hazeltop Mtn.

12.0 Pass blue-blazed Laurel Prong Trail on right. (Laurel Prong Tr. leads down 2.8m. to Camp Hoover. It passes through one of the few areas in the Park where rosebay rhododendrons (R. maximum) grow. About 1m. from the *AT* the Laurel Prong Tr. passes through Laurel Gap. Here the Cat Knob Tr. leads right, up Cat Knob, to end on the Jones Mtn. Tr.) *AT* continues to ascend.

12.5 Cross wooded summit of Hazeltop, el. 3812', highest point on the *AT* in the SNP. *AT* now descends gently.

13.0 Along a level area of the *AT* there is a fine stand of stiff gentians, mixed with purple and white asters, each autumn. Beyond this area the *AT* again descends.

14.0 Trail bears left, due west. From a rock to right of the *AT* at this turn is a good wintertime view of Doubletop and Fork Mtns. (Former President Hoover's Camp is in the Rapidan Valley between these peaks.)

14.4 Come into overgrown field. A cement post marks the Mill Prong Trail leading right from the *AT*. (This trail, of which the first 1.0m. is blue-blazed, leads 1.8m. to Camp Hoover. The latter 0.8m. of the trail is coincident with the Mill Prong Horse Trail.) A few feet farther, just south of Milam Gap, the *AT* crosses the Skyline Drive, SDMP 52.8. (This is the only crossing of the Drive in the central section of the Park.) Cross a field and enter woods.

15.3 Pass a spring 50 ft. to right of the *AT*.

15.5 Cross Tanners Ridge Fire Road. (To right, the fire road leads 0.1m. to the Drive, SDMP 51.6. To left, it leads down the mountain becoming Va. Sec. 682 outside the Park.) Cross open field with cemetery to the left. Here are fine views, back, of Hazeltop.

15.7 Cross Tanner Ridge Horse Trail. Cross the horse trail again in about 0.1m. Ascend gradually.

16.1 Pass outlet of housed-in Lewis Spring. Immediately beyond, cross Park service road. (To left of the *AT* the road leads down to a sewage disposal area. To reach Lewis Falls follow the road down for about 150 ft. to a small pumphouse on right of road. Turn left off the road here, onto a footpath that continues downhill 0.5m. to the falls.) (To the right of the *AT* the road leads about 0.3m. to the Skyline Drive, SDMP 51.4, 0.1m. south of the Big Meadows Wayside. Lunches are available at the wayside. Here too is located the Harry F. Byrd Sr. Visitor Center.) *AT* ascends steadily along west slope of ridge with occasional views from rocks to the left of the Trail.

16.5 Trail to right of *AT* leads 0.1m. to Blackrock Viewpoint and 0.2m. farther to Big Meadows Lodge. 0.2m. farther along the *AT*, pass under the sheer cliffs of Blackrock.

SOUTH TO NORTH

17.0 Trail intersection marked by two cement posts, *AT* is straight ahead. (Trail to left leads back 1.2m. to Lewis Falls. The Lewis Falls Tr. and *AT* together offer a 3.1m. circuit hike. To right of *AT*, a trail leads up to the Amphitheatre and Picnic Grounds. One can follow the exit road here as far as the campground registration office; then turn right and in a short distance take the Story of the Forest Nature Tr. left for 0.6m. Here a short spur trail leads to the Skyline Drive across from Dark Hollow Falls Parking Area.) *AT* now passes below the Big Meadows Amphitheatre.

17.1 A trail leads right 0.1m. to the Amphitheatre and Picnic Parking Area of Big Meadows. *AT* now skirts the northwestern and northern edge of the ridge.

17.3 Cross over small rocky knob, the Monkey Head, where there are views. Beyond *AT* skirts the north edge of the Big Meadows Campground. Several small unmarked trails lead right to the camping area. Openings along the *AT* give fine views north and west. (Hawksbill Mtn. in the foreground, Stony Man Mtn. farther away and, in the distance, Knob Mtn., The Neighbor, and across the Page Valley can be seen Signal Knob at the north end of the Massanutten range.)

17.6 A trail leads right from the *AT* coming into the Story of the Forest Tr. in 0.8m. (See Big Meadows inset on back of PATC Map No. 10.) 50 ft. to left of *AT* at the trail junction is David Spring. *AT* now descends. Pass through beautiful hemlock grove.

18.4 Pass to left of split rock.

18.5 Spur trail leads right 100 ft. to Fishers Gap Parking Overlook on the Skyline Drive.

18.6 Intersection with Red Gate Fire Road, 350 ft. west of the Skyline Drive, just north of the Fishers Gap Parking Overlook, SDMP 49.3, el. 3061'. (To left, fire road (gated) leads 4.8m. down the mountain to Va. Sec. 611 at a point about 4m. from Stanley. Across the Drive, the Rose River Fire Rd. (also gated) leads 6.5m. down the mountain, crossing, in 1.0m., Hogcamp Branch a few hundred feet below the Dark Hollow Falls. Also here is the northern end of the Dark Hollow Falls Loop Trail. See Chap. 5: "Side trails," Central Section. Also refer to PATC Map No. 10 and PATC publication: *Circuit Hikes in the Shenandoah National Park.*)

SUBSECTION:
FISHERS GAP TO SKYLAND
SOUTH TO NORTH

6.3 miles (10.1 kilometers) (PATC Map No. 10)

General description:

Most of the Blue Ridge in this area was at one time covered by a series of lava flows. Today this lava, in its present form of greenstone, is the rock seen in the various rock outcrops along the Skyline Drive and along the Appalachian Trail in this section. On the west side of the ridge, where the slope is very steep, the old layers of lava show as a series of vertical cliffs, one above another. The route of the *AT* at Franklin Cliffs, along Hawksbill, below Crescent Rocks (and farther north along Stony Man Mtn.) follows along shelves below one series of cliffs and above another, thus affording a very rugged and photogenic section of Trail.

Hawksbill Mtn. is the highest in the Park. The *AT* slabs along the northwestern slope of Hawksbill but side trails lead to the summit, el. 4050'. Red spruce and balsam fir are native at high elevations from Hawksbill to Stony Man Mtn. just north of Skyland. They do not grow along the *AT* north of this area until one reaches Vermont! (They do grow farther south but at much higher elevations and are found along the *AT* in SW Virginia on Mt. Rogers, el. 5729', and White Top nearby.)

Side trails:

The summit of Hawksbill Mtn. can be reached by several routes. The lovely Whiteoak Canyon-Cedar Run circuit hike is in this area. East of the main ridge of the Blue Ridge the rock-sculptured top of Old Rag Mountain beckons hikers. For details of these and other side trails see Chap. 5: "Side Trails", Central Section.

Accommodations:

The Big Meadows Developed Area, SDMP 51.2, (see PATC Map No. 10, inset on the back), just south of Fishers Gap, offers meals and lodging for 200 persons. It also contains a wayside, stables (wagon rides only), the Byrd Vistor Center, and a tremendous camping area with the standard facilities for campers—store, laundry, showers, etc. Big Meadows campground is open all year except Jan. & Feb. Public accommodations are also available at Skyland (See PATC Map No. 10, inset on back) from mid-April through November. The lodge and cottages can accommodate 350 persons. A stable is maintained here and a network of horseback trails are in the area. For information and lodging reservations write to the ARA Virginia Sky-Line Co., Inc., Box 727, Luray, Va. 22835.

One open-faced shelter, Rock Spring Hut, 1.9m., is available for the use of *AT* thru-hikers. Byrds Nest #2 (trails at both 2.2m. and 3.2m. lead about 1m. to the shelter which is located near the top of Hawksbill Mtn.) may be used for picnicking but not for camping. Considerably east of the Drive are two additional shelters, Byrds Nest #1, on the western ridge of Old Rag Mtn. and the Old Rag Shelter, 0.4m. SE of the junction of the Old Rag Rd. and Weakley Hollow Rd. via the Saddle Tr. up Old Rag Mtn. They are available for picnicking only. (See PATC Map No. 10 and Chap. 5: ''Side Trails'', Central Section; also Chap. 6: ''Picnic Shelters, Huts and Cabins''.)

One locked cabin, Rock Spring, 1.2m. (spur trail to cabin 0.2m.) is also available. Reservations for its use must be obtained in advance from PATC Headquarters. (See Chap. 6: ''Picnic Shelters, Huts and Cabins.'')

Detailed Trail data:

0.0 Intersection of the *AT* and the Red Gate Fire Road in Fishers Gap. (To the west, the fire road leads 4.8m. down the mountain to Va. Sec. 611 about 4m. east of Stanley. To the right of the *AT* the road leads 350 ft. to the Skyline Drive at a point just north of Fishers Gap Parking Overlook, SDMP 49.3, el. 3061 ′. The road through Fishers Gap was once the Gordonsville Turnpike. Across the Drive the road, now called the Rose River Fire Rd. on the east side of the Drive, leads 6.5m. down the mountain, in 1.0m. crossing Hogcamp Branch a few hundred feet below Dark Hollow Falls. Also at Fishers Gap is one end of the Rose River-Dark Hollow Falls Loop Trail. See Chap 5: ''Side Trails,'' Central Section; also PATC publication: *Circuit Hikes in the Shenandoah National Park.)*

0.2 Pass post marking spur trail, right, leading uphill 0.1m. to the south end of Franklin Cliffs Overlook, SDMP 49.0, el. 3135'. From here *AT* passes below the Franklin Cliffs, along a ledge above more cliffs. (Cliffs, composed of altered basaltic rock, are the result of the erosion of ancient lava beds, laid down in layers 100 to 250 ft. thick for a total thickness of two to three thousand feet and later tilted about 90°.)

0.5 Post marks obscure trail, right of the *AT*, which leads 0.3m. to the north end of the Franklin Cliffs Overlook. 100 ft. farther along the *AT* there is a wet weather spring 15 ft. to the left of the Trail. *AT* continues to slab along the west side of the ridge.

1.3 Spur trail, right, marked by post, leads 150 ft. uphill to Skyline Drive at Spitler Knoll Parking Overlook, SDMP 48.1, nearest parking spot for users of Rock Spring Cabin. *AT* now gradually ascends, passing old road at 1.5m. Trail soon levels off, then descends gently.

1.9 *AT* comes into a slightly open area. Here post marks spur trail which leads left 0.2m. downhill to Rock Spring Hut, for the use of thru-hikers, and Rock Spring Cabin, a locked building. (For its use, reservations must be obtained in advance from PATC Headquarters. See Chap. 6: ''Picnic Shelters, Huts and Cabins.'') A spring is 150 ft. north of the cabin. Twenty feet farther along the *AT* an old road, which serves as Park access road to the cabin, leads 0.2m. to the Drive, SDMP 47.8. The *AT* passes along an old orchard rapidly being overgrown with pine, sumac, and locust.

2.2 Reach sag between Hawksbill Mtn. and Nakedtop. (To right, trail leads 0.9m. to top of Hawksbill Mtn., highest point in the SNP, el. 4050 ft. Byrds Nest # 2, an open-faced shelter (picnicking only), is located just below the summit.) From the sag the *AT* slabs along the northern face of Hawksbill, passing below steep cliffs. Note balsam fir growing here. There are good views north of Ida Valley and Luray, and views ahead of Crescent Rock, Stony Man and Old Rag Mountain.

3.2 Reach Hawksbill Gap and a trail intersection. (To left, a trail leads down 0.1m. to a spring. To right, a trail leads uphill 300 ft. to Hawksbill Gap Parking Area on the Drive, SDMP 45.6, el. 3361'. On the east side of the drive here is the start of the Cedar Run Trail. (From the Hawksbill Gap Parking Area, the Hawksbill

SOUTH TO NORTH

Trail leads steeply uphill 0.8m to Byrds Nest #2 and the summit, el. 4050'. From the summit, the Hawksbill Tr. descends southward to the Upper Hawksbill Parking Area on the Drive, SDMP 46.7. The Nakedtop Tr. also starts at the shelter and descends the west ridge of Hawksbill, ending on the *AT* in 0.9m. See Chap. 6: "Picnic Shelters, Huts and Cabins.")

3.6 The *AT* passes under the cliffs of Crescent Rock. These, like those of Franklin Cliffs, are the eroded remnants of ancient lava beds.

3.7 A side trail, marked by cement post, leads right, uphill, 0.1m. to near the north end of the Crescent Rock Parking Overlook, SDMP 44.4, coming into a short trail, 0.3m., leading from the Overlook north to Bettys Rock. (In crannies along the exposed rocks of Bettys Rock one may find the three-toothed cinquefoil, a northern plant, blooming in late spring and early summer.)

4.5 Pass piped spring 4 ft. right of the *AT*.

4.6 Spur trail, right, leads uphill 300 ft. to Timber Hollow Parking Overlook on the Drive, SDMP 43.3. From the trail junction the *AT* parallels the Drive, passing through a thicket of mountain laurel, blooming time early June. Trail then ascends by switchbacks toward Pollock Knob, el. 3560'. There are good views here of Hawksbill Mtn. and Ida Valley.

5.0 Reach top of ridge with splendid views of Hawksbill Mtn. and Ida Valley. Trail now follows cliffs along the west side of Pollock Knob, with fine views west. From here Trail ascends slightly, then follows the corral fence to Skyland stables.

5.7 Horse trail leads right to Skyline Drive and beyond to Whiteoak Canyon and on to Big Meadows. The *AT* continues ahead and crosses the paved road at the stables, then proceeds through woods.

6.1 At top of hill reach paved road on open Skyland grounds. At the road, 200 ft. left of the *AT* crossing, the Millers Head Trail goes left. (Excellent views are available at the end of the 0.8m. Millers Head Trail. It is well worth the side trip.)

6.3 Come into paved path, where signboard marks route of the *AT*. This is the end of the subsection. (*AT* continues straight ahead on paved path. To right, the path leads 75 ft. to Skyland Dining Hall.)

SUBSECTION:
SKYLAND TO THORNTON GAP
SOUTH TO NORTH

9.4 miles (15.1 kilometers) (PATC Map No. 10)

General description:

This section is especially scenic. From Skyland the Trail passes through beautiful woods of white pine and then hemlock. It then skirts the cliffs along the west edge of Stony Man, following the original Passamaquoddy Trail constructed by George Freeman Pollock, founder of Skyland. Along Stony Man, as at Franklin Cliffs, the cliffs were formed by the erosion of layer upon layer of ancient lava. Beyond, the *AT* swings around the head of Nicholson (Free State) Hollow paralleling the Skyline Drive. The Trail route crosses the edge of the Pinnacles Picnic Grounds, then passes below the Jewell Hollow Overlook. From here the Trail climbs over The Pinnacle, el. 3730′, then follows the narrow ridge crest to the southern end of the Marys Rock outcrop. Here the *AT* starts its long steady descent, 1200 ft., to Thornton Gap. A spur trail leads to the northern tip of Marys Rock with its outstanding panoramic views. *AT* passes below Panorama Restaurant in Thornton Gap reaching U.S. 211 about 0.1m. west of the Skyline Drive.

There are no dependable springs along the *AT* in this subsection. Piped water is available "in season" at the Byrds Nest #3, the Pinnacles Picnic Area, and the Stony Man Mtn. Parking Overlook. The springs at Meadow Springs and Shaver Hollow are each 0.3m. downhill from the *AT*.

Side trails:

The Park is wide on the east side of the Drive in this area and there are many trails. In addition to the trails in the Skyland area, including the very popular *AT*-Stony Man Trail loop, there is one network of trails centered around Nicholson (Free State) Hollow and Corbin Cabin and another one, overlapping the first, that covers the "Hazel Country", that section near the Hazel River and Hazel Mountain. For details see Chap. 5: "Side Trails," Central Section.

SOUTH TO NORTH

Accommodations:

Skyland has an excellent restaurant, also a lodge and cottages which can accommodate 350 guests. A stable is maintained here and there is a network of horse trails in the area. At Panorama, in Thornton Gap, there is also a restaurant, closed in winter. Gasoline is available here. Nearest public campground is at Big Meadows, SDMP 51.2, about 9 miles south of Skyland.

There are no huts available for camping in this subsection. Byrds Nest #3, 3.0m., may be used for picnicking only. One and a half miles east of the Drive, SDMP 37.9, via the Corbin Cabin Cut-Off Tr., is Corbin Cabin, an old mountaineer cabin restored and maintained by the PATC. It is available for use by hikers but reservations must be made in advance at PATC Headquarters. See Chap. 6: "Picnic Shelters, Huts and Cabins."

Detailed Trail data:

0.0 This subsection of *AT* starts at wooden signboard at junction of paths about 75 ft. below the Dining Hall of Skyland (near northern entrance to Skyland, SDMP 41.7). At this junction the *AT*, coming from the south, comes into the paved Skyland path and follows it straight ahead. (To right, the paved path leads uphill to dining hall.) A few feet forward along the Trail, at a sharp bend to the left on the paved route, a spur trail leads right. (This trail leads to service road in the dormitory area of Skyland. Road can be followed uphill toward north entrance of Skyland, to where the Stony Man Trail begins. From the *AT* via this route, the Stony Man Cliffs are 0.9m., and Little Stony Man 1.3m. This route has steeper grades than the *AT* and is 0.2m. longer but must be taken if the summit of Stony Man, el. 4011', is to be reached. Little Stony Man Trail rejoins the *AT* in 1.5m. at a point on the *AT* 1.3m. from start of the section.)

0.1 Turn sharp right away from paved path. Continue through woods.

0.2 Cross paved Skyland road and descend through grove of old white pines and hemlock.

0.3 Turn right onto road at signpost. In 200 ft. turn into footpath. On the right of the *AT* the Furnace Spring Tr. leads 0.5m. uphill to its junction with the Stony Man Horse Tr. at the Stony

Man Nature Tr. Parking Area, at northern entrance to Skyland. (Road, which was the original road to Skyland, continues, left, downhill, for 3m. to the "foot of the mountain". Road is gated at Park boundary, where it becomes Va. Sec. 672, about 8m. from Luray.) *AT* now passes through beautiful hemlock grove.

0.4 Pass Skyland power line and housed Furnace Spring 25 ft. to right of trail. From here the route of the *AT* as it skirts around Stony Man and Little Stony Man Mtns. is a slight relocation of George Freeman Pollock's original Passamaquoddy Trail built in 1932. ("Passamaquoddy" is a Maine Indian word signifying "abounding in pollock".) This bit of *AT* is exceptionally beautiful as it follows the base of rocky cliffs and passes by hugh hemlock trees.

1.3 Little Stony Man Trail comes in on right. *AT* descends by switchbacks.

1.6 Spur trail, right, leads 150 ft. to Little Stony Man Parking Area on Skyline Drive, SDMP 39.1. *AT* drops well below the Drive, then parallels it, clinging to the steep western slopes of the main ridge. Trail route affords spectacular views of Page Valley, the Massanutten Range, New Market Gap and Luray. To the southeast is a near view of Little Stony ManCliffs and the "profile" of Stony Man Mtn.

2.0 Spur trail, right, leads 200 ft. to south end of Stony Man Mtn. Parking Overlook in Hughes River Gap, SDMP 38.6, el. 3097'. Drinking water and toilets here. *AT* now ascends.

2.4 Trail junction. (To right, the blue-blazed Nicholson Hollow Trail leads 0.1m. to Skyline Drive, SDMP 38.4, then crosses it diagonally and continues down into Nicholson Hollow, passing Corbin Cabin in 1.9m. See Chap. 5: "Side Trails", Central Section. Trail to left of *AT* here soon dead-ends.)

2.6 Intersection with the blue-blazed Crusher Ridge Tr. (This trail utilizes an old road known as Sours Lane. To left, the trail leads along Crusher Ridge, then descends into Shaver Hollow to near Va. Sec. 669. To right, the trail ends on the Nicholson Hollow Trail a few feet from the Skyline Drive.) *AT* descends, then passes over a slight rise and descends again.

3.2 To left a trail leads downhill 0.3m. to a spring near the location of the former Shaver Hollow Shelter. To right of the *AT* a

SOUTH TO NORTH

trail leads 150 ft. to Skyline Drive at a parking area, SDMP 37.9. Across the Drive here the Corbin Cabin Cut-Off Trail leads 1.5m. to Corbin Cabin and the Nicholson Hollow Trail. (See Chap. 6: "Picnic Shelters, Huts and Cabins".) From the intersection, the *AT* ascends.

3.3 Where *AT* switchbacks sharply to the left there is an excellent viewpoint. The *AT* is immediately above the Skyline Drive here and offers an unobstructed view of Nicholson (Free State) Hollow and Old Rag Mountain beyond. (The mountaineers who once lived in Nicholson Hollow were reputed to be so mean they were a "law unto themselves" and the local sheriffs were afraid to enter the area, hence the name "Free State". See the book *Skyland,* by George Freeman Pollock.)

3.6 Pass under power line. About 0.1m. farther, notice the impressive old white pine growing to the right of the *AT*. From here Trail ascends over knob, then descends to reach Pinnacles Picnic Grounds.

4.0 Come onto paved path in picnic grounds and bear left, following *AT* blazes. Turn left at drinking fountain (about 200 ft.), pass toilets and follow path between walls of laurel. Trail now follows picnic grounds path, paralleling the entrance road to the Pinnacles Area for about 0.1m.

4.3 Bear left, away from road. Descend gradually along narrow ridge crest. Fine views westward over Jewell Hollow.

4.4 Spur trail, right, leads 75 ft. to the Jewell Hollow Parking Overlook, SDMP 36.4. *AT* passes below the Overlook.

4.6 Pass a second spur trail leading back to the Overlook. Trail now ascends gently through some tall white pines.

4.7 Cross Leading Ridge Tr., blue-blazed. (This trail leads right 0.1m. to Skyline Drive. To left it climbs over Leading Ridge, then descends steeply toward the Shenandoah Valley and comes into Va. Sec. 669 outside the Park boundary, at a point about 2m. from U.S. 211 using the shortest route. See PATC Map No. 10.) *AT* now ascends, passing through thick growth of mountain laurel.

5.4 Pass to the right of highest point of The Pinnacle, el. 3730'. Trail now leads for a short distance along the level ridge crest with excellent views. Pass, on left, the jagged rocks forming the north peak of The Pinnacle. From here Trail descends to a sag at base of The Pinnacle.

5.6 Pass obscure trail, left, leading 100 ft. to fine view north. *AT* descends by switchbacks along a rocky, picturesque ridge.

6.4 Reach Byrds Nest #3. (Piped water available here during the warmer months. See Chap. 6: "Picnic Shelters, Huts and Cabins.") Beyond the shelter, *AT* follows access road for 180 ft., then turns left, away from the road. (Road leads 0.3m. to Skyline Drive, SDMP 33.9.) From road, *AT* ascends slightly by switchbacks on east slope of ridge, passing viewpoint at 6.7m, then bearing right along the ridge. Descend into slight sag.

7.0 Junction with Buck Hollow Trail. (Buck Hollow Trail leads right, downhill, passing Meadow Springs on its left in 0.3m. Buck Hollow Trail continues downhill crossing the Skyline Drive, SDMP 33.5, in 0.7m. and on down to reach U.S. 211 in 3.7m. at a point 3.4m. west of Sperryville.) From trail junction *AT* follows the ridge crest. Just before start of the large rock outcrop marking Marys Rock, swing to the right of the ridge and start to descend.

7.7 Spur trail leads left 0.1m. to the exposed northern tip of Marys Rock. (The view from this point is unsurpassed anywhere in the Park. Highest point, 3514', is reached by climbing to the top of the rock outcrop (granodiorite). It can be dangerous in icy, wet, or windy weather. Geologists believe the rock of Marys Rock is over one billion years old!) From trail junction the *AT* descends steadily all the way to Thornton Gap, at first through laurel and scrub oak. Here there are splendid views—of Hazel Mtn. to the southeast, of Oventop Mtn. with its many peaks to the northeast, and of the Blue Ridge as far north as Mt. Marshall.

9.3 Spur trail, right, leads into Panorama Upper Parking Area. The *AT* now passes to the left and below the Panorama Restaurant.

9.4 Junction with U.S. 211, about 0.1m. west of the Skyline Drive in Thornton Gap. (Skyline Drive at Thornton Gap, SDMP 31.5, el. 2307'.)

SUMMARY OF DISTANCES ALONG THE *AT*
Section VII Central
(for Skyline Drive mileages, see N to S)

	Miles	Kilometers
Swift Run Gap and U.S. 33	0.0	0.0
South River Falls Trail	3.0	4.8
Pocosin Cabin	6.3	10.1
Lewis Mtn. Campground	8.2	13.2
Bearfence Mtn. Hut	9.1+0.2	14.7+0.3
Hazeltop Mtn. summit	12.5	20.1
Skyline Drive, *AT* crossing at Milam Gap	14.4	23.2
Lewis Spring Service Rd.	16.1	25.9
Big Meadows—Amphitheatre area	17.0	27.4
Fishers Gap	18.6	30.0
Rock Spring Hut	20.5+0.2	33.0+0.3
Rock Spring Cabin	20.5+0.2	33.0+0.3
Byrds Nest #2 and Hawksbill Mtn. summit via Nakedtop Trail from *AT*	20.8+0.9	33.5+1.4
Hawksbill Gap	21.8	35.1
Whiteoak Canyon Trail	24.3	39.1
Skyland (area of Dining Hall)	24.9	40.1
Little Stony Man Parking Area	26.5	42.7
Stony Man Parking Overlook	26.9	43.3
Nicholson Hollow Trail	27.3	44.0
Pinnacles Picnic Grounds	28.9	46.5
Byrds Nest #3	31.3	50.4
Buck Hollow Trail	31.9	51.4
Marys Rock summit	32.6+0.1	52.5+0.2
Thornton Gap and U.S. 211	34.3	55.2

SECTION VI NORTHERN SHENANDOAH PARK
THORNTON GAP TO U.S. 522
SOUTH TO NORTH

27.4 miles (44.1 kilometers)　　　　　　　　(PATC Map No. 9)

Section VI of the Appalachian Trail in Virginia begins at U.S. 211 in Thornton Gap. Through most of the section the Trail and Skyline Drive parallel closely and there are many intersections, so that the *AT* throughout this section is easily accessible. However, the deep woods through which the Trail passes makes the Trail hiker feel remote from civilization. At Compton Gap the *AT* leaves the proximity of the Skyline Drive and continues north along the Blue Ridge crest following the old road from Compton Gap toward Chester Gap for a mile and three-quarters. It then descends the northwest side of the ridge, leaving the Shenandoah National Park near the top. It passes along easements first through private property in Harmony Hollow, then across land of the Northern Virginia 4–H Educational Center. For the last mile and a half before the end of the section at U.S. 522 the *AT* follows along an easement near the edge of property of the National Zoological Park Conservation Center.

Numerous side trails and fire roads in the northern area of the Park can be used in conjunction with the *AT* for a variety of walking trips including some circuit hikes.

For convenience, the trail description of this section has been divided into two subsections: Thornton Gap to Gravel Springs Gap and Gravel Springs Gap to U.S. 522.

Maps:

PATC Map No. 9. Also available are the USGS map of Shenandoah Park, Northern Section, 1969, scale 1:62,500 and 7½' quads for Front Royal, Bentonville, Chester Gap, Luray, Thornton Gap, and Washington, Va.

SOUTH TO NORTH

SUBSECTION:
THORNTON GAP TO GRAVEL SPRINGS GAP

14.6 miles (23.5 kilometers) (PATC Map No. 9)

General description:

From Thornton Gap the Trail climbs Pass Mountain, then makes several other smaller ascents as it follows the crest of the Blue Ridge. From Elkwallow Gap the Trail climbs over a thousand feet to reach the highest elevation in the northern section of the Park, the summit of the Second Peak of the Hogback, el. 3475'. From the Hogback peaks the route is downhill all the way to Gravel Springs Gap. South of Pass Mtn. and also near Range View Cabin, the Trail passes through areas where large oak trees with low widespreading branches are being crowded by slender young forest trees. The old oaks remind the hiker that these areas were open fields in the pre-National Park days during which these oaks grew to maturity.

Side trails:

At 10.8m. the *AT* connects with the Big Blue-Tuscarora Trail at its southern terminus. This trail offers a 220 mile route west of the *AT*, rejoining it northeast of Carlisle, Pa. From the junction in the SNP, the Big Blue descends along Overall Run for 4.5m., running concurrent with the Overall Run Tr., then bears right, crossing U.S. 340 just south of Bentonville. From there it crosses the two forks of the Shenandoah River and the Massanutten range which separates them, and continues on west as far as the Va.–W. Va. state line, whence it proceeds generally north-northeast, roughly paralleling the *AT* route far to the east. It crosses the Potomac at Hancock, Md. The Tuscarora section, that part of the Big Blue-Tuscarora Trail north of the Potomac, continues on in a northeasterly direction from Hancock to end at the *AT* near Carlisle, Pa.

The Thornton Gap-Gravel Springs area is rich in side trails, too many to enumerate here. See Chap. 5: "Side Trails," Northern Section; also the PATC publication: *Circuit Hikes in the Shenandoah National Park.*

122   APPALACHIAN TRAIL DATA

Accommodations:

Along this section two open-faced huts are available for use of thru-hikers: Pass Mtn. Hut, 1.2m. (follow Pass Mtn. Tr. 0.2m. from *AT*) and Gravel Springs Hut, 14.3m. (follow Bluff Tr. 0.2m.). There is also one locked cabin, Range View Cabin, 9.5m. (follow spur trail right for 0.1m.). Reservations for the use of the cabin must be obtained in advance from PATC Headquarters. See Chap. 6: "Picnic Shelters, Huts and Cabins."

Mathews Arm Campground, SDMP 22.2, offers extensive camping facilities. Meals are available at Panorama Restaurant at Thornton Gap and lunches can be purchased at the Elkwallow Wayside, SDMP 24.0. None of these facilities are available during the cold months.

Detailed Trail data:

0.0 Intersection with U.S. 211 at a point 0.15m. west of the Skyline Drive in Thornton Gap, SDMP 31.5, el. 2307'. Trail leads uphill through woods.

0.1 Cross to right side of Skyline Drive and follow service road for a few feet; then turn left, up the bank, into woods.

0.4 *AT* turns left onto service road, follows it about 150 ft., then turns left, away from the road. Trail now ascends gradually.

1.2 Pass Mtn. Tr. leads right 3.0m. to its lower terminus on U.S. 211. Pass Mtn. Hut is 0.2m. from *AT* down this trail. Spring is a few feet behind the shelter. (See Chap. 6: "Picnic Shelters, Huts and Cabins.")

2.0 Reach wooded summit of Pass Mtn., el 3052'.

2.4 The *AT*, descending, passes through rocky area with wintertime views west of Kemp Hollow, Neighbor Mtn. and Knob Mtn.

3.0 Intersection with yellow-blazed Rocky Branch Tr.

3.1 Trail crosses to left of the Skyline Drive, SDMP 28.6, at Beahms Gap.

3.3 A spur trail leads right 0.1m. to Beahms Gap Parking Overlook on the Skyline Drive, SDMP 28.5.

3.5 Trail on the left leads 100 ft. to a spring. A few feet farther along the *AT* a blue-blazed trail leads right 0.5m. to Byrds Nest #4. (Piped-in water is available here May through October.) The Trail now slabs the southwest side of the ridge.

4.2 Reach ridge crest and follow along it.

SOUTH TO NORTH

4.3 Reach top of rise. Two hundred feet farther reach junction with the yellow-blazed Neighbor Trail. (To the left the Neighbor Trail follows a side ridge almost along a contour line as far as the peak of "The Neighbor," 1.9m., and then descends steeply to Jeremys Run Trail, 4.6m. To the right the horse trail swings southward keeping between the *AT* and the Drive and passing near Byrds Nest #4; then it crosses the Drive to connect with the yellow-blazed Hull School Trail, SDMP 28.1.)

4.7 Spur trail leads right 0.1m. to Parking Area on Skyline Drive, SDMP 26.8. Beyond this junction the *AT* continues along the crest of a long narrow ridge for over two miles, then descends.

5.9 Junction with blue-blazed Thornton Hollow Tr. (This trail leads right, crossing the Skyline Drive in 0.3m. then continuing eastward to the Park boundary.)

7.8 There is a spring 5 yds. to the left of the *AT*, shortly after a sharp turn to the right. The Trail continues to descend.

8.0 Cross creek. 100 ft. beyond, where the *AT* turns sharply right, is intersection with the Jeremys Run Trail. (Jeremys Run Tr. leads left 6.5m. to Va. Sec. 611 at a point 3.5m. from Big Spring on U.S. 340. See Chap. 5: "Side Trails" for details of this trail and circuit hikes that can be made in this area; also see PATC publication: *Circuit Hikes in the Shenandoah National Park.*) *AT* now ascends.

8.1 On right of the *AT* a short trail leads to a spring.

8.3 A trail straight ahead leads 200 ft. to Elkwallow Picnic Grounds. *AT* turns sharply to the left here to swing around the developed area of the Elkwallow Picnic Grounds and Wayside.

8.5 Intersect the Elkwallow Trail. (To the left this trail leads 1.9m. to Mathews Arm Campground; to the right it leads 0.1m. to the Elkwallow Wayside. Lunches may be obtained here from mid-May through October.) At 250 ft. farther the *AT* crosses to the right of Skyline Drive, SDMP 23.9. Trail now ascends gently.

9.4 Cross service road to Range View Cabin. (To right road leads down 0.1m. to the cabin. About 100 ft. down this road the Piney Ridge Trail leads off to the right. See Chap. 5: "Side Trails." To the left road leads 0.6m. to Piney River Ranger Station and the Skyline Drive, SDMP 22.1.) 200 ft. farther along the *AT*, a spur trail leads right 0.1m. to Range View Cabin, a locked structure. (See Chap. 6: "Picnic Shelters, Huts and Cabins.")

9.5 Pass under power line. A trail to right follows power line 0.1m. to the cabin.

9.8 Turn right into access road and follow it a few feet before leaving it again as road bends to the left. Immediately ahead is junction with Piney Branch Trail which leads right from AT. (See Chap. 5: "Side Trails;" also see publication: *Circuit Hikes in the Shenandoah National Park.*) *ALERT: There are plans to relocate the next 3.5m. of AT keeping it on the east side of the Skyline Drive.*

10.1 Cross to left side of Skyline Drive, SDMP 21.9. Rattlesnake Point is to left of Trail as you reach the Drive. (50 yds. right of the *AT*, on the Drive, is Rattlesnake Point Overlook, el. 3105', with views east over Piney Branch. 0.2m. to left of the *AT*, along the Drive, is the entrance road to Mathews Arm Campground.) *AT* now ascends.

10.4 Spur trail on left leads 50 ft. to summit of Sugarloaf.

10.7 Junction with Big Blue-Overall Run Trail. (This is the southern terminus of the Big Blue-Tuscarora Trail which provides a 220m. route connected to the *AT* at each end. 5.6m. of the Big Blue Tr. lies within the Shenandoah Park. From the junction with the *AT* the Big Blue Trail, concurrent with the Overall Run Tr., descends to the left. At 0.7m. a trail leads left from it to Mathews Arm Campground. The trail passes near Overall Falls at 2.7m. At 4.5m. the Big Blue bears right, away from Overall Run and the Overall Run Tr. and at 6.6m. reaches U.S. 340 at a point on the highway 2.6m. south of Bentonville. See Chap. 5: "Side Trails.")

10.8 Side trail leads right 30 ft. to summit of the Fourth Peak of Hogback, el. 3440', with fine view south. Continue along ridge, descending slightly.

11.1 Cross to right of Skyline Drive, SDMP 21.1. Ascend over the Third Peak of Hogback, el. 3440'. Just beyond the top a side trail leads 15 ft. to a spot offering a splendid view north over Browntown Valley and Dickey Ridge. (Skyline Drive is directly below; there are enormous rocks here.) Descend.

11.4 Cross to left of Skyline Drive, SDMP 20.8. Follow tower

SOUTH TO NORTH

access road a few feet, then bear right off the road. (A spur trail leads right, here, 300 ft. to Skyline Drive.) In 400 ft. *AT* crosses to left of access road.

11.6 Trail follows road across its turn-around area, reaching the summit of the Second Peak of Hogback, el. 3475', highest point in northern section of the SNP; antenna towers are to left of Trail. Descend.

11.7 Graded trail to right leads 0.2m. downhill to a walled-in spring which is within sight of the Skyline Drive. *AT* now ascends.

11.9 Pass a few feet to the right of the First Peak of Hogback, el. 3420'. Continue along ridge crest, then descend steeply, by switchbacks, down the east face of the mountain.

12.6 Spur trail, at signpost, leads right 50 ft. to Little Hogback Overlook on the Skyline Drive, SDMP 19.7. *AT* veers left here, and climbs.

12.7 Reach top of Little Hogback where there is a fine outlook from ledge 30 ft. to left of Trail. *AT* now descends gradually.

13.0 Spur trail to right leads 100 ft. to Skyline Drive, SDMP 19.4, at junction of the Keyser Run Fire Road on east side of Drive. (Keyser Run Fire Rd. leads south along the east slopes of the Blue Ridge, passing the point known as "Four-Way" in 1.0m. See Chap. 5: "Side Trails," also PATC publication: *Circuit Hikes in the Shenandoah National Park*.)

13.2 Cross to right side of Skyline Drive, SDMP 18.9. Trail passes along an almost level area. *ALERT: North end of possible relocation of the AT previously mentioned (see note, 9.8m.) would be in this area.*

14.3 Junction with the Bluff Trail. *AT* turns sharply left, paralleling the old Browntown-Harris Hollow Rd. from here to the Drive. (Bluff Tr. starts here, descends by switchbacks to Gravel Springs, 0.2m., where it crosses the old Harris Hollow Rd. It continues on, slabbing the east sides of South and North Marshall Mtns. ending at the Mt. Marshall Trail in 3.8m. Gravel Springs Hut is 50 ft. from Gravel Springs, to the right of the Bluff Trail. See Chap. 6: "Picnic Shelters, Huts and Cabins.")

14.5 Cross to the left side of the Skyline Drive, SDMP 17.7, el. 2665', at its intersection with the old Browntown-Harris Hollow Rd. (Harris Hollow Rd., right of the Drive and *AT*, is utilized as a service road to the Gravel Springs Hut for 0.3m. The Harris Hollow Trail, yellow-blazed, follows the route of the old road down the mountain, except that it detours around Gravel Springs and the hut. Its lower end is on Va. Sec. 622 at a point 5.0m. from Washington, Va. The Browntown Trail, left of the Drive, leads northwest down the mountain for 3.4m. to reach Va. Sec. 631 at a point about 1m. south of Browntown. See Chap. 5: "Side Trails.")

SUBSECTION:
GRAVEL SPRINGS GAP TO U.S. 522

12.9 miles (20.8 kilometers)   PATC Map No. 9

General description:

From Gravel Springs Gap the Trail ascends South and North Marshall Mtns., then descends about 1000 ft. to Jenkins Gap. After a climb to Compton Peak and descent to Compton Gap the *AT* leaves the proximity of the Skyline Drive, which here swings to the west, and follows along the old Compton Gap Rd. toward Chester Gap still following the crest of the Blue Ridge. In one and three-quarter miles it turns left off the road and descends the northwest slopes of the ridge into Harmony Hollow, leaving the Shenandoah Park near the top. The *AT* comes into Va. Sec. 601 in 1 mile, then leaves it again immediately. Members of the PATC have constructed a small, primitive campground, the Tom Floyd Wayside, along the *AT* about halfway between the Park boundary and Rt. 601. A quarter of a mile north of Rt. 601 the trail enters the property of the Northern Virginia 4–H Educational Center following an *AT* easement and continues through this property until it reaches Va. Sec. 602 which it crosses. Beyond this point the *AT* is on an easement at the edge of property of the National Zoological Park Conservation Center all the way to U.S. 522 and beyond.

Viewpoints along the Trail in the northern section of the Park are limited to occasional rock outcrops. Fields on the 4-H and on the Zoological Park land offer nice vistas. Water is obtainable at several springs on or near the Trail along this 12.9 mile stretch.

SOUTH TO NORTH

Side trails:

The Browntown Tr., the Bluff Tr., the Mt. Marshall Tr., the Lands Run Fire Rd. and the Dickey Ridge Tr. offer good walking; so do the two short but interesting trails, Big Devils Stairs Tr. and the Peak Tr. For details on side trails see Chap. 5: "Side Trails." Also refer to the PATC publication: *Circuit Hikes in the Shenandoah National Park.*

Accommodations:

One open-faced shelter, Gravel Springs Hut, is available. From Gravel Springs Gap, follow *AT* south for 0.2m., then the Bluff Tr. east for 0.2m. to reach hut. See Chap. 6. "Picnic Shelters, Huts and Cabins."

South of Gravel Springs Gap, at SDMP 22.2, the Mathews Arm Campground with extensive camping facilities is open during the warmer months. There are many motels and restaurants in Front Royal, 4 miles northwest of the Trail intersection with U.S. 522; there are also a number of private campgrounds in the Front Royal area.

The Tom Floyd Wayside, a primitive camping area for thruhikers with a few tent sites and a rain shelter, is located on the *AT* about one-half mile north of the Park boundary (and 0.5m. south of Va. Sec. 601).

Detailed Trail data:

0.0 West side of the Skyline Drive at its intersection with the Browntown Trail (yellow-blazed), SDMP 17.7, el. 2666'. (The Browntown Tr. follows the route of the old Browntown-Harris Hollow Rd. northwest down the mountain for 3.4m. entering Va. Sec. 631 at a point about 1m. south of Browntown. East of the Drive the first 0.3m. of the old road serves as the Harris Hollow Tr. as well as an access road to Gravel Springs Hut. The Harris Hollow Trail (yellow-blazed) descends to Va. Sec. 622 at a point about 5m. from Washington, Va.) *AT* follows Browntown Tr. for a few feet, then turns right and ascends gradually. Ledges on left, near top of mountain, afford splendid views.

1.0 Reach summit of South Marshall, el. 3212'.

1.6 Cross to the right of the Skyline Drive, SDMP 15.9, el. 3087'. Parking for two cars here. Ascend North Marshall by switchbacks. Near top, where Trail jogs sharply left, the high cliffs on right are worth a scramble. At the next bend of the Trail there is an excellent view of the Blue Ridge to the south. (The cliffs of North Marshall are quite visible from the Skyline Drive south of the mountain.)

2.1 Reach crest of ridge. Cliffs to left of the trail offer many good views to the west.

2.2 Reach summit of North Marshall, el. 3368'. (The name of this mountain grows out of the fact that these lands were formerly a part of the Blue Ridge holdings of John Marshall, the noted Chief Justice of the United States from 1801-1835. See "Manor of Leeds" by Jean Stephenson in the April, 1934 PATC Bulletin.) Trail now descends gradually.

3.1 Pass Hogwallow Spring, 30 ft. on right. Continue to descend, very gently, through Hogwallow Flat.

3.7 Cross to left of Skyline Drive at Hogwallow Gap, SDMP 14.2, el. 2739'. Some parking available here. For half a mile the *AT* proceeds across relatively level terrain. Foundations of an old building can be seen on right at 3.9m. Trail now climbs unnamed mountain, passing through an area of old orchard, with many of the old fruit trees persisting, although now topped by black locust trees.

5.3 Cross abandoned road diagonally. (The old road leads left 0.1m. to an old quarry.)

5.4 Cross gravel road in Jenkins Gap. (To left the Jenkins Gap Tr., yellow-blazed, descends the mountain to Va. Sec. 634 at a point 2.2m. east of Browntown. To right trail leads 150 ft. to Skyline Dr., crossing it at SDMP 12.3, and continues for 0.5m. to the Mt. Marshall Trail. Some parking space available at Jenkins Gap. The Mt. Marshall Trail can be reached by walking south along the Skyline Drive for about 0.3m.) Trail now passes through a level area containing an extensive growth of mountain laurel (bloom early June) and pink azalea (bloom late May). Beyond, Trail ascends fairly steeply.

6.2 Pass Compton Springs. One spring is about 15 ft. to the left and below the *AT,* another is 50 ft. uphill on the right.

6.6 A signpost at top of climb marks short blue-blazed trails leading left and right to viewpoints. Though ungraded and offering

SOUTH TO NORTH

only rough footing, both trails are worthwhile. (Trail on right leads down 0.2m. to an interesting outcrop of columnar basalt. To see the columnar structure it is necessary to climb down below the rocks. The top of the outcrop affords a good view east. Trail on left leads over the crest of Compton Mtn., el. 2909', and down 0.2m. to a rocky ledge offering excellent views to west and north.) *AT* continues along the ridge of Compton Mtn. for about 0.2m., then descends, passing several large boulder-like outcrops of basalt. There is at least one clump of yellow lady-slipper (bloom in mid-May) and some white clintonia (bloom early June) along this stretch of Trail.

7.4 In Compton Gap cross to the right side of the Skyline Drive, SDMP 10.4, el. 2415'. Parking area here. The *AT* now follows the old Compton Gap-Chester Gap Road, both white and yellow blazes, continuing along the Blue Ridge crest. (The Skyline Drive swings northwest here along Dickey Ridge down which it descends into Front Royal.)

7.7 Intersection with the blue-blazed Dickey Ridge Trail (left) and service road (right) to Indian Run Maintenance Bldg. (Dickey Ridge Tr. begins here and leads northwest 9.2m. to the entrance to the Skyline Drive at the Front Royal town limits. Fort Windham Rocks are 0.2m. from the *AT* along this trail. The service road leads 0.4m. to the Indian Run maintenance structure, not available for camping. There is a spring 250 ft. to the left of the service road about 0.1m. before reaching the building.)

8.0 Springhouse Rd., yellow-blazed, leads left from the *AT* for 0.7m. coming into the Dickey Ridge Trail at a point 0.6m. north of its *AT* junction.

9.1 At the self-registration permit booth turn left from the Compton Gap Tr. onto a narrower footpath (white-blazed only). (Compton Gap Tr., yellow-blazed, continues 0.5 mi. downhill to Va. Sec. 610 at the Park boundary. It is 1.8m. farther, via Rt. 610, to U.S. 522 at Chester Gap. This was the route of the *AT* until 1974.)

9.3 A trail leads left 0.1m. to viewpoint at Possums Rest. A few steps farther the *AT* leaves Shenandoah National Park. It now follows a narrow easement over private property; STAY ON TRAIL! *AT* descends by switchbacks.

APPALACHIAN TRAIL DATA

9.7 Enter Tom Floyd Wayside, an area for primitive camping. No open fires permitted. A spur trail leads left 150 ft. to a rain shelter.

9.8 Spur trail leads left 800 ft. to Ginger Spring. Leave Wayside.

10.2 Bear right, diagonally, across old road. In 200 ft. cross small creek and pass through gap in rock wall.

10.3 Come into Va. Sec. 601 at a sharp corner of the road. (It is 0.4m. down Rt. 601 to a PATC parking area and 0.3m. farther to the main road through Harmony Hollow, Va. Sec. 604.) Immediately turn right onto farm road passing a white house on the right side of the *AT*. Follow farm road for about 750 ft., then turn left onto footpath. (Property to the left of the farm road and *AT* here belongs to the PATC.)

10.5 A trail leads left from the *AT* 0.2m. to a parking area, PATC owned, on Va. Sec. 601.

10.7 Cross through narrow gap in fence onto *AT* easement on property of the Northern Virginia 4–H Educational Center.

11.0 Come into field. There is a good view of Harmony Hollow and its fruit orchards from the center of this field.

11.3 Turn sharply right into woods and immediately cross wet weather creek.

11.5 Cross small creek, Moore's Run, and then dirt road, Va. Sec. 602. *AT* enters the property of the National Zoological Park Conservation and Research Center here following an *AT* easement. Trail now ascends.

12.0 Reach summit of hill. 100 ft. beyond, cross stile.

12.5 Enter field. From this vantage point and with the help of field glasses, the hiker may be able to spot various zoo animals in the fenced-in areas across the highway. The *AT* descends along the edge of fields, passing below the dam of Lake Front Royal.

12.9 Cross bridges over Sloan Creek Swamp and reach U.S. 522 at a point 3.2m. SE of its junction with Va. 55 in Front Royal. (The *AT* crosses the highway here and continues on an *AT* easement through property of the National Zoological Conservation and Research Center.)

SUMMARY OF DISTANCES ALONG THE *AT*
Section VI Northern

	Miles	Kilometers
Thornton Gap(U.S. 211)	0.0	0.0
Pass Mtn. Hut	1.2 + 0.2	1.9 + 0.3
Pass Mtn.	2.0	3.2
Skyline Drive crossing Beahms Gap	3.1	5.0
Byrds Nest #4 (no camping)	3.5 + 0.5	5.6 + 0.8
The Neighbor Trail	4.4	7.1
Thornton Hollow Trail	5.6	9.0
Jeremys Run Trail	8.0	12.9
Skyline Drive crossing Elkwallow Gap	8.6	13.8
Range View Cabin	9.4 + 0.1	15.1 + 0.2
Piney Ridge Trail	9.4	15.1
Piney Branch Trail	9.8	15.8
Big Blue Trail	10.7	17.2
Summit of Hogback, 2nd Peak	11.6	18.7
Gravel Springs Hut	14.3 + 0.2	23.0 + 0.3
Gravel Springs Gap	14.5	23.3
Summit of North Marshall	16.7	26.9
Jenkins Gap	19.9	32.0
Compton Gap	21.9	35.3
U.S. 522	27.4	44.1

For summary of distances by Skyline Drive to points on the *AT*, see end of write-up for "North to South, Section VI."

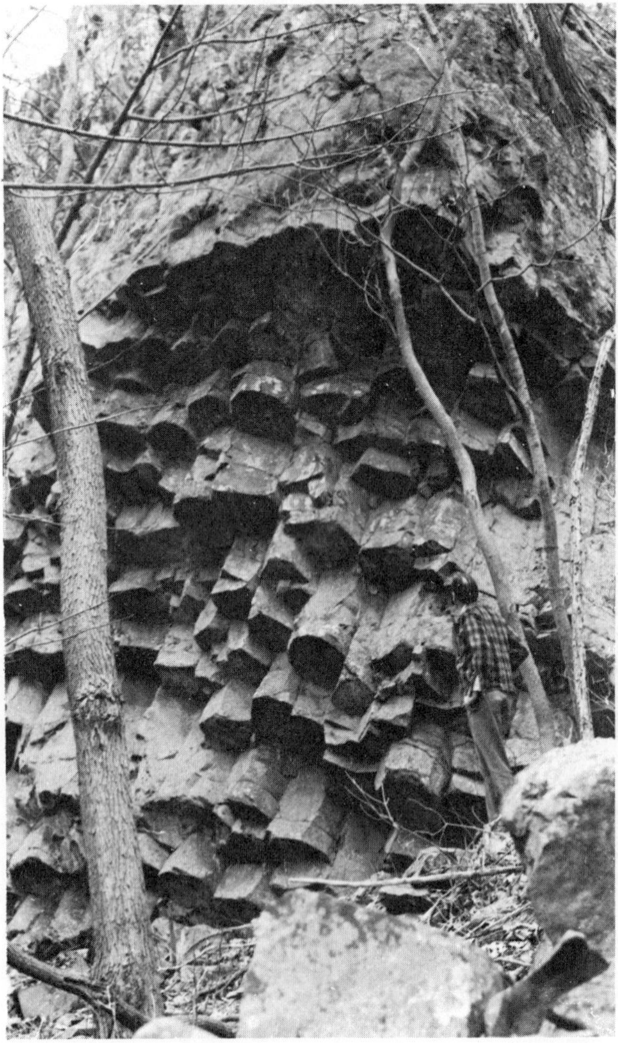

CHAPTER 5

SIDE TRAILS

Introduction to Side Trails
Trails, Northern Section:

Dickey Ridge Tr.	139
Fox Hollow (nature) Tr.	141
Snead Farm Rd.	142
Snead Farm Loop Tr.	142
Lands Run Fire Rd.	142
Hickerson Hollow Tr.	143
Jenkins Gap Tr.	143
Browntown Tr.	144
Compton Gap Fire Rd./Horse Trail—Va. Sec. 610	145

North and South Marshall Mtn. area:

Access	146
Mt. Marshall Tr.	147
Bluff Tr.	148
Jordan River Tr.	149
The Peak Tr.	149
Big Devils Stairs Tr.	150
Harris Hollow Tr.	151

Range View Cabin area:

Access	151
Keyser Run Fire Rd.	153
Little Devils Stairs Tr.	154
Pole Bridge Link Tr.	155
Piney Branch Tr.	156
Piney Ridge Tr.	157
Fork Mtn. Tr.	158
Thornton Hollow Tr.	158
Hull School Tr.	159
Hogback Spur Tr.	160

Mathews Arm-Elkwallow area:

Big Blue Tr.	160
Thompson Hollow Tr.	163
Overall Run Trail	163
Overall-Beecher Ridge Connector Tr.	164
Beecher Ridge Tr.	164

Mathews Arm Tr.	164
The Traces (interpretive) Tr.	165
Knob Mtn. Tr.	166
Heiskell Hollow Tr.	167
Weddlewood Tr.	168
Knob Mtn. Cut-off Tr.	169
Elkwallow Tr.	169
Jeremys Run Tr.	169
The Neighbor Mtn. Tr.	171
Rocky Branch Tr.	172
Pass Mtn. Tr.	172

Trails, Central Section:

Buck Hollow Tr.	174
Buck Ridge Tr.	174
Leading Ridge Tr.	174
Crusher Ridge Tr.	174

Nicholson Hollow-Hazel Country Trail network:

Access	176
Nicholson Hollow Tr.	177
Hannah Run Tr.	179
Hazel Mountain Tr.	180
Corbin Cabin Cut-Off Tr.	182
Sams Ridge Tr.	182
Hazel River Tr.	183
Broad Hollow Tr.	184
Pine Hill Gap Tr.	185
Hot-Short Mountain Tr.	186
Catlett Mountain Tr.	187
Catlett Spur Tr.	188
White Rocks Tr.	188

Skyland-Old Rag area:

Stony Man Nature Tr.-Little Stony Man Tr.	189
Stony Man Horse Tr.	190
Millers Head Tr.	190
Old Skyland Road Tr.	191
Furnace Spring Tr.	191
Whiteoak Horse Tr.	192
Whiteoak Canyon Tr.	192
Cedar Run Tr.	195

Cedar Run-Whiteoak Link Tr.	196
Weakley Hollow Fire Rd.	196
Berry Hollow Fire Rd.	196
Old Rag Fire Rd.	198
Limberlost Tr.	200
Corbin Mtn. Tr.	201
Indian Run Tr.	202
Corbin Hollow Tr.	202
Robertson Mtn. Tr.	202
Whiteoak Fire Rd.	203
Old Rag Mtn. circuit—includes Ridge Tr., Saddle Tr. and Weakley Hollow Fire Rd.	203
Skyland-Big Meadows Horse Tr.	206
Crescent Rock Tr.	207
Bettys Rock Tr.	208
Hawksbill Mtn. Tr.—Nakedtop Tr.—Byrds Nest #2 Service Rd.	208

Big Meadows-Hoover Camp area:

Red Gate Fire Rd.	210
Story of the Forest Nature Tr.	210
Lewis Spring Falls Tr.	211
Dark Hollow Falls-Rose River Loop Tr.	211
Rose River Fire Rd.	213
Stony Mountain Tr.	214
Upper Dark Hollow Tr.	214
Tanners Ridge Horse Tr.	215
Tanners Ridge Rd.	215
Rapidan Fire Rd.-Va. Sec. 649	215
Mill Prong Tr.	217
Mill Prong Horse Spur Tr.	217
Laurel Prong Tr.	218
Cat Knob Tr.	219
Graves Mill Fire Rd.	219
Fork Mountain Rd.	220
Staunton River Tr.	220
Fork Mountain Tr.	221
Jones Mountain Tr.	222
McDaniel Hollow Tr.	223
Nicholson Moonshine Tr.	223

Powell Mountain Tr.	223
West Naked Creek Fire Rd.	223
Meadow School Fire Rd.	224

Pocosin Cabin-South River area:
- Lewis Mtn. East Tr. 224
- Conway River Fire Rd. 224
- Bearfence Mtn. Loops 224
- Slaughter Tr. 225
- Pocosin Fire Rd. 225
- Pocosin Tr. 226
- Pocosin Hollow Tr. 226
- South River Falls Tr. 227
- South River Fire Rd. 228
- Saddleback Mountain Tr. 228

Big Bend Fire Rd. (abandoned) 229
Lewis Mountain West Tr. 229
Dry Run Falls Fire Rd. 229

Trails, Southern Section:

Hightop Hut Road 230
Smith Roach Gap Fire Road/Horse Trail 230
Simmons Gap Fire Road, both sides of the Skyline Drive 230
Rocky Mount Trail 231
Gap Run Tr. 231
Onemile Run Tr. 232
Ivy Creek Maintenance Bldg. Service Road 233
Deadening (nature) Trail 233
Doyles River Tr. 233
Browns Gap Fire Rd. 235

Big Run area:
- Big Run Portal Tr. 236
- Rocky Mountain Run Tr. 237
- Patterson Ridge Tr. 237
- Big Run Loop Tr. 237
- Madison Run Spur Tr. 238
- Rocky Mtn.-Brown Mtn. Tr. 239
- Rockytop Tr. 240
- Austin Mountain Tr. 242
- Lewis Peak Tr. 243
- Madison Run Fire Rd. 244
- Stull Run Fire Rd.-Crimora Fire Rd.-Lewis Run Fire Rd. 244

Trayfoot Mountain area:
- Trayfoot Mtn. Tr. 245

Blackrock Spur Tr.	247
Furnace Mtn. Tr., Furnace Mtn. Summit Tr.	247
Paine Run Tr.	248

Riprap area:
Riprap Tr.	249
Wildcat Ridge Tr.	250
Turk Gap Tr.	251

Turk Mountain Tr.	252
Moormans River Fire Rd.	252
Turk Branch Tr.	254
Bucks Elbow Mountain Fire Rd.	254
Gas Line Rd.	255

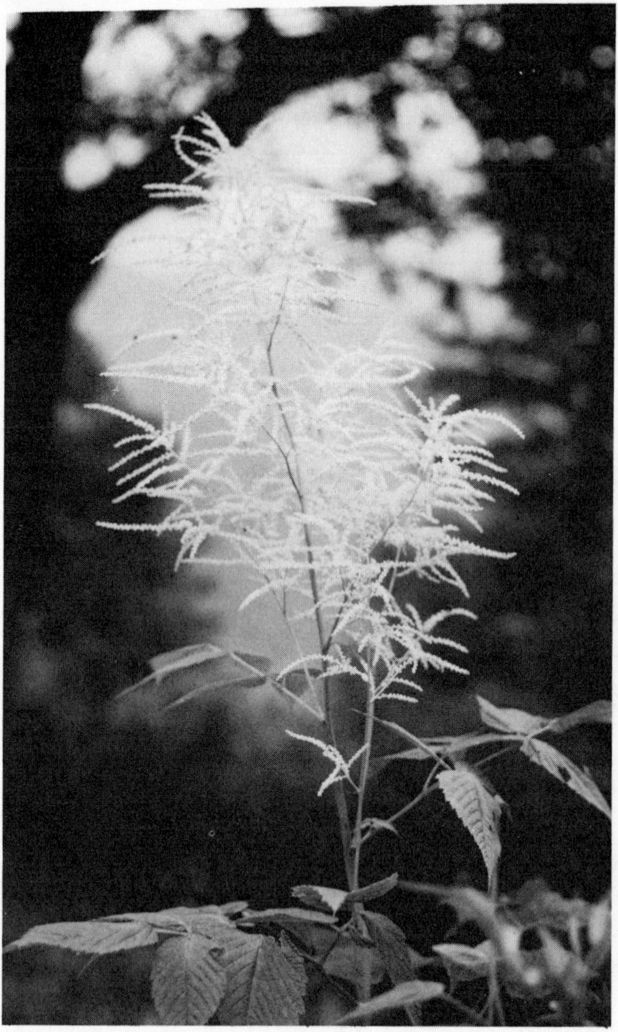

CHAPTER 5
INTRODUCTION TO SIDE TRAILS

In addition to the Appalachian Trail that traverses the Park from one end to the other, there are three classes of trails in the SNP. Those trails blue-blazed are for foot-travelers only; most of these, like the *AT* itself, are maintained by volunteers, members of the Potomac Appalachian Trail Club. Yellow-blazed trails, including fire roads, are classified as horse/foot trails; they are primarily maintained by Park personnel, although several horse-riding groups have been assigned maintenance for specific trails. Park-maintained nature trails and stroller trails, usually quite short, are not blazed but are marked by signposts.

For all trails the trailheads and trail junctions are marked by cement posts with aluminum bands which indicate direction and usually distance to the next trail junction or other landmark. It is wise, when hiking in a new area of the Park, to carry a guide book or map with you as the aluminum bands are sometimes removed by vandals.

Trail descriptions have been grouped according to area to facilitate the planning of hikes. The PATC publication, *Circuit Hikes in the Shenandoah National Park,* will also be found useful in hike planning. The three PATC maps of the Shenandoah Park: No. 9 Northern Section, No. 10 Central Section, and No. 11 Southern Section are valuable for use in conjunction with the Guide. USGS 7½′ quadrangle maps are available but are chiefly of value for bushwhacking and exploring.

In giving detailed trail data in this section, description is given in one direction only. The distances indicated on the left are those in the direction indicated. Those on the right are the distances in the reverse direction.

NORTHERN SECTION

DICKEY RIDGE TRAIL

9.2 miles (14.8 kilometers)   blue-blazed

This is a very popular trail because of its accessibility and gentle grade. The northern end is at the northern entrance to the Skyline Drive. The trail parallels the Drive much of the way, crossing it at SDMP 2.1, again at Low Gap, and yet again at Lands Run Gap. The southern terminus is on the Appalachian Trail just north of Compton Gap, SDMP 10.4. Most of the climb along Dickey Ridge is between the northern end and the summit of Dickey Hill and involves a change in elevation of about 1700 ft. The remainder of the route consists of gentle ups and downs.

There are few views from this trail. Where it climbs nearly to the top of Dickey Hill there are glimpses west of the Shenandoah Valley. (Summit has been cleared because of a federal navigational installation, Vortac.) Near the southern end of the trail, the Fort Windham Rocks are of considerable interest.

Detailed trail data:
   (N to S) Front Royal to the *AT* near Compton Gap
0.0-9.2 Southern side of U.S. 340, at the southern limits of Front Royal. Trail cuts across open area of the Shenandoah Park's northern entrance and crosses to the right side of the Skyline Drive at the Entrance Parking Area, SDMP 0.0. From here trail ascends very gently along a small creek. Although close to the Drive here, it is effectively isolated from it by trees and a jungle of Japanese honeysuckle. At about 1.4m. it turns sharply right away from the creek and climbs more steeply.

1.9-7.3 Cross to left of Skyline Drive, SDMP 2.1. Continue to ascend. In about one-half mile the trail comes quite close to the Drive at the Shenandoah Valley Overlook where there is a good view of Front Royal and Signal Knob in the Massanuttens. There is a large patch of Virginia bluebells right on the trail in this area, probably planted by a long ago resident of the area. Expect to find the bluebells in bloom the latter part of April.

4.0-5.2 The Skyline Drive is slightly above and to the right of the trail here. Cleared areas allow glimpses of Dickey Ridge Visitor Center and several side trails lead up to it. Among these is a Park interpretive trail, the Fox Hollow Tr., which cuts across the Dickey Ridge Tr. directly below the visitor center, descends about one-half mile to the former Fox Farm, then returns to the Dickey Ridge trail and follows it south about 0.2m. before turning up to the Drive. A self-guiding trail leaflet can be purchased at the visitor center.

4.5-4.7 Cross dirt road, Snead Farm Rd. (To right the road leads a few feet to the Drive, just opposite the exit road of the Dickey Ridge Picnic Grounds, SDMP 5.1. To left, road leads into old apple orchard and the site of the Snead Farm.)

5.3-3.9 Trail skirts along the ridge, just below the summit of Dickey Hill. Summit can be reached by a short scramble and offers sweeping views. From here trail descends gently.

5.7-3.5 Snead Farm Loop Tr. enters on the left. (The blue-blazed loop trail, 0.7m. long, has its lower end on the Snead Farm Rd., offering a nice circuit route.)

7.0-2.2 Reach Low Gap, SDMP 7.9. Cross to right of the Skyline Drive.

8.0-1.2 Reach Lands Run Gap, SDMP 9.2, and cross to left of the Drive. (To the right, and south, Lands Run Fire Rd. leads 2.0m. to Park boundary and Va. Sec. 622 at a point about 2 miles east of Browntown. To left and north, the yellow-blazed Hickerson Hollow Tr. leads 1m. down beyond the Park boundary to Va. Sec. 600 at a point about 3.5m. from U.S. 522.)

8.6-0.6 Here yellow-blazed Springhouse Rd. Trail leads left for 0.7m. to join the Compton Gap Rd. and *AT* at a point 0.3m. north of where the Dickey Ridge Tr. itself joins the *AT*.

9.0-0.2 Pass Fort Windham Rocks on the left. They are interesting to climb upon.

9.2-0.0 Junction with the *AT*, which is here coincident with the Compton Gap Rd/Horse Trail, at a point on the *AT* 0.3m. from Compton Gap, SDMP 10.4. (To left, *AT* follows the road for 1.5m. then turns left and descends into Harmony Hollow reaching U.S. 522 in 3.8 additional miles. Compton Gap Horse Trail itself leads down to the Park boundary. As Va. Sec. 610 it continues to U.S. 522 at Chester Gap. Distance from Dickey Ridge Tr. to Chester Gap via this route, 3.7m.)

FOX HOLLOW TRAIL

1 mile (1.6 kilometers)   not blazed

The interpretive trail starts from the Skyline Drive directly across from the Dickey Ridge Visitor Center. It descends about a half mile, then ascends through the former Fox Farm to complete the circuit. See PATC Map No. 9, inset on the back, or check map displayed outside the visitor center. A self-guiding leaflet, with map, can be purchased at the visitor center.

SNEAD FARM ROAD

0.6 miles (1.0 kilometer)　　　　　　　　　　　　　　not blazed

This road, along with the Snead Farm Loop Tr. and a segment of the Dickey Ridge Tr., can be used for a leisurely 2½ mile circuit starting from the Dickey Ridge Picnic Grounds. It intersects the Dickey Ridge Tr. in 300 ft. A short distance farther a road from the FAA installation atop Dickey Hill enters on the right.

Detailed trail data:

0.0 Snead Farm Rd. leaves the Skyline Drive, SDMP 5.0, just across from the exit road of the Dickey Ridge Picnic Grounds.

0.3 A road leads left, downhill, from Snead Farm Rd., soon coming to a dead end.

0.7 Reach the Snead homesite at end of the road. The house is gone but the barn has been renovated. A cement post at the road's end marks the lower end of the Snead Farm Loop Tr.

SNEAD FARM LOOP TRAIL

0.7 miles (1.1 kilometers)　　　　　　　　　　　　　blue-blazed

The lower end of this trail is at the end of the Snead Farm Road. Its upper end is on the Dickey Ridge Trail, joining the latter at a point about 0.3m. south of the summit of Dickey Hill. From here via the Dickey Ridge Tr. it is 1.2m. north (to the right) to return to the Snead Farm Rd. and Skyline Drive.

LANDS RUN FIRE RD.

2.0 miles (3.2 kilometers)　　　　　　　　　　　　yellow-blazed

Lands Run Fire Rd. leaves the Skyline Drive, SDMP 9.2, in Lands Run Gap and descends the west side of the Blue Ridge to the Park boundary where it connects with Va. Sec. 622, a narrow

NORTHERN SECTION 143

graveled road, at a point on the latter about 2m. NE of Browntown. About a half-mile from the Skyline Drive the road crosses Lands Run. The creek immediately below the road here is very pretty, falling rapidly in a series of cascades.

To reach the lower end of the Lands Run Fire Rd., drive to Browntown (which is about 6 miles east of Bentonville via Va. Sec. 613 and 7 miles SW of Front Royal on Va. Sec. 649). Turn east in Browntown onto Va. Sec. 634. In 1 mile turn left onto Va. Sec. 622. Reach fire road in 1 mile from this junction.

HICKERSON HOLLOW TRAIL

1.2 miles (1.9 kilometers)   yellow-blazed

This trail leads from Lands Run Gap, SDMP 9.2, northward down one of the branches of Happy Creek into Harmony Hollow. It ends outside the Park where it meets Va. Sec. 600 at a point on the road about 0.5m. from Va. Sec. 604, the main road through Harmony Hollow. (The land is posted along the stretch of trail between the Park boundary and Va. Sec. 600.) A circuit hike could include the *AT* from Va. Sec. 601 in Harmony Hollow uphill to its junction with the Dickey Ridge Trail, that trail to Lands Run Gap, and the Hickerson Hollow Tr. back down the mountain, then a road walk down Rts. 600 and 604, and up 601 to the start, for a total distance of about 7 miles.

JENKINS GAP TRAIL

1.5 miles (2.4 kilometers)   yellow-blazed

From the end of Va. Sec. 634, about 2 miles east of Browntown, this trail climbs the west side of the Blue Ridge, crosses the Skyline Drive at Jenkins Gap just north of the Jenkins Gap Overlook, SDMP 12.3, then continues on to the Mt. Marshall Tr.

About 1 mile of the trail is west of the Drive. This section has a nice gradient and is particularly attractive when the mountain laurel, which is quite plentiful along the trail, blooms around the first week in June. The lowest 0.2m. is outside the Park. Remember that access to the Park boundary across private land depends upon the goodwill of the landowner. Posted trail closures must be respected. The trail intersects the *AT* about 0.1m. west of the Drive.

East of the Drive the trail descends, passes below the Jenkins Gap Overlook, then climbs back to reach the Mt. Marshall Tr. joining it at a point on the latter 0.1m. from Skyline Drive.

BROWNTOWN TRAIL

3.4 miles (5.5 kilometers)　　　　　　　　　　　　yellow-blazed

This trail utilizes the western portion of the route of the pre-Park Browntown-Harris Hollow Rd. From Gravel Springs Gap, SDMP 17.7, it runs down the west side of the Blue Ridge, descending in switchbacks. The grade is gentle and there are occasional glimpses of Hogback Mtn. and Gimlet Ridge through the trees.

Access:

The upper trailhead is on the Skyline Drive at Gravel Springs Gap, SDMP 17.7. In 50 ft. it intersects the *AT*.

The lower end of the trail can be reached by driving to Browntown (6m. east of Bentonville via Va. Sec. 613 and 7m. SW of Front Royal via Va. Sec. 649). From Browntown follow Va. Sec. 631 for about 1 mile. Here, where Rt. 631 turns sharply right, the old Browntown Rd. is straight ahead. There is room for two cars to park. Do not drive up the old Browntown Rd. but start hiking here.

Detailed trail data:

From Rt. 631 to Skyline Drive

0.0-3.4 Junction with Va. Sec. 631. Follow old road along creek, Phils Arm Run. Land is posted on both sides of road so stay on road.

0.2-3.2 Take right fork and immediately cross creek. (Left fork leads through a gate into field.)

0.8-2.6 Where road forks, take right fork straight ahead. In a few yards road forks again, and again take right fork straight ahead. (Avoid other roads to right which are gated.) Road soon begins to climb.

1.1-2.3 Cross into SNP. Road, now trail, is gated here. Continue to climb. It soon begins a series of switchbacks. There are occasional views of Hogback Mtn. and Gimlet Ridge.

3.4-0.0 Pass gate. In a few feet intersect the *AT* and a few feet farther reach the Skyline Drive, SDMP 17.7. (East of the Drive here the Harris Hollow Trail, yellow-blazed, descends into Harris Hollow reaching Va. Sec. 622 in about 2.5 miles.)

COMPTON GAP FIRE ROAD—COMPTON GAP HORSE TRAIL—VA. SEC. 610

4.0 miles (6.4 kilometers) white- (*AT* portion) and yellow-blazed

This fire road-horse trail leads NE along the Blue Ridge crest from Compton Gap, SDMP 10.4, for 2.2 miles. Here it leaves the Park and becomes Va. Sec. 610, which continues another 1.8m. to Chester Gap where U.S. 522 crosses the mountain (the last 340 ft. of road is Va. Sec. 665). The *AT*, until 1974, followed this route from Compton Gap to Chester Gap and continued across U.S. 522 following at first near the mountain crest, then on through woods to reach Mosby Shelter in another 2.5m. The present route of the *AT* follows the fire road from Compton Gap for 1.7m., then turns north away from it.

Detailed trail data:
 Compton Gap to U.S. 522

0.0-4.0 Junction with Skyline Drive, SDMP 10.4, el. 2415'. *AT* hikers traveling north will cross the Drive at this junction after descending Compton Mtn. From here the *AT* and fire road/horse trail are coincident for the next 1.7m.

0.3-3.7 Intersection with Dickey Ridge Trail (left) and service road (right) leading to Indian Run Maintenance Bldg. and a spring. (Dickey Ridge Tr. leads north 9.2m. to entrance to Skyline Drive at Front Royal town limits. Fort Windham Rocks are 0.2m. from the fire road along this trail. Access road leads 0.4m. to Indian Run Maintenance Bldg. Spring is 250 ft. from the service road, on the left, about 0.1m. before reaching the building.)

0.6-3.4 Yellow-blazed Springhouse Rd. leads left 0.7m., coming into the Dickey Ridge Trail at a point 0.6m. north of its junction with the fire road. Beyond this point the horse trail is blocked to motorized vehicles.

1.7-2.3 The *AT* turns left, away from the horse trail here.

Beyond this junction horse trail is yellow-blazed only.

2.2-1.8 Pass gate and leave Park. Beyond this point road is Va. Sec. 610 and is paved. Rt. 610 is blue-blazed.

3.9-0.1 Take left fork of road, Va. Sec. 665, and descend a short distance.

4.0-0.0 Reach U.S. 522 in Chester Gap. To the left along U.S. 522 it is 1.5m. to the *AT* crossing and 3.2m. farther to the junction of U.S. 522 with Va. 55 in Front Royal.

SIDE TRAILS IN THE NORTH AND SOUTH MARSHALL MOUNTAINS AREA

This group of trails includes the Mt. Marshall Trail (part of which is also fire road), the Bluff Trail, the Peak Trail, Jordan River Tr., Big Devils Stairs Tr. and Harris Hollow Tr.

Access:

From *Skyline Drive* there are two points of access. The yellow-blazed Mt. Marshall Tr. enters the Drive at milepost 12.6, just south of Jenkins Gap Overlook. (Horses may prefer using the Jenkins Gap Tr. which leaves the Drive just north of the overlook, SDMP 12.3.)

At Gravel Springs Gap, SDMP 17.7, the yellow-blazed Harris Hollow Tr. descends eastward paralleling the *AT* for a short distance and in 0.4m. intersects the Bluff Tr. near Gravel Springs. One can also follow the *AT* from the gap and reach the start of the Bluff Tr. in 0.2m.

From the *east*, main access to the area is through the town of Washington, Va. From the main corner of the town go north one block on Va. Sec. 628, then turn left on Va. Sec. 622. *To reach the Mt. Marshall Tr.* follow Rt. 622 for 2.4m., then turn right onto Va. Sec. 625 and follow it about 1.0m. to the end of state maintenance. There is room for 1 or 2 cars here. Sign and a blue arrow mark trail which leads right from the road. In about 250 yds. turn left onto old roadbed. Trail is not blazed until it enters the Park. *To reach bottom of Big Devils Stairs Tr.* follow Va. Sec. 622 for 4.0m. from Washington, Va. and 0.1m. west of stream crossing. *To reach bottom of the Harris Hollow Tr.* follow Va. Sec. 622 for about 5 miles from Washington to the head of Harris Hollow. Trail starts just before reaching the highest elevation of Rt. 622. There is a small sign saying "Trail" but no blazes outside the Park.

The lower end of the Jordan River Tr. is reached by turning west in Flint Hill, Va. onto Va. Sec. 641. Continue ahead on Va. Sec. 606 for about 1 mile, then turn right on Va. Sec. 628 and, at a "T" turn left on graveled road, Va. Sec. 629. Follow Rt. 629 on up the Jordan River to where it is gated. Park here and continue up the road on foot. In about 0.1m. enter the SNP.

Trail accesses across private property depend upon the goodwill of the landowners. Posted trail closures must be observed.

MT. MARSHALL TRAIL

5.7 miles (9.1 kilometers)   yellow-blazed

This trail is valuable in providing access to the Bluff Tr., the Jordan River Tr. and the Peak Tr., also for use in several circuit hikes. The upper 4 miles are almost level. The trail is not blazed outside the Park but is marked at its lower end on Va. Sec. 625.

Detailed trail data:

Skyline Drive to Harris Hollow (Va. Sec. 625)

0.0-5.7 Intersection with Skyline Drive, SDMP 12.6, just south of Jenkins Gap Overlook.

0.1-5.6 To left the yellow-blazed Jenkins Gap Tr. leads 0.5m. to where it crosses the Skyline Drive. It continues another mile to the west Park boundary.

0.9-4.8 Trail enters wilderness area.

3.5-2.2 Junction with yellow-blazed Bluff Trail. (Bluff Tr. leads right 3.8m. to end on the *AT* near Gravel Springs Gap.)

3.9-1.8 On the left the Jordan River Tr., yellow-blazed, leads down the mountain 1.3m. following a branch of the Jordan River to Va. Sec. 629. A few feet farther along the Mt. Marshall Tr. a second cement post marks the blue-blazed Peak Tr. which leads left 0.8m. to "The Peak".

5.1-0.6 Pass chain across road near Park boundary. Yellow blazes end here. Travel across private land beyond this point depends upon the goodwill of the landowner. Posted trail closures must be respected.

5.3-0.4 Pass through wooden gate.

5.5-0.2 Turn right off roadbed and descend.

5.7-0.0 Trail junction with Va. Sec. 625 at end of state maintenance. From here it is 1.0m. via Rt. 625 to the main road through Harris Hollow, Va. Sec. 622.

BLUFF TRAIL

3.8 miles (6.1 kilometers)   first 0.3m blue-blazed
remainder yellow-blazed

"Bluff" was a local name for Mt. Marshall. The trail slabs around the southern and eastern slopes of the mountain with a very gentle grade. It provides access to the Big Devils Stairs Trail and the Peak Trail and is also useful in circuit hikes.

Detailed trail data:
  AT to Mt. Marshall Trail, S to N

0.0-3.8 Junction with *AT*, 0.2m. south of Gravel Springs Gap, SDMP 17.7.

0.2-3.6 Intersection with access road for Gravel Springs Hut. Hut is 100 ft. to right. See Chap. 6: "Picnic Shelters, Huts and Cabins."

0.3-3.5 Harris Hollow Tr. enters from left. At this junction blue blazes end, yellow blazes start. Bluff Tr. and Harris Hollow Tr. are concurrent here.

0.4-3.4 Bluff Tr. bends sharply left as the Harris Hollow Tr. continues straight ahead.

1.6-2.2 Junction with Big Devils Stairs Trail which leads right, downhill, for 0.5m., then makes a sharp left turn where it climbs up to the north rim of the canyon, before descending again to end on Va. Sec. 622 in Harris Hollow.

3.4-0.4 Trail turns sharply right, soon followed by sharp turn to the left.

3.8-0.0 Reach Mt. Marshall Trail. (To left it is 3.5m. to Skyline Drive, SDMP 12.5, at Jenkins Gap; to right it is 0.4m. to the Peak Tr. and Jordan River Tr. and 2.2m. to the lower end of the Mt. Marshall Tr. on Va. Sec. 625.)

NORTHERN SECTION

JORDAN RIVER TRAIL

1.3 miles (2.1 kilometers)   yellow-blazed

Although this trail is primarily used by horsemen, it is a pleasant walk for hikers along an abandoned road; it is the shortest route to "The Peak".

To reach the lower end of this trail first take U.S. 522 to Flint Hill and turn west onto Va. Sec. 641. Continue ahead on Va. Sec. 606 for about 1 mile, then turn right on Va. Sec. 628 and, at a "T" turn left on graveled road, Va. Sec. 629. Follow Rt. 629 on up the Jordan River to where it is gated and park. Continue beyond the gate on foot. Access to the Park boundary across private land depends upon the goodwill of the landowner. Posted trail closures must be respected. In about 0.1m. enter the SNP.

The upper end of the trail is on the Mt. Marshall Tr. in Thorofare Gap. To the north it is 0.4m. to the Bluff Tr. and 3.5m. to Skyline Drive. The start of The Peak Tr. is only 25 ft. to the south.

About 0.1m. inside the Park boundary there are two very tall chimneys just across the river, all that is left of what was once a large home. Much higher on the trail there are the ruins of a simpler home.

THE PEAK TRAIL

1.5 miles (including loop) (2.4 kilometers)   blue-blazed

The route involves a short but steep climb with a loop at the summit. The shortest foot access to this trail is via the yellow-blazed Jordan River Tr.

Detailed trail data:

0.0 Junction in Thorofare Gap with Mt. Marshall Tr. at a point on the latter 3.5m. from Skyline Drive at Jenkins Gap and 2.2m. from Va. Sec. 625 in Harris Hollow. The upper end of the Jordan River Tr. is only about 25 ft. north of The Peak Tr. junction. The lower end of the Bluff Tr. is 0.4m. farther north.

0.4-1.5 Reach trail fork where loop begins (description given in clockwise direction). Ascend left fork, being careful of loose rock.

0.8-1.1 Reach wooded summit of The Peak. (Side trail on left leads to viewpoint.) Continue along crest of ridge, then bear right descending.

1.1-0.8 Turn sharp right downhill onto old road. (To left old road leads 250 ft. to excellent viewpoint.)

1.5-0.4 Reach end of loop.

BIG DEVILS STAIRS TRAIL

2.3 miles (3.7 kilometers)   blue-blazed

The Big Devils Stairs canyon is one of the most impressive features of the Shenandoah Park. There is no trail through the canyon but, with caution, one can climb along the stream all the way through. The present trail after a 0.5m. hike into the canyon, follows the rim on the eastern side of the canyon. It is not suitable for young children. If parking in Harris Hollow *please do not park in someone's driveway*. Access to the Park boundary depends upon the goodwill of the landowner. Trail closures must be observed.

Detailed trail data:
   Bluff Tr. to Harris Hollow (Va. Sec. 622)

0.0-2.3 Junction with Bluff Trail, 1.6m. from the *AT* near Gravel Springs Gap.

0.2-2.1 Enter canyon area. Trail descends steeply along creek. (Creek is a branch of the Rush River.)

0.3-2.0 Trail turns sharply left and climbs up east side of canyon.

0.6-1.7 Trail now descends along the rim, following close to the cliff edge. There are excellent views across the canyon and toward the south. Once past the cliffs the trail descends by switchbacks.

1.6-0.7 Cross the creek and in a few feet pass the Park boundary.

2.3-0.0 Junction with Va. Sec. 622 in Harris Hollow at a point about 0.1m. west of the creek and 4.0m. from Washington, Va. *Do not block driveways*. Remember access to the Park boundary across private propety depends on the goodwill of the landowner. Trail closures must be respected.

NORTHERN SECTION

HARRIS HOLLOW TRAIL
2.8 miles (4.5 kilometers)　　　　　　　　　　　yellow-blazed

A circuit hike of about 7½m. can be made using this trail, the Bluff Tr. and Big Devils Stairs Tr. and a mile of road walking along Va. Sec. 622. A longer circuit, 11½m., would use the Bluff Tr., the Mt. Marshall Tr. and a road walk along Rts. 625 and 622.

If starting at the lower end of the Harris Hollow Tr. park along Rt. 622 wherever one can pull off the road. *Please do not block a private driveway.* Trail is not blazed outside the Park but a small sign on Rt. 622 says "Trail" Where it leaves the gravel road it is again marked by a sign saying "Trail". Remember, access to the Park boundary across private land depends on the goodwill of the landowner. Trail closures must be respected.

Detailed trail data:
  Skyline Drive to Va. Sec. 622

0.0-2.8 Junction with Skyline Drive at Gravel Springs Gap, SDMP 17.7. Trail follows access road toward Gravel Springs Hut.

0.3-2.5 Turn left off access road.

0.4-2.4 Come into Bluff Tr. and follow it left. The two trails are coincident for 0.1m.

0.5-2.3 Continue straight ahead where Bluff Tr. bends sharply to the left.

0.7-2.1 Reach roadbed of former Harris Hollow Rd. and turn left along it. (To the right here Gravel Springs Hut Tr., blue-blazed, leads 0.1m. up to Gravel Springs Hut.)

1.4-1.4 Cross Park boundary. There are no blazes beyond this point. Continue down old road. Land is posted on both sides so stay on road.

2.6-0.2 Reach gravel road and follow it to the right. Where the gravel road bends to the left continue straight ahead on old rutted road.

2.8-0.0 Junction with Va. Sec. 622 at a point 5m. from Washington, Va. (Trailhead of Big Devils Stairs Tr. is 1m. to left along Rt. 622; Mt. Marshall Tr. is 3½m. via Rts. 622 and 625.)

TRAILS IN THE RANGE VIEW CABIN AREA
EAST OF THE SKYLINE DRIVE

The Keyser Run Fire Road, Piney Branch Trail and Hull School

Trail are the major routes in the area. Trails that intersect one or more of these include the Piney Ridge Tr., the Little Devils Stairs Tr., the Pole Bridge Link, the Fork Mtn. Tr., the Thornton Hollow Tr., and, of course, the *AT*. Many different circuit routes are possible.

Range View Cabin is ideally situated for campers who wish to hike in this area or in the adjacent Mathews Arm-Elkwallow area. Cabin reservations must be made in advance at PATC Headquarters; see Chap. 6: "Picnic Shelters, Huts and Cabins".

Access to the area:

I. From the Skyline Drive there are five points of access:

a. *SDMP 19.4:* Here is the upper end of the Keyser Run Fire Road. Also at this mile post, but across the Drive from the fire road, a spur trail goes west to connect with the *AT* in 100 ft. One mile down the fire road is "Four-Way", the point where the Little Devils Stairs Trail goes off to the left (east) and the Pole Bridge Link Trail goes to the right.

b. *SDMP 21.9:* The *AT* crosses the Drive here, just south of the Rattlesnake Point Overlook. Follow the *AT* south for 0.4m. to reach the upper end of the Piney Branch Trail and another 0.4m. to reach the intersection with the service road to Range View Cabin.

c. *SDMP 22.1:* Here a service road (gated) leads by Piney River Ranger Station and on east to Range View Cabin, intersecting the *AT*. Both the Piney Branch Trail and the Piney Ridge Trail have their upper ends on this road (and on or near the *AT*). The upper end of the Piney Ridge Trail is a few feet down the road from this intersection.

d. *SDMP 25.4:* Thornton Hollow Tr. crosses the Drive.

e. *SDMP 28.1:* Hull School Tr. descends eastward from Beahms Gap.

II. From the Piedmont north of Sperryville there are three points of access:

a. *Lower end of Piney Branch Trail:* To reach this point turn northwest from U.S. 522-211 onto Va. Sec. 612 at a point just north of the Thornton River bridge north of the town. In 1.3m. continue ahead on Va. Sec. 600 following the Piney River. Reach a junction with Va. Sec. 653, which enters from the left, when 3.3m. from U.S. 522-211. Park car near this junction. Continue along Rt. 600 on foot to its end, about 0.1m. Here the Piney Branch Tr. leads left, crossing the Piney River, then continuing up the river for 0.6m. before entering the Park. The Piney Branch Trail is yellow-blazed from the Park boundary as far as the Hull School Trail. Above this point it is blue-blazed.

Fords of the Piney River along the lower stretch of the Piney Branch Trail may be difficult in wet weather. The Hull School Tr. and the lower end of the Piney Ridge Trail are easily reached by this access route.

b. *Lower end of the Thornton Hollow Trail:* Turn off U.S. 522-211 as described above but continue on Va. Sec. 612 where it forks left at its junction with Va. Sec. 600. About 3.2m. from the junction reach the end of state maintenance and park. Continue up the road on foot and, in 0.1m, enter the Park. This road, now the Thornton Hollow Tr., here yellow-blazed, continues up the North Fork of the river for 1.4m. to its junction with the Hull School Trail. One can then follow the Hull School Trail, right, to reach the Fork Mtn. Tr., the Piney Branch Tr., and Keyser Run Fire Road. Using this route there are no fords of creeks except where the Hull School Tr. crosses Piney River. Above Hull School Tr. the Thornton Hollow Trail is blue-blazed.

c. *Lower ends of the Little Devils Stairs Trail and Keyser Run Road:* From U.S. 522-211 at the southwest side of the bridge over the Covington River, about 2.5m. north of Sperryville, turn west onto Va. Sec. 622. Follow Rt. 622 for 2.0m. to just past the bridge over the Covington River. There take the left fork which is Va. Sec. 614 and follow it about 3.0m. to the start of the Little Devils Stairs Trail and a parking area. A do-it-yourself backcountry permit booth is located here for those who intend to backpack in this area. Keyser Run Fire Rd. is a continuation of Va. Sec. 614 and is gated about 0.2m. beyond the parking area.

KEYSER RUN FIRE ROAD

4.5 miles (7.2 kilometers)   yellow-blazed

This is a pleasant road to hike with an easy gradient most of the way. It is also an important route as it offers access to the Little Devils Stairs Tr., Pole Bridge Link, Piney Branch Tr., and other trails in the area. Across the Drive from its upper end a short spur trail leads west to the *AT*, thus extending the number of circuit hikes for which the fire road can be used.

Access:

The upper end starts at the Skyline Drive, SDMP 19.4, at the east base of Little Hogback Mtn. A short spur trail (100 ft.) between the *AT* and a point on the Drive directly opposite the fire road gives access from the *AT*.

Access from U.S. 522-211 is via Va. Sec. 622 and 614. (See "Access to Trails in the Range View Cabin area")

Detailed trail data:

Skyline Drive to Va. Sec. 614

0.0-4.5 From south or "east" side of the Skyline Drive, SDMP 19.4, the fire road drops very gradually, passing around the head of the hollow containing Little Devils Stairs.

1.0-3.5 Reach "Four-Way". To left the Little Devils Stairs Tr. leads 2.0m. down to Va. Sec. 614. To right Pole Bridge Link leads 0.8m. to Piney Branch Trail.

3.3-1.2 The Hull School Tr. leads right here, reaching Piney Branch Tr. in 0.4m. and crossing Piney River 0.1m. farther. On the left of the Keyser Run Fire Rd. here is the walled-in Bolen Cemetery.

4.3-0.2 Road is gated.

4.5-0.0 Reach Va. Sec. 614, at end of state maintenance. Little Devils Stairs trailhead is here at parking area.

LITTLE DEVILS STAIRS TRAIL

2.0 miles (3.2 kilometers)   blue-blazed

This trail follows up Keyser Run into the canyon known as Little Devils Stairs. The canyon area is steep, wild and picturesque. Its sheer cliffs are outstanding; they offer a challenge to rock climbers. The trail's upper end is at "Four-Way" on the Keyser Run Fire Road, 1.0m. from the Skyline Drive and the *AT*. The lower end is reached via Va. Sec. 622 and 614 from U.S. 522-211. (See "Access to Trails in the Range View Cabin area")

The trail route is dangerous in wet or icy weather and even in

NORTHERN SECTION 155

good weather must be negotiated with care. For a circuit hike it is wise to ascend the Little Devils Stairs Trail, and to descend via the Keyser Run Fire Road.

Detailed trail data:
  Va. Sec. 614 to Keyser Run Fire Rd. at "Four-Way"
  0.0-2.0 From parking area at end of state maintenance of Va. Sec. 614 trail heads north, immediately crossing two small creeks. (The road (614) continues into the Park as Keyser Run Fire Rd. It is gated 0.2m. beyond the parking area.)
  0.6-1.4 Trail approaches Keyser Run, the stream that cut the Little Devils Stairs canyon. Here there is an old rock wall, part of a former dam or bridge. From here the trail crosses the run frequently as it climbs steeply.
  1.7-0.3 Trail makes a sharp left turn and climbs steeply away from the run.
  1.8-0.2 Trail crosses a rock-edged terrace, a former homesite.
  2.0-0.0 Reach Keyser Run Fire Rd. at "Fourway." Directly across the road is the Pole Bridge Link which joins the Piney Branch Tr. in 0.8m. To the right the Keyser Run Fire Rd. leads to the Skyline Drive (and *AT*) in 1.0m. To the left it leads 3.5m. down to Va. Sec. 614 at the Little Devils Stairs trailhead.

POLE BRIDGE LINK

0.8 miles (1.3 kilometers)   blue-blazed

This trail links the Keyser Run Fire Rd. and Little Devils Stairs Trail with the Piney Branch Trail.

Detailed trail data:
  Keyser Run Fire Rd. to Piney Branch Trail
  0.0-0.8 "Four-Way" intersection on Keyser Run Fire Rd., 1.0m. from Skyline Drive (and the *AT*). Little Devils Stairs Trail also starts here, from the opposite side of the fire road.
  0.8-0.0 Intersection with Piney Branch Trail. (To right, via Piney Branch Trail, the *AT* is 1.4m. and Range View Cabin 0.4m. farther. To left the Hull School Tr. is 2.8m. and the lower end of the Piney Ridge Trail is 2.4m.)

PINEY BRANCH TRAIL

6.5 miles (10.5 kilometers) blue-blazed between the *AT* and Hull School Tr., yellow-blazed from Hull School Tr. to Park boundary

This trail, with the Piney Ridge Trail, provides an 8 mile circuit hike from Range View Cabin. Another circuit could be the *AT* between the Piney Ridge Tr. junction and Keyser Run Rd., the fire road down to "Four-Way", then the Pole Bridge Link, and back up Piney Branch Tr. and on to the Range View Cabin.

Another favorite circuit (7¾m.) starts from Va. Sec. 614. Climb up Little Devils Stairs, then follow the Pole Bridge Link, descend the Piney Branch Tr. to the Hull School Tr. Then follow the Hull School Tr. left and descend the Keyser Run Fire Rd. to the start. A study of PATC Map No. 9 will show other possible circuits.

Access:

The upper end of the trail starts at the *AT* and the service road leading to Range View Cabin. (See PATC Map No. 9, inset of Range View Cabin area.) Start of the trail is 0.4m. north of Range View Cabin and 0.4m. from the Skyline Drive at Rattlesnake Point, SDMP 21.9, via the *AT*, and about 0.3m. from the Drive via the service road at Piney River Ranger Station, SDMP 22.1. The lower end of the trail is on Va. Sec. 600. See "Access to Trails in the Range View Cabin area" for details.

Detailed trail data:

AT to Va. Sec. 600 and 653

0.0-6.5 Intersection with *AT*, 0.4m. north of Range View Cabin and 0.4m. south of Skyline Drive at Rattlesnake Point. Trail leads east at signpost. It follows an old road down the mountain. Follow blue blazes.

1.3-5.2 Cross headwaters of Piney Branch.

1.4-5.1 Junction with Pole Bridge Link Tr. which comes in from the left. (Via Pole Bridge Link it is 0.8m. to "Four-Way" on Keyser Run Fire Rd.) Turn right at this junction.

NORTHERN SECTION

4.0-2.5 Junction with Piney Ridge Trail which enters from right. (Range View Cabin is 3.4m. from this junction via Piney Ridge Tr.)

4.3-2.2 Cross Piney Branch.

4.4-2.1 Junction with the Hull School Tr. Blue blazes end here. Turn right. The Piney Branch Tr. and Hull School Tr. are coincident for the next 0.2m.

4.6-1.9 Cross Piney River, then turn left from the Hull School Tr. and descend old road along the Piney River following yellow blazes.

5.8-0.7 Leave the Park and continue down road to Va. Sec. 600.

6.5-0.0 Reach junction of Va. Sec. 600 and 653.

PINEY RIDGE TRAIL

3.3 miles (5.3 kilometers)   blue-blazed

This trail used along with the Piney Branch Trail provides a circuit hike from the Range View Cabin.

Access:

The upper end of the Piney Ridge Trail may be reached by following the service road from the Skyline Drive, SDMP 22.1, past the Piney River Ranger Station south about 0.7m., crossing the *AT* a few feet before reaching the start of the Piney Ridge Trail which leads right from the road. (The trailhead is within sight of the Range View Cabin at the road's end.) One can also start at Rattlesnake Point Overlook and follow the *AT* south for 0.8m. to its intersection with the service road, then turn left onto the road toward the cabin and, in a few feet, reach the start of the Piney Ridge Trail. See inset map of area, on back of PATC Map No. 9. The lower end of the Piney Ridge Trail is on the Piney Branch Tr. 0.4m. on that trail from the Hull School Tr.

Detailed trail data:

Range View Cabin Service Rd. (near *AT*) to Piney Branch Trail.

0.0-3.3 Junction with service road, just west of Range View Cabin. Trail bears south, descending along crest of the ridge.

2.0-1.3 Pass old cemetery to right of the trail; a few feet beyond take left fork (east) at trail intersection. (Straight ahead the blue-blazed Fork Mtn. Tr. continues along the ridge, reaching the Hull School Tr. in about 1.2m.) As one descends one may find traces of an old homesite.

3.3-0.0 Reach Piney Branch Trail at a point on that trail 0.4m. from its junction with the Hull School Tr.

FORK MTN. TRAIL

1.2 miles (1.9 kilometers) blue-blazed

This short trail leads along the Fork Mtn. ridge from the Piney Ridge Trail southeastward to its intersection with the Hull School Tr. It makes a useful link in circuit hikes.

THORNTON HOLLOW TRAIL

5.2 miles (8.4 kilometers) yellow-blazed east of Hull School Tr., blue-blazed to the west

From Va. Sec. 612 the trail follows an old road up the North Fork of the Thornton River to the Hull School Tr. (See "Access to Trails in the Rangeview Cabin area.") It then continues on up Thornton Hollow crossing on a diagonal the Skyline Drive at SDMP 25.2. It continues on to end at the *AT*.

Detailed trail data:
   Junction of Va. Sec. 612 and 653 to the *AT*.

0.0-5.2 From junction of Rts. 612 and 653 continue up Rt. 612 on foot.

0.6-4.6 State road maintenance ends.

0.7-4.5 Road gated at Park boundary. There is a spring to right of the road just beyond the gate. The trail is yellow-blazed from Park boundary to Hull School Tr.

2.0-3.2 Junction with Hull School Tr. Follow road a few feet beyond its sharp turn to the right. Thornton Hollow Tr. (blue-blazed from here on) then turns left away from road. Trail crosses river 3 times in next 0.6m. Difficult in wet weather.

NORTHERN SECTION

3.4-1.8 Cross a branch of the river. The valley is wide here and there are numerous indications of old homesites, traces of old roads, etc., even an old car!

3.6-1.6 From here the trail climbs gently but steadily upward through open woods.

4.9-0.3 Reach Skyline Drive, SDMP 25.4. Cross Drive diagonally to the left.

5.2-0.0 Reach *AT* at a point on the *AT* 1.2m north of The Neighbor Mtn. Parking Area.

HULL SCHOOL TRAIL

4.4 miles (7.1 kilometers)   yellow-blazed

This trail makes use of a number of roads that existed before the Park was established—the Beahms Gap Rd., the North Fork (of the Thornton) Rd., a bit of the Keyser Run Rd. and a short section long known as "PLD". One end is on the Skyline Drive at Beahms Gap, SDMP 28.1; the lower end is on the Keyser Run Rd. at the Bolen Cemetery. Trails that intersect it include the Thornton Hollow Tr., Piney Branch Tr. and Fork Mtn. Tr.

Detailed trail data:

Skyline Drive to Keyser Run Fire Rd.

0.0-4.4 Skyline Drive, SDMP 28.1. Trail follows route of old Beahms Gap Rd., occasionally detouring right or left of it where erosion has damaged the old roadbed.

1.5-2.9 Enter area of old homesites. Find double daffodils in bloom the first week of April.

1.9-2.5 Find an old homesite on the right. More double daffodils.

2.2-2.2 Cross Thornton River and reach Thornton Hollow Tr. Hull School Tr. now follows route of former North Fork Rd. over the ridge of Fork Mtn.

2.9-1.5 Reach summit of Fork Mtn. ridge. (Fork Mtn. Tr., blue-blazed, leads left for about 1.0m. to end on the Piney Ridge Tr.)

3.5-0.9 Junction with Piney Branch Tr. (To right Piney Branch Tr., yellow-blazed, leads out of the Park to Va. Sec. 600.) Cross Piney River.

3.7-0.7 Piney Branch Tr., here blue-blazed, leads left 4.2m. to the *AT*.

4.4-0.0 Reach Keyser Run Fire Rd. Just up the fire road from the junction is the walled-in Bolen Cemetery. (To the right, Keyser Run Rd. leads 1.2m. downhill to the parking area for the Little Devils Stairs Tr. on Va. Sec. 614. To the left the fire road leads 3.3m. to the Skyline Drive (and *AT*) passing "Fourway" in 2.3m.)

HOGBACK SPUR TRAIL

0.3 miles (0.5 kilometers)   blue-blazed

This short trail runs from the Skyline Drive, SDMP 20.4, up to the *AT*. There is a spring near its lower end. The upper terminus is less than 0.1m. north of a hang glider launching area, so that the main use of this trail is for hang glider enthusiasts.

TRAIL NETWORK IN THE MATHEWS ARM-ELKWALLOW AREA (WEST OF SKYLINE DRIVE)

This trail network includes about a dozen trails from the Big Blue Tr. and Mathews Arm Tr. on the north to Neighbor Mtn. Tr. on the south. A study of the PATC Map No. 9 will suggest a number of possible circuit hikes of varying length.

Historical note: Mathews Arm was part of a grant of land made by Lord Fairfax to Israel Mathews. Many of Israel's descendents still live in Warren County.

BIG BLUE TRAIL

7.8 miles (12.6 kilometers)   blue-blazed

The Big Blue-Tuscarora Trail extends about 220 miles, with its southern terminus on the Appalachian Trail on Hogback Mountain in the SNP and its northern terminus, also on the *AT*, near Duncannon, Pa. West of U.S. 340 its route crosses the south branch of the Shenandoah River at the Bentonville Low Water Bridge, then climbs west over the ridges of the Massanutten, crosses the main Shenandoah Valley in the area of Toms Brook, climbs Little

NORTHERN SECTION 161

North Mountain and zigzags its way west to the Va.-W. Va. state line where it runs generally northeast.

For much of its length within Shenandoah Park the Big Blue follows Overall Run and is coincident with the Overall Run Tr. Just off the trail, at a point 3.1m. from the *AT* and 4.6m. from U.S. 340 via the Big Blue Tr., is the beautiful cascade, Overall Run Falls. This is one of the prettiest spots in the northern section of the Park. The falls here is considered the highest in the Park. Caution: The Big Blue Tr. is extremely steep near here and the side trail to the base of the falls is very rough.

Access:

To reach the southern end of the Big Blue Trail, follow the *AT* south for 0.4m. from the *AT* crossing of the Skyline Drive at SDMP 21.1 or follow the *AT* north 0.6m from crossing of the Drive at SDMP 21.9, just south of Rattlesnake Point Overlook which provides parking space. Cement post on the *AT* identifies the trail here as the Big Blue Tr.

To reach the NW end of this section of the Big Blue Tr., drive along U.S. 340 to a point about 1.5m. south of Bentonville (and 300 yds. south of Va. Sec. 628) and 1.1m. north of Overall. There is room for parking on the west side of U.S. 340 here. Directly across the highway the Big Blue Trail heads eastward along a farm road.

Detailed trail data:

AT to U.S. 340

0.0-7.8 Junction with *AT*. The Big Blue Tr. descends to the west. (Big Blue Tr. and Overall Run Tr. are coincident for the first 4.8m.)

0.7-7.1 Turn sharply right. Straight ahead a short, connecting trail leads 250 ft. to Traces Interpretive Tr., and beyond to the northern part of the Mathews Arm Campground. (Follow the Traces Trail to the left for 0.5m. to reach parking area and the entrance road to the campground.) The Big Blue Tr. continues to descend gently, skirting a swampy area known as Bearwallow.

2.3-5.5 Come into Mathews Arm Tr., yellow-blazed. Continue ahead on the road for 240 ft., then turn left following blue blazes and descend.

2.5-5.3 Several short paths lead left to views of Overall Run Falls and the valley below. Beyond these the trail becomes very steep.

3.1-4.7 Blue-blazed spur trail leads left 0.2m. to foot of Overall Falls. (Spur trail is very rugged; dangerous in icy weather.) Beyond the junction the main trail continues to descend via several switchbacks.

3.7-4.1 Trail crosses to south side of the creek.

4.1-3.7 Trail recrosses creek (to north bank).

4.8-3.0 Concrete post marks separation point of Big Blue and Overall Run Trails. The Big Blue turns sharply right here and ascends toward Thompson Hollow.

5.0-2.8 Turn 90° to left. (Blue-blazed Thompson Hollow Tr. continues straight ahead.) Big Blue now follows the trace of an old road.

5.5-2.3 Take left fork of the old road, heading northwest, then bear around or over several hills with relatively little change in elevation.

6.3-1.5 Begin descent.

6.5-1.3 Make a sharp right turn. (An old trail continues ahead, reaching Park boundary in about 100 ft.) Trail now descends along the Park boundary, crossing in and out several times.

6.7-1.1 Cross creek and turn left. 200 ft. farther, leave Park. Ascend gradually along old road.

6.8-1.0 Turn back sharply to the right while continuing to climb.

6.9-0.9 Again turn right, returning to the Park boundary and following it a short distance. Then descend gradually through pines, passing a pasture on the left.

7.3-0.5 Cross gate and turn sharply left, following the southwest edge of pasture. At lower corner of pasture, nearly under power-line, bear right downhill, heading directly toward railroad underpass in the hollow. (Trail through meadow is marked with stakes, blue-blazed.)

7.6-0.2 Reach farm road and turn left onto it. Pass through railroad underpass.

7.8-0.0 Reach U.S. 340 at a point on the highway 1.5m. south of Bentonville and 1.1m. north of Overall.

NORTHERN SECTION

THOMPSON HOLLOW TRAIL

0.4 miles (0.6 kilometers)　　　　　　　　　　　　　blue-blazed

One end of this short trail is at the Park boundary at the end of Va. Sec. 630 in Thompson Hollow south of Bentonville. Turn east on Va. Sec. 613. In about ¾m. turn south on Va. Sec. 630 and drive to the end of state maintenance. *Do not block road access.* Follow trail through privately owned land a short distance to reach Park boundary and look for post marking the trail. Access to the Park boundary across private land depends upon the goodwill of the landowner. Posted trail closures must be respected.

The upper, or southern, terminus of the trail is on the Big Blue Tr. at a point on the latter 2.8m. from U.S. 340 and 0.2m. from Overall Run.

Now that the Overall Run Tr. has no outside access, this Thompson Hollow Tr.-Big Blue Tr. route is the shortest approach to Overall Run Falls.

OVERALL RUN TRAIL

5.4 miles (8.7 kilometers)　　　　　　　　　　　　　blue-blazed

Most of what was earlier called the Overall Run Trail is now coincident with the Big Blue Tr. Only the lowest section along the run, below the point where the Big Blue Tr. turns away from it, remains separate. At present there is no access to the lower end of the Overall Run Tr. from U.S. 340, so the trail is not maintained west of the Overall-Beecher Ridge Connector Tr. A pleasant circuit hike can be made starting at the Mathews Arm Campground by descending Mathews Arm Tr., going left on Beecher Ridge Tr. and right on the Overall-Beecher Ridge Connector Tr., then ascending via the Overall Run Tr., the Big Blue Tr. and Mathews Arm Tr. (See PATC Map No. 9.)

Detailed trail data:

East to west

0.0-5.4 See description of the Big Blue Tr. for the first 4.8 miles.

4.8-0.6 Overall Run Tr. continues straight ahead. Big Blue Tr. turns right toward Thompson Hollow. (This point is 2.5m. from

Mathews Arm Tr. and 3.0m. from U.S. 340 via the Big Blue Tr.)

4.9-0.5 Lower falls of Overall Run is a few feet left of the trail.

5.4-0.0 End of maintenance. (Trail is closed to the public outside the Park.) Overall-Beecher Ridge Connector Tr., blue-blazed, leads left, crossing the run and ascending the ridge.

OVERALL-BEECHER RIDGE CONNECTOR TRAIL

0.7 miles (1.1 kilometers)　　　　　　　　　　　blue-blazed

The upper terminus of this trail is on the Beecher Ridge Tr., 2.3m. down from its upper end on the Mathews Arm Tr. The lower terminus is on the Overall Run Tr. at its lower end. (Note: Overall Run Tr. is no longer maintained below this point as there is no hiker access from outside the Park at present.)

BEECHER RIDGE TRAIL

3.1 miles (5.0 kilometers)　　　　　　　　　　　yellow-blazed

This trail leaves the Mathews Arm Tr. at a point 0.9m. from the northern end of the Mathews Arm Campground (1.4m. from the campground registration station) and descends along the crest of Beecher Ridge. It comes into the Heiskell Hollow Tr. at a point on the latter 2.5m. below its upper terminus on the Knob Mtn. Tr. and 1.5m. from its lower end on Va. Sec. 697. The Overall-Beecher Ridge Connector Tr., blue-blazed, connects the Overall Run Tr. near its lower end (The Overall Run Tr. is not maintained below this junction.) with the Beecher Ridge Tr., joining it 2.3m. from Mathews Arm Tr. From the Mathews Arm Campground registration station a circuit hike including Beecher Ridge and Overall Run Trails would be about 9.5m., the circuit hike using Beecher Ridge and Heiskell Hollow Trails about 7.5m. (See PATC Map No. 9.)

MATHEWS ARM TRAIL

4.4 miles (7.1 kilometers)　　　　　　　　　　　yellow-blazed

This old road, most of which is now classified by the Park as trail, leads north from the Mathews Arm Campground. After

NORTHERN SECTION

crossing Overall Run it continues along the long ridge, Mathews Arm, from which the campground takes its name. Outside the Park, the road is closed to the public, including foot-travelers.

Access:

From the Skyline Drive, SDMP 22.2, drive down paved entrance road to the Mathews Arm Campground and park in the lot near the registration station. Note large map at the station indicating the camp layout and select any route desired to Tent Area B. Distance from Drive to Tent Area B is 1.1m. (When campground is closed one must walk the full distance. One can follow the abandoned section of the Mathews Arm Rd. from the Drive to the registration station and avoid some of the paved road walking.) Trail description below starts at the camp road in Tent Area B.

Detailed trail data:

0.0 Mathews Arm Trail is gated as it leaves paved camp road in Tent Area B. Descend gently.

0.1 The "Traces" Tr. intersects the road here.

0.4 Weddlewood Tr. leads left. (Weddlewood Tr. leads 1.3m. to end on the Heiskell Hollow Tr.)

0.9 Beecher Ridge Tr. leads left down the Beecher Ridge and over to the Heiskell Hollow Tr. (The Overall Run-Beecher Ridge Connector Tr. runs from low on Beecher Ridge to Overall Run.)

1.3 Cross Overall Run and turn right.

1.4 Intersection with the Big Blue Tr. (From this junction it is 2.3m. right, via the Big Blue Tr., to the *AT;* to the left via the Big Blue Tr. it is 5.2m. to U.S. 340.)

2.7 Trail descends steeply. In 0.6m. turn sharp left off the ridge crest.

4.4 Reach Park boundary. Trail closed to hikers outside the Park.

THE TRACES INTERPRETIVE TRAIL

1.7 miles (2.8 kilometers)   not blazed

This trail, which loops around the Mathews Arm Campground, emphasizes the traces that remain of the pre-Park days of this land. It starts at the upper end of the parking area (near the Entrance

SIDE TRAILS

Station) and circles the campground in a counter-clockwise direction.

Detailed trail data:

0.0 Sign at edge of parking area.

0.5 Cement post marks spur trail to campground. 50 ft. farther a second post marks spur trail which leads right 0.1m. to the Big Blue Trail.

1.1 The interpretive trail intersects the Mathews Arm Rd. at a point on the latter about 0.1m. from the northern end of the campground.

1.3 There is a viewpoint on right.

1.6 Reach camp road at lower end of parking area.

1.7 Completion of loop at trail's start.

KNOB MTN. TRAIL

7.6 miles (12.2 kilometers)   yellow-blazed

From Mathews Arm Campground this trail follows a portion of the graveled road leading to the sewage treatment plant. Near this area the trail goes left and follows the ridge, passing over the peak of Knob Mtn., descending along the ridge crest, then dropping down to Jeremys Run.

Access:

To reach the upper end of trail and road turn west from the Skyline Drive, SDMP 22.2, onto the entrance road to Mathews Arm Campground and drive a half-mile to the parking area at the entrance station. (In winter the entrance road to the campground is closed so it is necessary to walk down from the Drive. One can avoid the paved road by following an abandoned section of the Mathews Arm Fire Rd. which parallels the entrance road a few feet to the south.) From the parking area follow on foot the paved road leading left to the trailer sewage disposal area. Knob Mtn. Tr. starts at the far side of the paved road's turnaround loop. (See inset map of Mathews Arm area, back of PATC Map No. 9.) Start of trail is 0.9m. from the Skyline Drive.

The lower end is reached via the Jeremys Run Trail. See description of that trail.

Detailed trail data:

Mathews Arm Campground to Jeremys Run

0.0-7.5 From loop in paved campground road, follow graveled road beyond chain.

0.4-7.1 Heiskell Hollow Tr. junction. (This yellow-blazed trail leads right 4.0m. down to Va. Sec. 697 near the town of Compton.)

2.2-5.3 To left, the Knob Mtn. (Jeremys Run) Cut-Off Trail, marked with blue blazes, leads 0.5m. steeply down to Jeremys Run Tr. at a point on the latter 0.8m. from the *AT*. (A six mile circuit hike would include the 2.2m. of Knob Mtn. Tr., the Knob Mtn. Cut-Off Tr., the upper portion of Jeremys Run Tr., the *AT* back to Elkwallow Gap, then the Elkwallow Tr. back to Mathews Arm Campground.)

4.3-3.2 The trail continues as a much narrower footway, immediately climbing over the highest peak of Knob Mtn, el. 2865′, then descending along the ridge crest, finally dropping steeply toward Jeremys Run.

7.5-0.0 Cross Jeremys Run and, 50 ft. beyond, reach the Jeremys Run Trail. (From this junction it is 0.8m., right, down the Jeremys Run Tr. to the Park boundary. To the left, the Jeremys Run Tr. intersects the Neighbor Tr. in 50 ft. The *AT* is 5.4m. from this junction via the Jeremys Run Tr. and 4.6m. via the Neighbor Tr. See PATC Map No. 9.)

HEISKELL HOLLOW TRAIL

4.0 miles (6.4 kilometers)   yellow-blazed

This trail can be used in combination with others in the area—Mathews Arm Tr., Weddlewood Tr., Beecher Ridge Tr. and the Big Blue (Overall Run) Tr.—for some excellent circuit hikes. (See PATC Map No. 9.)

Access:

To reach the "upper" or easternmost trailhead follow the Knob Mtn. Trail from Mathews Arm Campground. In 0.5m. from the registration station reach trailhead on the right. To reach the "lower" or western trailhead follow U.S. 340 to Compton, about 4½m. south of Bentonville and 1¾m. north of Rileyville. Turn east on Va. Sec. 662. In 0.4m. turn left onto Va. Sec. 697 and follow it 0.6m. to its end. There is room for parking here but don't block driveway. As first 0.2m. of trail is on private property and necessitates passing through barnyard it is courteous to ask permission before starting. Trail access to the Park boundary depends upon the goodwill of the landowner. Trail closures must be observed. Trail roughly follows along the south side of Compton Run (or Dry Run) to the Park boundary.

Detailed trail data:
Knob Mtn. Tr. to Va. 697

0.0-4.0 Trailhead on Knob Mtn. Tr. 0.5m. from Mathews Arm Registration Station. Descend.

0.7-3.3 Junction with yellow-blazed Weddlewood Tr. (Weddlewood Tr. leads right 1.3m. to end on the Mathews Arm Tr.)

2.5-1.5 Just after crossing Compton (or Dry) Run reach junction with the Beecher Ridge Tr., yellow-blazed also. Within the next mile the trail crosses the run 4 times.

3.8-0.2 Pass gate into pasture. Continue to parallel creek until reaching barnyard.

4.0-0.0 Reach Va. Sec. 697.

WEDDLEWOOD TRAIL

1.3 miles (2.1 kilometers)   yellow-blazed

The eastern (upper) end of this short trail is at a point on the Mathews Arm Tr. 0.5m. north of the paved campground road (and 1.0m. north of the campground registration station) and 1.0m. south of the Big Blue Tr.-Mathews Arm Tr. junction. Its western (lower) terminus is at a point on the Heiskell Hollow Tr. 0.7m. west of the latter's upper end on the Knob Mtn. Tr. (and 1.2m. from the Mathews Arm Campground Registration Station) and 3.3m. east of its end on Va. Sec. 697. The Weddlewood Tr. utilizes an old roadbed and the slope is a gentle one. Thanks to this trail one can start outside the Park using either the Big Blue Tr. or Heiskell Hollow Tr. and make a circuit hike avoiding the campground area.

NORTHERN SECTION

KNOB MTN. (JEREMYS RUN) CUT-OFF TRAIL

0.5 miles (0.8 kilometers)   blue-blazed

This is a short, very steep trail that connects the Jeremys Run Trail to the Knob Mtn. Trail. It is useful in circuit hikes. One end is on the Knob Mtn. Trail 2.2m. from the Mathews Arm Campground; the other is on the Jeremys Run Trail, 0.8m. from its upper end on the *AT* near Elkwallow Picnic Grounds.

ELKWALLOW TRAIL

2.0 miles (3.2 kilometers)   blue-blazed

This short trail leads from the Elkwallow Wayside over to the registration area (and parking area) of the Mathews Arm Campground, roughly paralleling the Skyline Drive. It crosses the *AT* near the edge of the wayside area. It is useful in circuit hikes. One such hike, about 5m., would include the *AT* from Elkwallow Gap north 2.1m. to its junction with the Big Blue (Overall Run) Trail. Descend the Big Blue for 0.7m. Turn left on spur trail toward Mathews Arm Campground. Bear left along the Traces Tr., entering paved entrance road to the campground at the upper end of the parking area. The beginnning of the Elkwallow Trail, with sign post so indicating it, is directly across the entrance road here. Follow this back to Elkwallow Wayside. Another possible circuit would include the upper portions of the Jeremys Run and Knob Mtn. Trails, the Knob Mtn. Cut-Off Tr. and a short stretch of *AT*.

JEREMYS RUN TRAIL

6.2 miles (10.0 kilometers)   upper 5.4m. blue-blazed
                                                                              lower 0.8m. yellow-blazed

Jeremys Run Trail is one of the most delightful routes in the Park. From the Park boundary at the base of the western slope of the Blue Ridge, it leads up Jeremys Run in a deep gorge between two projecting spurs, Knob Mtn. and Neighbor Mtn., to the Appalachian Trail at a point 0.3m. from the Elkwallow Picnic Grounds. The whole of this valley is beautifully forested; the run itself is a continual series of cascades and pools. The hiking is generally easy, with a gentle rise in elevation and numerous rockhopping crossings of the stream. The exception is one very steep stretch, the lowest 0.5m. to the Park boundary. The valley abounds with wildlife. Deer are frequently seen and bear scat can be found on the trail, though the bears themselves are seldom sighted. Jeremys Run is considered one of the fine trout streams in the park.

Access:

The upper or northeast end of the trail can be reached by following the *AT* south 0.6m. from the Skyline Drive crossing in Elkwallow Gap, SDMP 23.9, or by following a short spur trail from the Elkwallow Picnic Grounds to the *AT* and then down the *AT* 0.3m.

To reach the lower or southwestern end of the trail turn east from U.S. 340 at Big Spring (5m. north of Luray) onto Va. Sec. 654. In 1.4m. turn left onto Va. Sec. 611. Follow Rt. 611 for about 1 mile to Jeremys Run but do not cross bridge. Trail access to the Park boundary depends upon the goodwill of the landowner. Posted trail closures must be observed.

Detailed trail data:

AT downhill

0.0-6.2 Junction with *AT*, 0.3m. south of Elkwallow Picnic Grounds (and 0.6m. south of the Skyline Drive at Elkwallow Gap via the *AT*).

0.8-5.4 Junction with Knob Mtn. Cut-Off Trail. (A possible circuit hike of about 6m. would include the 0.8m. of Jeremys Run Tr., the Knob Mtn. Cut-Off Tr., the upper portion of the Knob Mtn. Tr., the Elkwallow Tr. and the 0.6m. stretch of *AT*.) One hundred yards beyond the junction, cross the first of the many fords of Jeremys Run.

3.1-3.1 Cross the 11th ford of the creek at the halfway point of the trail.

4.8-4.1 Pass the largest of the waterfalls on Jeremys Run.

5.4-0.8 Junction with the Neighbor Trail which enters from the left. 50 ft. farther the Knob Mtn. Trail enters from the right.

5.5-0.7 Cross the 16th and final ford.

6.2-0.0 Reach Park boundary.

NORTHERN SECTION

THE NEIGHBOR MTN. TRAIL

5.6 miles (9.0 kilometers)   yellow-blazed

The upper end of this trail is on Skyline Drive, SDMP 28.1, directly across from the Hull School Trail, also yellow-blazed. The Neighbor Mtn. Tr. follows the service road toward the Byrds Nest #4, circles around to the east and north of this picnic shelter, then bears northwestward as far as its intersection with the *AT*. Hikers may prefer parking in the grassy Neighbor Mtn. Tr. Parking Area, SDMP 26.8, and either following the short spur trail to the *AT* and thence south along the *AT* for 0.3m. to the Neighbor Mtn. Trail junction; or they can follow the "spur" horse trail, yellow-blazed, for 0.3m. from the parking area to the Neighbor Mtn. Tr.

From the *AT* west the trail follows the long, almost level, ridge to beyond the peak of "The Neighbor". It then descends steeply to Jeremys Run where it connects with the Jeremys Run Tr. and the Knob Mtn. Tr., offering a choice of circuit hikes.

Detailed trail data:

Skyline Drive to Jeremys Run Tr.

0.0-5.6 From Skyline Drive, SDMP 28.1, just opposite the Hull School Tr., the Neighbor Mtn. Tr. follows the service road toward Byrds Nest #4.

0.1-5.5 A blue-blazed trail leads left for 0.1m. to the *AT*.

0.4-5.2 Turn right off service road and circle east and north of Byrds Nest #4. Water available at the shelter during the summer.

0.9-4.7 At trail junction a yellow-blazed spur trail leads 0.3m. to the Neighbor Mtn. Trail Parking Area.

1.0-4.6 Cement post marks intersection with the *AT*. (Via the *AT* this point is 3.9m. south of Elkwallow Picnic Grounds and 1.2m. north of Beahms Gap.)

2.0-3.6 Pass curious rocks known as "The Gendarmes".

2.9-2.7 Reach peak of "The Neighbor". Trail now descends steeply with switchbacks.

4.7-0.9 Spur trail leads right 50 ft. to Dripping Spring.

5.6-0.0 Junction with Jeremys Run Trail. (To left Jeremys Run Tr. leads 0.8m. to Park boundary, passing junction with Knob Mtn. Tr. in 50 ft. To right Jeremys Run Tr. continues uphill 5.4m.

ROCKY BRANCH TRAIL

3.2 miles (5.2 kilometers) yellow-blazed

From its trailhead 50 ft. west of the Skyline Drive, SDMP 28.1, on the Hull School Tr. this trail heads south, crossing the *AT* in 0.4m. Two miles from its start it crosses the Drive and descends eastward. It ends on Va. Sec. 666 at the point on the road where state maintenance begins.

To reach the lower terminus of the Rocky Branch Trail turn off U.S. 211 just west of Shenandoah Park Headquarters onto Va. Sec. 674. Turn right in 0.2m. onto Va. Sec. 658; then, in 0.4m., turn left onto Va. Sec. 612. Follow Va. Sec. 612 for 1.3m., then turn right onto Va. Sec. 666 and continue to the end of the drivable road and park. Blazed trail starts here.

PASS MTN. TRAIL

3.0 miles (4.7 kilometers) blue-blazed

This trail starts at the *AT* at a point 1.2m. north of Thornton Gap and furnishes access to the Pass Mtn. Hut. It descends eastward to a deep sag between Pass Mtn. and Oventop Mtn. (There is no longer a maintained trail along the ridge of Oventop Mtn.) Here it turns sharply right and descends to U.S. 211 reaching it at a point on the highway directly across from the former Piedmont Picnic Area (approximtely 4½m. west of Sperryville and 2½m. east of Thornton Gap).

Detailed trail data:
   AT to U.S. 211

0.0-3.0 Junction with the *AT* at a point on the latter 1.2m. north of Thornton Gap and 1.9m. south of Beahms Gap, SDMP 28.6.

0.2-2.8 Pass to the right of Pass Mtn. Hut. (See Chap. 6: "Picnic Shelters, Huts, and Cabins.")

0.5-2.5 Come into old road and follow it downhill.

2.4-0.6 Trail turns 90° to the right. (The Oventop Tr., no longer maintained, continued straight ahead here.) The Pass Mtn. Tr. now follows the route of the former Butterworth Branch Tr. and descends along an old road to end on U.S. 211.

CENTRAL SECTION

BUCK HOLLOW TRAIL

3.7 miles (6.0 kilometers) blue-blazed

This trail starts from U.S. 211 at a point about 3½m. west of Sperryville, climbs to the Skyline Drive in 3m., crossing it near the junction of the Hazel Mtn. Tr. with the Drive. Continuing to climb, the trail reaches the *AT* on the crest of the Blue Ridge, for a total gain in altitude of 2270 ft. The Buck Ridge Tr., also blue-blazed, runs from a point low on the Buck Hollow Tr. to the Hazel Mtn. Tr. making a circuit hike possible.

Detailed trail data:
 U.S. 211 to *AT* (north to south)

0.0-3.7 U.S. 211, at a point 3.4 west of its junction with U.S. 522 in Sperryville and 4.6m. east of Thornton Gap. From U.S. 211 trail passes through a brushy area.

0.1-3.6 Cross Thornton River. 200 ft. farther cross Buck Hollow stream.

0.2-3.5 Buck Ridge Tr. leads left for 2.4m. climbing rather steeply to reach the Hazel Mtn. Tr., joining it at a point about 0.4m. from Skyline Drive.

1.3-2.4 Just beyond a crossing of Buck Hollow stream an old road leads off to the left. Beware of this road when coming downhill. (The trail when we checked it could easily be missed.) For the next 0.3m. the trail is close to the stream and very attractive.

1.6-2.1 When climbing one reaches a Y where an old road goes left, the trail (also following an old roadbed) goes right. Watch for blazes. No problem for those heading downhill. The trail is quite pretty all the way to the Drive, sometimes passing through areas with large hemlock, sometimes following the stream.

3.0-0.7 Intersection with Skyline Drive, SDMP 33.5. (Parking area on west side of Drive here. Hazel Mt. Tr. junction is just south of here. Buck Ridge Tr. leads off the Hazel Mtn. Tr.in ⅓m.) Trail crosses Drive diagonally, then climbs, quite steeply at first.

3.4-0.3 Pass Meadow Spring, to right of trail. (Here was site of former PATC's Meadow Spring Cabin which burned in 1946.)

3.7-0.0 Reach Appalachian Trail. (Via the *AT* it is 2.4m. right to Thornton Gap, and 0.6m. left to Byrds Nest #3.)

BUCK RIDGE TRAIL

2.4 miles (3.9 kilometers) blue-blazed

This steep trail has its lower end on the Buck Hollow Trail about 0.2m. from the lower end of the latter on U.S. 211. Its upper end is on the Hazel Mtn. Tr. about 0.4m. from the Skyline Drive, SDMP 33.5. It can be used along with the Buck Hollow Tr. for a circuit hike.

LEADING RIDGE TRAIL

1.3 miles (2.1 kilometers) blue-blazed

This trail leads NW from the Skyline Drive, SDMP 36.2, and crosses at the *AT* in a few hundred feet. It then climbs to a small knob about 0.1m. west of the *AT* intersection before descending steeply along a ridge, finally coming into Jewell Hollow and passing through private property to reach Va. Sec. 669. To reach the trail from the valley turn south from U.S. 211 at a point about 1.0m. east of Park Headquarters and 2½m. west of Thornton Gap. In 0.5m. turn left onto Va. Sec. 669 and drive about 0.8m. Access across private land at the Park boundary is by goodwill of the landowner. Posted closures must be respected.

CRUSHER RIDGE TRAIL

approx. 2½ miles (4 kilometers) blue-blazed

The trail starts on the Nicholson Hollow Trail a few feet "west" of the Skyline Drive and heads north along Crusher Ridge following an old road once known as Sours Lane. It crosses the *AT* about 0.1m. from the Drive. In about 1½m. it leaves the ridge and descends into Shaver Hollow, continuing outside the Park. Access across private land at the Park boundary is by goodwill of the landowners. Posted closures must be respected.

CENTRAL SECTION 175

NICHOLSON HOLLOW—HAZEL COUNTRY TRAIL NETWORK

This area was well populated before the creation of the Shenandoah National Park. Now most of the old cabins are gone, but a few, in ruins, can be seen along the trails. There is one cluster, still quite interesting, along the Hannah Run Trail; two can still be seen along the Broad Hollow Trail and another on the Hot-Short Mtn. Trail. Corbin Cabin, on the Nicholson Hollow Trail, has been restored and is maintained in good condition by the PATC. It is available for use by hikers but reservations must be made in advance at PATC Headquarters. The cabin is to be nominated to the National Register of Historic Places. Its location is ideal for anyone wanting to explore the many trails of the area. Most of the present trails were orginally roads that served the mountain community. There are many other signs of the formerly well-populated area—small orchards, rock walls and the remains of chestnut rail fences, walled springs, even bits of rusting metal. Sometimes one discovers an old family cemetery with the only markers thin slabs of local rock, set vertically into the ground. Very often periwinkle was planted around the graves and its bright shiny greenery helps one spot the cemetery plots today.

Nicholson Hollow was named after the Nicholson clan that had homes along the Hughes River. It was also called "Free State" Hollow, reputedly because law enforcement officers avoided entering the hollow because of its ill-tempered and lawless inhabitants. George F. Pollock, in his book, *Skyland,* gives a vivid description of some of the Nicholsons who lived here. The old USGS Stony Man Quadrangle map, surveyed in 1927, indicated the location of many of the mountain cabins. A series of articles by H.T. Dockerty, published in the Washington Times and preserved in the PATC scrap books, recorded many legends of the "Free State" Hollow.

Three major trails cross through the area—the Nicholson Hollow Trail which leads up the Hughes River, the Hannah Run Trail, and the Hazel Mtn Trail. Other trails in the area include the Catlett Mtn. Tr., Hot-Short Mtn. Tr., Sams Ridge Tr., Broad Hollow Tr., Corbin Cabin Cut-Off Tr., Corbin Mtn. Tr., Catlett Spur Tr., and Indian Run Tr., all blue-blazed; also White Rocks Tr., Hazel River Tr., and Pine Hill Gap Tr., which are yellow-blazed horse-foot trails. See PATC Map No. 10 and the PATC publication: *Circuit Hikes in the Shenandoah National Park*.

Access:

The upper ends of the Hazel Mtn. Tr., Hannah Run Tr. and Corbin Cabin Cut-Off Tr. are on the Skyline Drive and the Nicholson Hollow Tr. which starts on the *AT*, crosses the Drive. The Hazel Mtn. Tr. leaves the Drive at SDMP 33.5, diagonally opposite the Meadow Spring Parking Area. The Hannah Run Tr. starts from the Drive, SDMP 35.1, at Pinnacles Parking Overlook. The Corbin Cabin Cut-Off Tr. begins at SDMP 37.9, just opposite the Shaver Hollow Parking Area. The Nicholson Hollow Tr. starts on the *AT*, crossing the Drive at SDMP 38.4. Parking for this trail is in the Stony Man Overlook-Hughes River Gap Parking Area 0.2m. farther south.

The upper ends of the Buck Ridge Tr., White Rocks Tr., Sams Ridge Tr., Broad Hollow Tr., Hazel River Tr. and Pine Hill Gap Tr. are all on the Hazel Mtn. Tr., as are the lower ends of the Catlett Mtn. Tr. and Catlett Spur Tr. The Buck Hollow Tr. crosses the Drive at the upper end of the Hazel Mtn. Tr.

From the east, access is primarily from Va. 231 south of Sperryville. To reach the lower ends of Sams Ridge Tr., Hazel River Tr., Broad Hollow Tr. and Pine Hill Gap Tr. turn west from Va. 231 onto Va. Sec. 681. (The road junction is about 4m. south of the U.S. 522-Va. 231 junction and is just north of the bridge over the Hazel River.) In about 1m. reach road fork. For Broad Hollow and Pine Hill Gap Trails go left on Rt. 681. Reach lower end of Broad Hollow Trail in about 1½m. Beyond this point road is not passable by car so continue on foot another ½m. to start of Pine Hill Gap Tr. For Sams Ridge Tr. and Hazel River Tr. take right fork which is Va. Sec. 600. In about 1m., where Rt. 600 crosses the Hazel River, walk up road south of the river to reach the Hazel River Tr.'s lower end at the Park boundary and the lower end of the Sams Ridge Trail.

The Buck Hollow (and Buck Ridge) Trail takes off from U.S. 211 about 3½m. west of Sperryville.

NICHOLSON HOLLOW TRAIL

5.9 miles (9.3 kilometers)   blue-blazed

This trail leads down through the hollow formed by the Hughes River. Reputedly, the mountaineers, mostly members of the Nicholson clan, who once lived in cabins scattered through the hollow, were so feared by the valley folks that the Madison Co. sheriffs and their deputies avoided entering the hollow, hence the name "Free State Hollow." Corbin Cabin, located on the Nicholson Hollow Trail, was the pre-Shenandoah Park home of George Corbin. It has been restored and is now maintained by the PATC. Reservations for its use must be made with PATC Headquarters. See Chap. 6: "Picnic Shelters, Huts and Cabins." From the *AT* west of the Drive the Nicholson Hollow Trail, blue-blazed, soon crosses the Skyline Drive, SDMP 38.4, near Hughes River Gap and continues in generally southwest direction to Va. Sec. 600 at its junction with the old Weakley Hollow Rd. (This is where the Brokenback Run joins the Hughes River.) Difficulty may be experienced in crossing Brokenback Run and the numerous fords of the Hughes River when the water is high. Trails connecting with the Nicholson Hollow Trail include the Hannah Run Tr., Hot-Short Mtn. Tr., Corbin Mtn. Tr., Indian Run Tr., and the Corbin Cabin Cut-Off Tr., all blue-blazed.

Detailed trail data;
  AT to Va. Sec. 600 (west to east)

0.0-5.9 Trailhead, marked by a cement signpost, is at a point on the *AT* 7.0m. south of Thornton Gap and 0.3m. north of Stony Man Mtn. Overlook. The Nicholson Hollow Trail leads southeast toward the Skyline Drive.

0.1-5.8 To left of the trail the blue-blazed Crusher Ridge Tr. leads north, crossing the *AT* in 0.1m. In a few feet reach the Skyline Drive and cross it diagonally to the left. The Nicholson Hollow Trail here is marked with a cement post. Descend bank and turn left along an old road which leads through an area of scrub oak and soon descends

0.5-5.4 To right of trail is good walled-in Dale Spring.

1.7-4.2 Cross a creek.

1.8-4.1 Here the Indian Run Tr. leads right. (This trail leads uphill for 1.7m. to end on the Corbin Mtn. Tr. The latter trail has its western terminus on the Old Rag Fire Rd. in another 0.6m.) Nicholson Hollow Tr. continues downhill, soon following the Hughes River.

1.9-4.0 Junction with the Corbin Cabin Cut-Off Tr. which leads left, climbing 1.4m. to the Skyline Drive, SDMP 37.9. (To the right of the trail here is Corbin Cabin, operated by the PATC for the use of campers. There are accommodations for 12 persons. Reservations must be made at PATC headquarters in advance. See Chap. 6: "Picnic Shelters, Huts and Cabins.")

2.0-3.9 Pass overgrown field on right. This was once the site of Madison Corbin's cabin. 250 ft. farther, on left of trail, is a marked spring.

2.1-3.8 Old road leads left to the Hughes River. Just below the road, across the river, are the ruins of Aaron Nicholson's cabin. An unmarked path here connects with the Corbin Cut-Off Tr.

3.5-2.4 Cross to left side of the Hughes River at base of deep pool.

4.0-1.9 Junction with Hannah Run Trail which leads left 3.7m. to Skyline Drive at SDMP 35.1. There are some giant hemlocks near the junction.

4.1-1.8 Cross Hannah Run.

4.2-1.7 Junction with Hot-Short Mtn. Trail which follows an old road, to the left, up a valley between Short Mtn. and Hot Mtn. and comes into the Hazel Mtn. Tr. in 2.1m.

4.6-1.3 To right of the trail the Corbin Mtn. Tr. leads across the Hughes River and climbs 4.4m. to end on the Old Rag Fire Rd.

5.1-0.8 To left of trail is a walled-in spring.

5.6-0.3 Leave SNP.

5.8-0.1 Cross to right of Hughes River. 150 ft. farther cross Brokenback Run. Beyond, turn left onto dirt road.

5.9-0.0 Reach Va. Sec. 600 at point where Weakley Hollow Rd. leads right toward Old Rag Mtn. There is automobile parking here and a SNP parking lot up the Weakley Hollow Rd. Both areas may be crowded on weekends. The Park Service has opened an overflow parking area 0.5m. east of the trail on Rt. 600.

CENTRAL SECTION

HANNAH RUN TRAIL

3.8 miles (6.1 kilometers) blue-blazed

This trail extends from the Skyline Drive down to the Nicholson Hollow Trail on the Hughes River, with a descent of about 2000 ft. It passes by the ruins of several old mountain cabins. The Catlett Mtn. Tr. serves as a link between Hannah Run Tr. and the Hazel Mtn. Tr. (Catlett Spur Tr. also links the same trails.) The Hot-Short Mtn. Trail, with its lower end just a short distance, 0.2m., down the Nicholson Hollow Tr. from the lower end of the Hannah Run Tr., also connects with the Hazel Mtn. Tr. so that an easy circuit hike can be made. One other circuit hike might be mentioned here. Leaving the car at the Pinnacles Overlook, follow the trail down to the Nicholson Hollow Tr., follow up this trail to Corbin Cabin, a distance of 2.1m., then take the Corbin Cabin Cut-Off Tr. 1.5m. to the Drive. Directly across the Drive a short spur trail connects with the *AT*. Follow the *AT* north for 1.2m., turning off on a spur trail which leads a few feet to the Jewell Hollow Parking Overlook. From here it is about 1.3m. along the Drive back to your car, for a total distance of just under 10 miles.

Detailed trail data:
Skyline Drive to Nicholson Hollow Tr.

0.0-3.8 East side of Skyline Drive, SDMP 35.1, at the Pinnacles Overlook Parking Area. Trail descends steeply with switchbacks. There are wintertime views to the east over Hazel Country, with Hazel Mtn. as the dominant feature.

1.3-2.5 Reach trail intersection in deep sag, with low knob ahead. Here the Catlett Mtn. Tr. leads 1.2m. to the Hazel Mtn. Tr. (A short distance along the Catlett Mtn. Tr., Catlett Spur Tr. leads left from it and also joins the Hazel Mtn. Tr. but 1½m. farther north.) At the intersection the Hannah Run Tr. turns sharply right and again descends.

1.7-2.1 Here trail is exceedingly steep, dropping 500 ft. in 0.2m.

1.9-1.9 Cross Hannah Run. After climbing out of ravine, pass ruins of a cabin on the left.

2.3-1.5 Pass between ruins of cabins. There is a spring on the right and an old apple orchard. Trail descends along Hannah Run but does not cross it.

3.8-0.0 Cross small stream; 200 ft. farther, reach Nicholson Hollow Tr. (Left from this junction via the Nicholson Hollow Tr. it is 0.2m. to the Hot-Short Mtn. Tr., 0.6 to the Corbin Mtn. Tr., and 1.9m. to its lower end at Va. Sec. 600. To the right it is 2.1m. to Corbin Cabin and 1.8m. farther to Skyline Drive, but only 1.5m. to the Drive via the Corbin Cabin Cut-Off Tr.).

HAZEL MTN. TRAIL

4.5 miles (7.2 kilometers)   yellow-blazed

This road is gated where it leaves the Skyline Drive, SDMP 33.5, diagonally across from the Meadow Spring Parking Area. The old road might well be called the hemlock trail for it passes through hemlock for much of the way; many of the trees are quite young but in the low areas, along the headwaters of the Hazel River, there are much larger trees, so that it is a veritable "limberlost." For the first two miles trail descends gently along one branch of the Hazel River. It then heads southward and climbs along another branch of the river. From here it passes through a broad level area for another 1½ miles.

At the Drive a signpost just north of the Hazel Mtn. Tr. marks the Buck Hollow Tr. In about 0.3m. the Buck Ridge Tr. leads north. A mile or so farther along there is a fork. The left fork, leading northward, is the White Rocks Tr. Still farther along the Hazel Mtn. Tr. are the junctions with the Catlett Spur Tr., Hazel River Tr., Sams Ridge Tr., Broad Hollow Tr., Catlett Mtn. Tr., Hot-Short Mtn. Tr., and Pine Hill Gap Tr. The old Hazel School which served the area in pre-Shenandoah Park days was situated near the junction of the Hazel Mtn. Tr. with the Sams Ridge-Broad Hollow Trails.

Detailed trail data:
   Skyline Drive to Pine Hill Gap Tr.
   0.0-4.5 Trail leaves Skyline Drive, SDMP 33.5, at a point diagonally across from the Meadow Spring Parking Area. (Buck

CENTRAL SECTION

Hollow Tr. crosses the Drive here and is marked by cement post.) Trail is gated at the Drive.

0.4-4.1 Where trail turns sharply to the right, the Buck Ridge Tr. leads east down Buck Ridge and comes into the Buck Hollow Tr. a short distance from that trail's lower end on U.S. 211.

1.6-2.9 Reach road fork. Take right branch. (Left fork is the White Rocks Tr. which continues 2.4m. first north, then east, to end on the Hazel River Tr.

1.7-2.8 Cross bridge over a branch of the Hazel River.

2.2-2.3 Junction with Catlett Spur Tr. (Spur Tr. leads right 1.1m. to come into the Catlett Mtn. Tr. just short of the latter's junction with the Hannah Run Tr.) Immediately beyond junction, ford creek, then in 250 ft. ford a second creek; both are branches of Hazel River. The old road now climbs, paralleling the last creek. Hemlocks are lovely here.

2.9-1.6 Junction with Hazel River Tr. (Hazel River Tr. leads left 2.8m. to Park boundary at a point about 0.4m. west of Va. Sec. 600.) Beyond the junction the trail passes to the right of the bulk of Hazel Mtn.

3.1-1.4 Cement post marks junction with the Sams Ridge-Broad Hollow Trails which are coincident here. (The Sams Ridge Tr. leads 2.2m. east down to Va. Sec. 600 where the Hazel River crosses that road. The Broad Hollow Tr. leads 2.4m. southeastward, coming into Va. Sec. 681.)

3.4-1.1 Unmarked trail on left leads 0.2m. to Broad Hollow Tr.

3.6-0.9 Junction with Catlett Mtn. Tr. (Catlett Mtn. Tr. leads right 1.2m. to junction with Hannah Run Tr. at a point on the latter 1.2m. from its junction with Skyline Drive.)

4.1-0.4 Junction with Hot-Short Mtn. Tr. (The Hot-Short Mtn. Tr. leads 2.1m. to the Nicholson Hollow Tr. at a point on the latter 0.2m. below its junction with the Hannah Run Tr.)

4.5-0.0 To left, the Pine Hill Gap Tr. leads to Park boundary and beyond to Pine Hill Gap where old road, not passable by auto, but a continuation of Va. Sec. 707 to the south and Rt. 681 to the NE, crosses the Gap. Beyond this point the Hazel Mtn. Tr. has been abandoned.

CORBIN CABIN CUT-OFF TRAIL

1.4 miles (2.3 kilometers)   blue-blazed

This is the shortest route from the Skyline Drive to Corbin Cabin. It is an old, old trail used by the mountain folk in Nicholson Hollow long before there was a Skyline Drive. Parking space is available directly across the Drive from the trail's start, at the Shaver Hollow Parking Area, SDMP 37.9. Trail is quite steep, descending 1000 ft. in the 1.5m.

Detailed trail data:

Skyline Drive to Corbin Cabin

0.0-1.4 From Skyline Drive, SDMP 37.9, directly opposite Shaver Hollow Parking Area, descend along blue-blazed trail.

0.5-0.9 Trail turns sharply to the left here.

0.7-0.7 Trail here switchbacks to right. The footway is rough and rocky for the next 250 ft.

1.1-0.3 Ruins of one of the Nicholson cabins to the left of the trail here.

1.3-0.1 A path leads right 180 ft. to a graveyard. Only unmarked, upended stones mark the graves, as is true of most of the old family cemeteries in the Park.

1.4-0.0 Cross Hughes River. Beyond come into Nicholson Hollow Trail just below Corbin Cabin which is to the right. (Corbin Cabin was once the home of George Corbin, and is typical of the mountain cabins which were once numerous in the hollows. It has been restored and may be rented by hikers. It is equipped for 12 persons. Reservations for its use must be made in advance at PATC Headquarters. See Chap. 6: "Picnic Shelters, Huts and Cabins.")

SAMS RIDGE TRAIL

2.2 miles (3.5 kilometers)   blue-blazed

This trail is one of the trails leading into Hazel Country from east of the mountains. It can be used with one of the others—the Broad Hollow Trail, also blue-blazed, or the yellow-blazed Hazel River or Pine Hill Gap Trails—for a relatively short circuit hike, for all these trails have upper ends on the Hazel Mtn. Tr. and all

CENTRAL SECTION

have their lower ends on either Va. Sec. 681 or Va. Sec. 600 which forks from Rt. 681.

Detailed trail data:

Va. Sec. 600 to Hazel Mtn. Trail (east to west)

0.0-2.2 Junction with Va. Sec. 600. (To reach this point by car, turn west off of Va. 231 onto Va. Sec. 681 at a point just north of the bridge over the Hazel River. Follow Rt. 681 for about 1m. to road fork. Take right fork which is Va. Sec. 600 and continue to where Rt. 600 crosses Hazel River. Walking begins here.) Follow old road up the south side of the Hazel River.

0.4-1.8 Reach Park boundary. Trail turns left away from road. (Road, within Park, becomes the Hazel River Tr., yellow-blazed.) Trail now tends away from the Park, climbing the slope of the ridge through private property. It then follows up the crest of the ridge.

0.6-1.6 Enter SNP, continuing up Sams Ridge.

1.5-0.7 Pass site of mountaineer home. The stone foundation, scattered apple trees, and rose bushes are the only evidences of former habitation. Here is a good view to the north of the Hazel River Valley. There is a spring 200 ft. to left of the trail.

2.0-0.2 Junction with Broad Hollow Trail which comes in from left. From here the two trails are coincident.

2.2-0.0 Junction of Sams Ridge-Broad Hollow Tr. with Hazel Mtn. Tr. (To left via the Hazel Mtn. Tr. it is 0.5m. to the Catlett Mtn. Tr., 1.0m. to Hot-Short Mtn. Tr., and 1.4m. to Pine Hill Gap Tr. To right it is 0.2m. to Hazel River Tr. and 1.5m. to the White Rocks Tr.) The old Hazel School was located near this junction. There is a spring 200 ft. to right of junction down abandoned Sams Run Tr.

HAZEL RIVER TRAIL

3.4 mile (5.5 kilometers)   yellow-blazed

This horse-foot trail offers yet another route into Hazel Country from the east. Its lower end is at the Park boundary, about 0.4m. up the Hazel River from Va. Sec. 600. It follows up the Hazel River for over a mile before swinging left up a subsidiary creek and climbing over a shoulder of Hazel Mtn. to reach its upper end on the Hazel Mtn. Tr. at a point on the latter 0.2m. NW of the Sams Ridge-Broad Hollow Tr. junction. Be prepared to wade the river at trail crossings after heavy rains.

Detailed trail data:
   Va. Sec. 600 to Hazel Mtn. Tr. (east to west)

   0.0-3.4 Start hike where Va. Sec. 600 crosses the Hazel River. On foot follow private road up south side of Hazel River. Where road turns right and crosses river *stay* on the south side of the river.

   0.4-3.0 Enter Park. Blue-blazed Sams Ridge Tr. turns left here.

   0.9-2.5 Within the next 0.6m. the trail crosses the river four times.

   1.8-1.6 Reach trail junction. (Caution: When we checked on these trails this junction was not marked with a cement post, nor clearly blazed, so could easily be missed.) Here the Hazel River Tr. turns left up a side creek and climbs. (The trail straight ahead, yellow-blazed White Rock Tr., soon crosses the river and climbs 2.4m. to end on the Hazel Mtn. Tr. at a point on the latter 1.3m. north of the upper end of the Hazel River Tr.)

   3.4-0.0 Junction with Hazel Mtn. Tr. at a point on the latter 0.2m. NW of the Sams Ridge-Broad Hollow Tr. junction and 1.3m. south of the junction with the White Rocks Tr.

BROAD HOLLOW TRAIL

2.4 miles (3.8 kilometers)   blue-blazed

Like the Sams Ridge Trail this trail offers access into Hazel Country from the east and can be used in combination with that trail or with the Pine Hill Gap Tr. or Hazel River Tr. for a circuit hike. The Broad Hollow Tr. ascends about 1400 ft., with its lower end on Va. Sec. 681 and its upper end coincident with the Sams Ridge Trail end on the Hazel Mtn. Trail. It passes several abandoned cabins along its route.

Detailed trail data:
   Va. Sec. 681 to Hazel Mtn. Trail (east to west)

   0.0-2.4 Junction with Va. Sec. 681. (To reach this point by car, turn west off Va. 231 onto Va. Sec. 681 at a point just north of the bridge over the Hazel River. Follow Rt. 681 for about 2½m. Trailhead on the right of the road.) In about 50 ft. trail crosses Broad Hollow Run. 250 ft. farther an old road takes off to the right of the trail.

0.3-2.1 Trail crosses run.

0.5-1.9 Trail recrosses run, continuing up the hollow for some distance farther.

0.7-1.7 Two old trails, about 250 ft. apart, lead left to the remains of two log buildings. Continue to ascend steadily, with several sharp turns in the trail.

1.0-1.4 Pass a rocked-up spring and, 150 ft. beyond it, a ruined cabin with shingled sides.

1.5-0.9 Pass a roofless cabin here, and another in about a quarter mile.

2.1-0.3 Unmarked trail leads left about 0.2m. to the Hazel Mtn. Tr., coming into the latter at a point about 0.2m. north of the Catlett Mtn. Tr. junction.

2.2-0.2 Junction with Sams Ridge Trail which comes in from the right. The two trails coincide for the next 0.2m.

2.4-0.0 Junction with Hazel Mtn. Tr. near the site of the old Hazel School. (To left via the Hazel Mtn. Tr. it is 0.5m. to the Catlett Mtn. Tr., 1.0m. to the Hot-Short Mtn. Tr., and 1.4m. to Pine Hill Gap Tr. To the right it is 0.2m. to Hazel River Tr. and 1.5m. to the White Rocks Tr. There is a spring 200 ft. to right of junction, down abandoned Sams Run Tr.)

PINE HILL GAP TRAIL

about 1.4m. (2.2 kilometers)   yellow-blazed

This trail leads from Pine Hill Gap to the Hazel Mtn. Tr., coming into that trail at a point 0.4m. south of the Hot-Short Mtn. Trail junction. To reach the lower end of the trail at Pine Hill Gap either drive up Va. Sec. 681 as far as is passable by car or follow Va. Sec. 707 from Nethers as far as is drivable; by either route continue on foot to the Gap, where trail starts. This trail is useful for circuit hikes.

HOT-SHORT MTN. TR.

2.1 miles (3.4 kilometers) blue-blazed

This is an interesting stretch of trail along the valley between Hot and Short Mountains. It connects the Nicholson Hollow Trail with the Hazel Mtn. Tr. From its lower end this trail involves a considerable climb with a change in elevation of about 1300 ft. It follows up a stream much of the way, utilizing old roads and passing several old homesites.

Detailed trail data:

Nicholson Hollow to Hazel Mtn. Trail

0.0-2.1 This trail begins on Nicholson Hollow Trail at a point 1.7m. from the latter's intersection with Va. Sec. 600 where it is joined by the Weakley Hollow Rd.

0.1-2.0 Turn left and follow trail between stone walls. From here trail ascends.

0.4-1.7 Continue to ascend, along a road, with ravine to left.

0.7-1.4 Reach an outcropping of rocks where there is a splendid view of Corbin and Robertson Mtns. across Nicholson Hollow.

0.9-1.2 Notice old farmhouse across stream to left. In 200 ft. cross stream and follow up it. 250 ft. farther, turn sharp left and ascend steeply. Then turn right and cross overgrown clearing.

1.3-0.8 Cross stream and continue to ascend.

1.4-0.7 Trail leads through overgrown field with apple trees. To right is view of Hot Mtn.

1.6-0.5 Cross stream again.

1.9-0.2 There is an old chimney worthy of notice about 100 ft. to right of trail.

2.0-0.1 Enter old road and continue through level section.

2.1-0.0 Junction with Hazel Mtn. Tr. (To left on Hazel Mtn. Tr. it is 0.5m. to Catlett Mtn. Tr., 1.0m. to Broad Hollow—Sams Ridge Trails, and 4.1m. to the Skyline Drive; to right it is 0.4m. to the Pine Hill Gap Tr.)

CATLETT MTN. TR.

1.2 miles (1.9 kilometers) blue-blazed

This blue-blazed trail connects the Hannah Run Trail with the

CENTRAL SECTION

Hazel Mtn. Tr. It affords a pleasant, easy walk along the north slope of Catlett Mtn. through woods, abandoned orchards, and small clearings. A good 10 mile hike could start at the end of Va. Sec. 600 west of Nethers. From here follow the blue-blazed Nicholson Hollow Tr. for 1.7m., then the Hot-Short Mtn. Tr. for 2.1m. Turn left on Hazel Mtn. Tr. and follow 0.5m. to the Catlett Mtn. Tr. Then follow this trail over to the Hannah Run Tr., 1.2m. and take the Hannah Run Tr. down 2.5m. to the Nicholson Hollow Tr., then 1.9m. down this trail back to the start at Va. Sec. 600.

Detailed trail data:

Hannah Run Tr. to Hazel Mtn. Tr.

0.0-1.2 Junction with Hannah Run Trail at a point on the latter 1.2m. from the Skyline Drive. Follow old roadbed, descending slightly. In 200 ft. reach another trail junction. Catlett Mtn. Tr. turns right here. (The trail straight ahead is the Catlett Spur Tr., also blue-blazed. It leads to Hazel Mtn. Tr. joining it 1.4m. nearer the Skyline Drive than the Catlett Mtn. Tr.-Hazel Mtn. Tr. junction. See PATC Map No. 10.)

0.1-1.1 Bear right around a pit; remnants of old stone wall to right of trail. Climb gently.

0.3-0.9 Cross worn road. For some distance trail is level; summit of Catlett Mtn. is to the right of trail.

0.7-0.5 Trail crosses over the shoulder of Catlett Mtn. From here it descends gradually through pine and abandoned orchard.

1.0-0.2 Cross stream and ascend.

1.2-0.0 Junction with Hazel Mtn. Tr. at a point on the latter 0.5m. north of the Hot-Short Mtn. Tr. and 0.5m. SW of the junction with the Sams Ridge-Broad Hollow Trs.

CATLETT SPUR TRAIL

1.1 miles (1.8 kilometers)   blue-blazed

One end of this trail is on the Catlett Mtn. Tr. a short distance from the Hannah Run Tr., the other is on the Hazel Mtn. Tr. Follow the Hannah Run Tr. from the Skyline Drive, reach the junction with the Catlett Mtn. Tr. in 1.2m. (Here the Hannah Run Tr. turns right.) Follow the Catlett Mtn. Tr., also blue-blazed, for about 200 ft. At a trail junction, presently marked by a metal post, the Catlett Mtn. Tr. turns right, whereas the Catlett Spur Tr. goes straight ahead following an old roadbed. It descends gently along one of the Hazel River tributaries, coming into the Hazel Mtn. Tr. at a point 2.2m. east of the Skyline Drive. This end of the Catlett Spur Tr. is 1.4m. nearer the Drive than the Catlett Mtn.-Hazel Mtn. Tr. junction.

WHITE ROCKS TRAIL

2.4 miles (3.9 kilometers)   yellow-blazed

This horse-foot trail leads east from the Hazel Mtn. Tr., first following an old roadbed (former Old Hazel Rd.) for 0.9m., then along the crest of the White Rocks Ridge. At 1.4m. the White Rocks will be to the right of the trail. Still following the ridge crest, the trail soon starts descending and at 2.1m. reaches a gap. Here trail turns to the right and descends to the Hazel River, 2.3m., crosses it and ends on the Hazel River Tr. 0.1m. downstream from the crossing.

The White Rocks Tr.-Hazel River Tr. is one of the five routes down the mountain from the Hazel Mtn. Tr. to the eastern Park boundary so can be used in combination with any one of the other four—Hazel River, Sams Ridge, Broad Hollow or Pine Hill Gap Trail—for a circuit hike.

TRAILS IN THE SKYLAND-OLD RAG AREA

Skyland is situated almost in the center of the Shenandoah Park. The story of Skyland's early days, from about 1890 to the formation of the SNP in the 1930's, and of its charismatic founder, George Freeman Pollock, has given the whole area around Skyland a romantic aura. Who can help smiling at the thought of Pollock's guests, elegant Washingtonians, rubbing elbows with rough mountain characters such as those who lived in the hollow once known as "Free State"? But what is Skyland today? A lodge and dining hall, some cottages and dormitories, a recreation room and stables—all these but much, much more. At the northern entrance to Skyland the Skyline Drive reaches its highest elevation, 3680 ft. Surrounding Skyland is as great a variety of

CENTRAL SECTION

fascinating places to explore as one could ask for. To start, listing them in clockwise order, there is that "Free State" Hollow (Nicholson Hollow), once home of the reputedly fierce and lawless Corbins and Nicholsons; then the unique Old Rag Mountain with its ragged top; next, the magnificent Whiteoak Canyon with its series of cascades; Hawksbill Mtn. that towers over the rest of the Park; then fearsome Kettle Canyon, immediately below Skyland; and, lastly, Stony Man Mtn. whose "profile" is so visible when traveling south along the Drive. Small wonder that the Shenandoah Park's most popular trails are here.

STONY MAN NATURE TRAIL

0.4 mile plus 0.4 mile loop   marked by signs

LITTLE STONY MAN TRAIL

0.6 mile (1 kilometer)   blue-blazed

The Park Service has constructed a nature trail (self-guiding with leaflet) leading from the Stony Man Nature Tr. Parking Area near the northern entrance to Skyland to Stony Man Mtn., where the trail loops around the summit and offers a view from the top of the cliffs that form the Stony Man's profile. Branching from the Nature Trail is another trail that leads on to the cliffs of Little Stony Man, then descends to the *AT*. By returning to Skyland via the *AT*, which follows a shelf below the cliffs, a good circuit hike can be made.

The cliffs of Stony Man and Little Stony Man are the weathered remnants of ancient beds of lava. (See Chap. 3, "Geology of the SNP".) From 1845 to the turn of the century a copper mine operated near the top of Stony Man Mtn. Overgrown culm banks and tree-masked workings on the cliff-face, with green rock showing the presence of copper, mark the place. The ore was smelted at Furnace Spring, the site of which is on the *AT* just north of Skyland. After operations were discontinued the mine was still a spot of much interest to visitors. The shaft, however, became a hazard and was filled up. There is now no trail to the spot.

Detailed trail data:

0.0 Nature Trail Parking Area, near the northern entrance to Skyland, SDMP 41.7.

0.4 Trail junction. Straight ahead the Nature Tr. continues and in 250 ft. starts a 0.4m. loop around the summit of Stony Man Mtn. To left, a spur trail connects with the Skyland-Stony Man Mtn. Horse Trail. Turn right here to continue on toward Little Stony Man, following blue blazes.

0.8 Reach the cliffs of Little Stony Man. The *AT* is directly below the cliffs here. From here trail descends steeply by switchbacks.

1.0 Reach *AT* at a point 0.3m. south of the Little Stony Man Parking Area, SDMP 39.1. From this point it is 1.2m. via the *AT* to paved Skyland Rd. (which leads uphill to Nature Trail Parking Area) and 1.3m. to where a short spur trail leads to paved service road which also can be followed to the parking area.

STONY MAN HORSE TRAIL

1.4 miles (2.3 kilometers)   yellow-blazed

This trail leads northeastward from the Skyland stables, crossing the northern entrance road to Skyland at the first road fork, in 0.8m. It then skirts the western side of the parking area for the Stony Man Nature Trail and continues on to the summit of Stony Man.

The upper end of the yellow-blazed Furnace Spring Tr. is on the Stony Man Horse Tr. just west of the Stony Man Nature Trail Parking Area. The upper (or northern) end of the Whiteoak Horse Tr. is just across the Drive.

MILLERS HEAD TRAIL

0.8 miles (1.3 kilometers)   blue-blazed

This short but rewarding trail leads over Bushytop Mtn. and on out the ridge to a lower peak known as Millers Head. The ridge forms the southern wall of the deep Kettle Canyon. A stone platform on Millers Head offers a superb view of the Shenandoah Valley, the Massanuttens and mountains farther west, Kettle Canyon, the buildings of Skyland, and, to the southwest, Buracher Hollow.

CENTRAL SECTION

Access:

Park at the southern entrance to Skyland, SDMP 42.5, and walk up the Skyland road toward the stables (left fork) only a few feet to reach the *AT*. Follow *AT* to the right to where it crosses the paved Skyland Rd. Turn left along the road for 200 ft. Sign indicates start of Millers Head Trail.

Detailed trail data:

0.0 Trail sign on paved Skyland Road. (The gravel road to left of trail here rejoins trail on summit of Bushytop, where it ends.)

0.2 Summit of Bushytop. (There is a microwave installation here.) 100 ft. farther along the trail is an excellent viewpoint on the right, with Kettle Canyon below and the Skyland buildings quite visible above the canyon.

0.8 Reach the Millers Head.

OLD SKYLAND ROAD TRAIL

3.2 miles (5.2 kilometers) yellow-blazed

As one walks this road it is fun to imagine what a trip to the "top of the mountain" was like in Pollock's day when it was only just barely usable for horse-drawn vehicles. The road climbs 2200 ft. following up the ridge between Kettle Canyon and Dry Run Hollow and is gated at the Park boundary and again just below Furnace Spring, located at the head of Dry Run and close by the *AT*. The lower end of the yellow-blazed Furnace Spring Trail is on the Old Skyland Road Tr. just above the gate.

To reach the lower end from Luray, head south on U.S. 340. Just south of the town turn left onto Va. Sec. 642. Follow Rt. 642 for about 1.6m., then turn right onto Va. Sec. 689 and follow for another 2 miles. Turn left on Va. Sec. 668 for 0.9m., then right on Va. Sec. 672. State maintenance ends in 0.6m. and road continues as the Skyland Rd. soon entering the Park.

FURNACE SPRING TRAIL

0.5 miles (0.8 kilometers) yellow-blazed

The upper end of the trail is on the Stony Man Horse Tr. at a point just north of the northern entrance road to Skyland and west of the parking area for the Stony Man Nature Tr. The horse trail then zigzags down toward the northwest, ending on the Old Skyland Road Tr. just above where it is gated (and where the *AT* and Old Skyland Road Tr. merge, a few feet from Furnace Spring.)

Hikers making the circuit using the Stony Man, Little Stony Man Trails and the *AT* may find the short trail a pleasant way to return to the parking area, rather than walking up the paved road.

WHITEOAK HORSE TRAIL

1.1 miles (1.8 kilometers)   yellow-blazed

The trail extends from Skyline Drive, directly across from the northern entrance to Skyland, down to the Old Rag Fire Rd. near the Whiteoak Ranger Station. It serves as a segment of an "over the mountain" route for horsemen (using the Old Skyland Road Tr., Furnace Spring Tr., Whiteoak Horse Tr. and Old Rag Fire Rd.).

From the stables area of Skyland an easy circuit, for horses or hikers, would include the Stony Man Horse Tr. as far as the upper entrance road to Skyland, the descent along the Whiteoak Horse Tr., and a return up the Skyland-Big Meadows Horse Tr. (and Old Rag Fire Rd.). See PATC Map No. 10 for other circuits utilizing this trail.

WHITEOAK CANYON TRAIL

5.1 miles (8.2 kilometers)   blue-blazed

Whiteoak Canyon is one of the scenic gems of the Shenandoah National Park. Whiteoak Run gathers waters from a number of streamlets gushing from as many springs located just below the Skyline Drive in the Skyland area. The broad area where these headwaters gather is covered with a virgin hemlock forest and is still called the "Limberlost," the name given to it by Mr. Pollock as it reminded him of the locale of Gene Stratton Porter's novel, *Girl of the Limberlost*.

Below the Limberlost, Whiteoak Run has cut a deep canyon in its rush to Old Rag Valley far below. There are six cascades, each more than 40 ft. high, along its route. (See Waterfall chart.) The falls occur between layers of the ancient lava beds, now tilted vertically, because the less resistant rock could withstand the creek's erosive powers much less than the basaltic rock. From the start of the Whiteoak Canyon Trail to the base of the sixth or lowest cascade there is a loss in elevation of 2000 ft. The trail drops another 350 ft. before reaching the Berry Hollow Rd. (Va. Sec. 600). The canyon is lined with towering trees—white oak, hemlock, tulip and ash.

A few miles to the south Cedar Run forms a canyon paralleling Whiteoak Canyon. A very popular hike includes a trip down one canyon and up the other with the stretch of the *AT* between Skyland and Hawksbill Mtn. completing the circuit.

Access:

The Whiteoak Canyon Trail starts at the parking area directly across the Skyline Drive from the south entrance to Skyland. To reach the lower end of the trail by car, follow Va. 231 to about 5m. north of Madison and turn west of Va. Sec. 670 which passes through the community of Criglersville. Five miles beyond Criglersville, at Syria, turn right on Va. Sec. 643. In 0.8m. turn left on Va. Sec. 600. (One can also reach this point by turning west off Va. 231 at Etlan onto Va. Sec. 643 and reaching the junction of Va. Sec. 600 in about 4 miles.) Follow Rt. 600 north, up the Robinson River, for 3.6m. Just beyond the fording of Cedar Run turn left into a large parking area divided into two sections by Cedar Run but connected by a low-water bridge. Trailhead is at the end of the parking area most distant from Rt. 600.

Detailed trail data:

Skyline Drive at Skyland to Old Rag Valley

0.0-5.2 Trail begins at parking area, east of the Drive and almost directly across from the southern entrance to Skyland, SDMP 42.5. Trail descends. (*AT* is 0.1m. from trailhead, on west side of Drive.)

0.5-4.7 Cross a branch of Whiteoak Run.

0.6-4.6 Cross Old Rag Fire Rd. (To right road leads 0.2m. to a parking area and 0.1m. farther to the Skyline Drive. To left it leads down the mountain 4.7m. to the Old Rag Valley at the top of the rise where the Weakley Hollow Fire Rd. and Berry Hollow Fire Rd. come together.) Trail soon enters the Limberlost area.

SIDE TRAILS

0.8-4.4 At trail junction the Limberlost Trail leads right 0.8m. to the parking area near the beginning of the Old Rag Fire Rd. To the left a spur trail leads 0.1m. over to Old Rag Fire Rd. Whiteoak Canyon Tr. descends more and more steeply from here.

2.2-3.0 Turn sharp left and cross footbridge over Whiteoak Run. (Just below the present bridge is the location of Mr. Pollock's "Middle Bridge." This was the site of his famous barbecues in the old "Skyland Days" and a favorite spot of his Skyland guests.) A few feet farther the trail intersects the Skyland-Big Meadows Horse Trail. (Horses must ford the Run. West of the Run the horse trail follows the Whiteoak Fire Rd. up the mountain. Hikers making the Cedar Run Canyon–Whiteoak Canyon circuit may "short-cut" the climb up Whiteoak Canyon from here by following this fire road 1.8 miles to the Skyline Drive, SDMP 45.0, at a point on the Drive only 0.6m. from the upper end of the Cedar Run Trail.)

2.3-2.9 To right is excellent viewpoint over the Upper Whiteoak Falls, the first of the six cascades in the canyon. From here the trail descends very steeply.

2.4-2.8 A spur trail on the right leads back 250 ft. along Whiteoak Run to near the base of the Upper Falls. The canyon trail continues its steep descent, remaining on the northeast side of the run. There are occasional views of the various falls as the trail switchbacks down the canyon.

3.7-1.5 Cross side creek, Negro Run. (There is a falls on this creek visible from the trail.) Trail now comes quite close to Whiteoak Run at a point just below the lowest or sixth cascade.

4.3-0.9 Junction with Cedar Run/Whiteoak Link Tr. which leads to the right, fording the Whiteoak Run, then continuing almost level until it reaches Cedar Run Tr. in 0.8m. (It is another 2.7m. via Cedar Run Tr. to Skyline Drive at Hawksbill Gap.)

4.8-0.4 Cross Whiteoak Run.

5.0-0.2 Cedar Run Tr. leads to the right, soon crossing Cedar Run and climbing, to reach Skyline Drive, SDMP 45.6, at Hawksbill Gap in 3.1 miles

5.1-0.1 Cross Cedar Run.

5.2-0.0 Reach parking area, just off of Va. Sec. 600. (To the right on Rt. 600 it is about 3.6m. to Rt. 643 and another 0.8m. to

CENTRAL SECTION

Syria. To the left, up Berry Hollow, it is about 1.7m. to the junction of Berry Hollow, Weakley Hollow and Old Rag Fire Roads.)

CEDAR RUN TRAIL

3.1 miles (5.0 kilometers)　　　　　　　　　　　　　blue-blazed

Cedar Run flows southeast, paralleling Whiteoak Run which it joins near the Berry Hollow Rd., Va. Sec. 600. The two canyons are separated by a high ridge along which the former Half-Mile Cliffs Trail extended. The Cedar Run Canyon is deep and wild with tall trees. While the stream has a lesser flow of water than Whiteoak Run, it has several high falls, sheer cliffs and deep pools.

The Cedar Run Trail is often used in conjunction with the Whiteoak Canyon Trail. The full circuit, starting at Hawksbill Gap, would be to descend the Cedar Run Tr., follow the Cedar Run/Whiteoak Link Tr., ascend the Whiteoak Canyon Tr. all the way to the Drive, cross to the *AT* and follow the *AT* back to Hawksbill Gap, a distance of 10.5m. A shorter circuit which would still include the deep canyon area of the Whiteoak Canyon Trail would be to descend as before, then to ascend the Whiteoak Tr. to just above the Upper Falls; turn left across the Run and follow the Whiteoak Fire Road up the mountain to the Drive; then walk along the Drive the 0.5m. back to Hawksbill Gap, for a total distance of 7.8m. (If starting from Va. Sec. 600 it is necessary to add ¾m. to the total distances.)

Access:

The upper end of the Cedar Run Tr. is directly across the Drive from the Hawksbill Gap Parking Area, SDMP 45.6. The lower end of the trail is reached from Berry Hollow by following the Whiteoak Canyon Trail from the parking area near Va. Sec. 600 for 0.2m. to the Cedar Run Trailhead.

Detailed trail data:

Hawksbill Gap to Berry Hollow

0.0-3.1 East side of the Skyline Drive at Hawksbill Gap, SDMP 45.6, across from parking area. Pass gate in 200 ft.

0.1-3.0 Cross the Skyland-Big Meadows Horse Trail. Trail soon descends along north side of Cedar Run.

1.1-2.0 To the right is the uppermost cascade of Cedar Run.

1.6-1.5 Cross to the right of Cedar Run and swing away from it.

1.8-1.3 Trail again comes near Cedar Run at a point near its highest falls. Across the creek here tower the sheer Half-Mile Cliffs.

2.5-0.6 Here trail turns left and fords the run immediately below a falls. (Old road which follows down the right side of the run passes through private property to reach Va. Sec. 600.)

2.7-0.4 At trail fork, right branch is the Cedar Run Tr.; left one is the Cedar Run/Whiteoak Link Trail which leads 0.8m. to the Whiteoak Canyon Tr., joining it just below the lowest falls.

3.1-0.0 Reach lower end on the Whiteoak Canyon Rd. about 0.2m. west of the parking area near Va. Sec. 600.

CEDAR RUN/WHITEOAK LINK TRAIL

0.8 miles (1.3 kilometers)   blue-blazed

This trail connects the Whiteoak Canyon Tr. and Cedar Run Tr. near their lower ends. It is almost level. The northern terminus is at a point on the Whiteoak Canyon Tr. just below the lowest falls and about 0.9m. from its lower end at the parking area near Va. Sec. 600. The southern end is on the Cedar Run Tr. 0.4m. from its lower end.

The trail is part of the popular Cedar Run Canyon-Whiteoak Canyon circuit hike.

WEAKLEY HOLLOW FIRE ROAD

2.5 miles (4.0 kilometers)   yellow-blazed

BERRY HOLLOW FIRE ROAD

0.8 miles (1.3 kilometers)   yellow-blazed

Prior to the establishment of the Shenandoah National Park, Old Rag Valley was an extensive mountain community. The state road that is now Va. Sec. 600 went from the village of Nethers through

CENTRAL SECTION

this valley and on out to Syria. A log building, the Old Rag Post Office, was located at the highest spot on this road, at its junction with a road coming down the Blue Ridge from Skyland. The section of the old highway, now in the Park, that lies northeast of the junction is now known as the Weakley Hollow Fire Rd., whereas southwest of the junction it is called the Berry Hollow Fire Rd. These two fire roads along with their extensions outside the Park (Va. Sec. 600 in both directions) are very valuable for access purposes; both the Ridge Trail and Saddle Trails up Old Rag Mountain start from here, the lower termini of the Whiteoak Canyon Tr. (and access to the Cedar Run Trail) and Nicholson Hollow Trail are on this old route, as is the Old Rag Fire Rd. The Robertson Mtn. Tr. and the Corbin Hollow Tr. also have their lower ends on this former state road.

The Weakley Hollow Fire Rd. is an important link for completing a circuit of Old Rag Mtn. The Park Service has constructed a parking area on this road just within the Park. There is also an "overflow" parking area 0.8m. back on Va. Sec. 600. The Berry Hollow Rd. is often used to complete a circuit along with the Whiteoak Canyon Trail and the Old Rag Fire Rd.

Access:

To reach the Weakley Hollow Fire Road turn west off Va. 231 (south of Sperryville) onto Va. Sec. 602 at a point just south of the bridge over the Hughes River. Continue up the river on Va. Sec. 707 where Rt. 602 ends. About 4 miles from Va. 231, where Rt. 707 turns right and crosses the river, continue on the paved road, Rt. 600, which follows on up the river. In one mile the road turns sharply to the left uphill. 0.3m. farther reach the Park boundary and parking area just beyond.

To reach the Berry Hollow Rd., turn west off Va. 231 onto Va. Sec. 670 at a point about 5 miles north of Madison. Continue on Rt. 670 through Criglersville and on to Syria, about 3.5m., then turn right onto Va. Sec. 643, and very shortly turn left onto Va. Sec. 600. Rt. 600 follows up the Robinson River and Berry Hollow 4.8m. to the Park boundary. Parking space is very limited along this road. Parking is provided at the lower end of the Whiteoak Canyon Trail.

Detailed trail data:
NE to SW

0.0-3.3 Parking area just beyond end of Rt. 600. (Nicholson Hollow Trailhead is 0.3m. down Rt. 600 from here.) Ridge Trail over Old Rag Mtn. leads south from here.

1.2-2.1 Corbin Hollow Tr. leads right, crossing Brokenback Run then following up the creek.

1.3-2.0 To the right the Robertson Mtn. Tr. leads up the ridge.

2.5-0.8 Road junction. (To the right the Old Rag Fire Rd. leads northwest to the Skyline Drive joining it just south of Skyland at SDMP 43.0. Berry Hollow Fire Rd. is straight ahead here. To the left, the Saddle Trail leads 1.9m. to the summit of Old Rag Mtn., passing the Old Rag Shelter in 0.4m. and the Byrds Nest #1 in 1.5m.) From the junction the Berry Hollow Fire Rd. descends.

3.3-0.0 Reach Park boundary and Va. Sec. 600. (0.9m. farther, down Rt. 600, is the lower end of the Whiteoak Canyon Trail and access to the Cedar Run Trail.)

OLD RAG FIRE RD.

5.0 miles (8.0 kilometers)   yellow-blazed

In pre-Shenandoah Park days, a road led from Skyland down the east slope of the Blue Ridge to the Old Rag Valley, coming into the road through the valley at its highest point. The Old Rag Post Office was located at this junction. Now the building that served as post office is gone, as is the community it served. But the lower 4 miles of the present fire road follows pretty much the route of the old road down the mountain. Above Comer's Deadening, the present road continues almost due west and reaches the Skyline Drive about a mile SW of where the original road crossed the Drive.

The Old Rag Fire Rd. can be used in conjunction with the Whiteoak Canyon Trail and the Berry Hollow Fire Rd. for a circuit trip of about 11.5m. From the Skyline Drive the fire road is the shortest route to the start of the Saddle Trail up Old Rag Mtn. The fire road also serves for access to the Corbin Mtn. Tr. (and via the latter to the Indian Run Tr.), the Corbin Hollow Tr. and the Robertson Mtn. Tr.

CENTRAL SECTION

Detailed trail data:

Skyline Drive to Weakley Hollow and Berry Hollow Fire Rds.

0.0-5.0 Skyline Drive, SDMP 43.0, el. 3360'. Fire road leads eastward.

0.1-4.9 Parking area to left of road. To right of road is upper end of Limberlost Trail which leads 0.8m. through the area of virgin hemlocks to its end on the Whiteoak Canyon Trail. Ahead the fire road is gated. Just beyond the gate the Skyland-Big Meadows Horse Trail enters the road from the left and follows down it.

0.3-4.7 Whiteoak Canyon Trail crosses the fireroad. (To the left it is 0.6m. to the Skyline Drive at the southern entrance to Skyland, SDMP 42.5. To the right it is 0.2m. to the lower end of the Limberlost Trail, 1.6m. to the viewpoint above the upper falls and 4.5m. to Va. Sec. 600 in Berry Hollow.)

0.5-4.5 Spur trail leads right 0.1m. to Whiteoak Canyon Tr. entering at the junction of the Whiteoak Canyon and Limberlost Trails.

0.7-4.3 Cross Whiteoak Run.

1.0-4.0 Reach the area known as Comer's Deadening. (Here the Skyland-Big Meadows Horse Trail turns right leaving the fire road, and in 1.7m. reaches the Whiteoak Run just above the Upper Falls. 100 ft. farther along the fire road the Whiteoak Horse Trail, marked by cement post, comes in from the left. It leads about 1m. to Skyline Drive, at a point just opposite the northern entrance to Skyland.)

1.1-3.9 Pass Ranger cabin on right. Beyond here the fire road descends steadily.

1.8-3.2 Corbin Mtn. Tr., 4.4 miles long, leads left following an old road down to a sag near Thorofare Mtn., then turns eastward to reach Corbin Mtn. From here it descends northward to end on the Nicholson Hollow Tr. at a point 0.4m. below the Hot-Short Mtn. Tr. junction. (From the sag the Indian Run Tr. leads left (NW, then N) 1.7m. to end on the Nicholson Hollow Tr. 0.1m above Corbin Cabin.)

2.3-2.7 Corbin Hollow Tr., blue-blazed, leads left for 2.0m., following down Brokenback Run to reach the Weakley Hollow Fire Rd. at a point 1.2m. above the parking area at Va. Sec. 600.

2.4-2.6 Robertson Mtn. Tr., blue-blazed, leads left for 2.4m.

climbing over Robertson Mtn., el. 3296', then descending to Old Rag Valley entering the Weakley Hollow Fire Rd. at a point 1.3m. above the parking area on that road, at the start of Va. Sec. 600.

5.0-0.0 Junction with the Weakley Hollow and Berry Hollow Fire Roads, at the top of the gap between Old Rag Mtn. and the main Blue Ridge (elevation here 1913 ft.). Directly ahead is the start of the Saddle Trail. (Via the Saddle Trail it is 0.4m. to the Old Rag Shelter, 1.5m. to Byrds Nest #1, and 1.9m. to the summit of Old Rag.) From the junction of the fire roads it is 2.5m. via the Weakley Hollow Fire Rd. to the parking lot at the Park boundary and 0.3m. farther, via Va. Sec. 600, to the lower end of the Nicholson Hollow Trail. To the right, via the Berry Hollow Fire Rd. it is 0.8m. to the Park boundary and 0.9m. farther along Va. Sec. 600 to the lower end of the Whiteoak Canyon Trail.

LIMBERLOST TRAIL

0.8 miles (1.3 kilometers)   blue-blazed

This trail leads through a very beautiful forest of virgin hemlock and some spruce, called by George Freeman Pollock the "Limberlost" because of its supposed similarity to the woods in the novel by Gene Stratton Porter entitled *Girl of the Limberlost*. There is little change in elevation on this trail.

From the Limberlost Trail Parking Area on Old Rag Fire Rd. 0.1m. east of Skyline Drive, SDMP 43.0, the trail leads gently down, toward the south, for 0.4m. Here at a trail junction the Crescent Rock Tr. leads right for 1.1m. to the Skyline Drive at Crescent Rock Overlook. From the trail junction the Limberlost Tr. swings to the east and ends on the Whiteoak Canyon Trail in another 0.4m.

For a short circuit hike, follow the Limberlost Tr. down to the Whiteoak Canyon Tr.; turn left and follow the Whiteoak Canyon Tr. up for 0.2m. to its intersection with the Old Rag Fire Rd., then follow the fire road left for 0.2m. back to the parking area.

Another circuit, about 4m. in length, would include the upper 0.4m. of the Limberlost Tr., the Crescent Rock Tr., the *AT* back to Skyland, and the short section of the Skyland-Big Meadows

CENTRAL SECTION

Horse Tr. between the *AT* and the Limberlost Parking Area. See write-up of the Crescent Rock Tr. for a slightly different circuit.

CORBIN MTN. TRAIL

4.4 miles (7.2 kilometers)   blue-blazed

This trail has one terminus low on the Nicholson Hollow Tr.; its other is on the Old Rag Fire Rd. There is a change in elevation of over 1800 ft. The trail route passes through a once-populated area and one can find house ruins and other indications of past human occupancy.

There are a number of good all-day circuit trips that can be made utilizing this trail. Start from Va. Sec. 600 (above Nethers) by hiking up Nicholson Hollow Tr. for 1.3m. to reach this trail; then follow the Corbin Mtn. Tr. which ascends steadily. One return route would be via the Indian Run and Nicholson Hollow Trs., about 11m. A shorter return route would be to descend via Old Rag Fire Rd., Corbin Hollow Tr. and the Weakley Hollow Fire Rd., about 9½m. roundtrip.

Detailed trail data:
Nicholson Hollow Tr. to Old Rag Fire Rd.

0.0-4.4 Trailhead is marked with a cement post on the Nicholson Hollow Tr. 0.4m. below the Hot-Short Mtn. Tr. junction and 1.3m. NW of Va. Sec. 600. Cross the Hughes River (be prepared to wade) and ascend along a small tributary. (At the first bend to the right, a faint trail leads left to a very pretty waterfall.)

1.2-3.2 Pass ruins of a house. Trail crosses the run just beyond the ruins.

3.8-0.6 In a sag just below the summit of Thorofare Mtn. trail turns sharply to the left. At the turn the Indian Run Tr. leads right, reaching the Nicholson Hollow Tr. 0.1m. above Corbin Cabin in 1.7m.

4.4-0.0 Reach Old Rag Fire Rd. Skyline Drive is 1.8m. to the right via the fire road; the upper end of the Corbin Hollow Tr., blue-blazed, is 0.5m. to the left.

INDIAN RUN TRAIL

1.7 miles (2.7 kilometers)　　　　　　　　　　　　blue-blazed

This short trail connecting the Nicholson Hollow Tr. with the Corbin Mtn. Tr. and, via the latter, with Old Rag Fire Rd. widens the hiking opportunities for users of Corbin Cabin. A number of circuit routes are available using Indian Run Tr. as a segment. See PATC Map No. 10.

From Skyline Drive, SDMP 43.0, follow the Old Rag Fire Rd. 1.8m. to reach the upper end of the Corbin Mtn. Tr., blue-blazed. Follow the latter 0.6m. to a sag where that trail makes a sharp right turn. Here a post marks the upper end of the Indian Run Tr. The lower end is on the Nicholson Hollow Tr. at a point 0.1m. west of Corbin Cabin and 1.7m. east of Skyline Drive (or 1.8m. east of the *AT*).

CORBIN HOLLOW TRAIL

2.0 miles (3.2 kilometers)　　　　　　　　　　　　blue-blazed

This trail is not hard to follow. Its upper end is on the Old Rag Fire Rd. at a point 2.3m. from the Skyline Drive, SDMP 43.0, and 2.7m. on the fire road from the Weakley Hollow Fire Rd. The lower end is on the Weakley Hollow Fire Rd. 1.3m. on that road NE of its junction with the Old Rag Fire Rd. and 1.2m. SW of the parking area at the Park boundary. The trail follows Brokenback Run through Corbin Hollow. This area was formerly the location of a very primitive and poverty-stricken mountain community.

The upper terminus of this trail is 0.5m. east of the upper end of the Corbin Mtn. Tr. and 0.1m. west of the upper end of Robertson Mtn. Tr. It can be used with either of these for a circuit route.

ROBERTSON MTN. TRAIL

2.4 miles (3.9 kilometers)　　　　　　　　　　　　blue-blazed

This trail offers some excellent views of Corbin Hollow and Old Rag Mtn. Its upper end is on the Old Rag Fire Rd. at a point 2.4m. east of the Skyline Drive, SDMP 43.0, via the fire road, and 2.6m. northwest of the Weakley Hollow Fire Rd. via the road.

CENTRAL SECTION

The lower end is on the Weakley Hollow Fire Rd. at a point 1.3m. up the road from Va. Sec. 600 at the Park boundary (and parking area) and 1.2m. down the road from its junction with the Old Rag Fire Rd. The upper ends of the Robertson Mtn. Tr. and Corbin Hollow Tr. are about 0.1m. apart; so are their lower ends.

From the Old Rag Fire Rd. the Robertson Mtn. Tr., starting at an elevation of about 2800 ft., climbs for 0.8m., with many switchbacks, to the top of Robertson Mtn., el. 3296'. From the summit it descends eastward, again with many switchbacks. Where it joins the Weakley Hollow Rd. the elevation is only 1532 ft.

WHITEOAK FIRE ROAD

1.8 miles (2.9 kilometers)   yellow-blazed

The chief use of this road, for hikers, is as a link to complete the circuit when descending Cedar Run Trail and ascending Whiteoak Canyon as far as the Upper Falls. The Skyland-Big Meadows Horse Trail also utilizes this road, following it from Whiteoak Run to just short of the Skyline Drive. The lower end of this road is at the Whiteoak Run, just above the Upper Falls at the site of G. F. Pollock's Middle Bridge. (Via the Whiteoak Canyon Trail it is 2.3m. to the Skyline Drive, SDMP 42.5.) The upper end is on the Skyline Drive, SDMP 45.0, about 0.6m. "north" of Hawksbill Gap and the upper end of the Cedar Run Trail.

OLD RAG MTN. CIRCUIT

(Includes the Ridge Trail, 2.7m., blue-blazed, the Saddle Trail, 1.9m., blue-blazed, and the Weakley Hollow Fire Rd., 2.5m., yellow-blazed.)

7.1 miles (11.4 kilometers)

To hikers Old Rag Mountain has a very special character. The only other mountains in the East that can compete with it are Mt. Katahdin in Maine and Grandfather Mountain in North Carolina. And of the three, Old Rag has the advantage, or disadvantage, of being the most accessible. Old Rag is the favorite hike of many youth organizations of the Washington area, so that every weekend finds one or more large groups of youngsters camping or hiking on the mountain, as well as family groups, novice hikers, and veteran walkers. Those who survive the steep climb up the Ridge Trail are rewarded by the fascinating walk over and around the tremendous rocks and by the outstanding views, first one direction, then another.

Old Rag stands apart from the main Blue Ridge, separated from it by the narrow Old Rag Valley. It consists of a long, rocky ridge composed primarily of granite. However, long ago, lava welled up in cracks in the granite and formed a series of basaltic dykes, varying in thickness from a few feet to fifty. This basaltic material has weathered more rapidly than the surrounding granite, creating some of the rock features that give the mountain its ragged appearance. At one place on the Ridge Trail there is a regular staircase, with high vertical walls of granite and "steps" formed by the characteristic weathering of columnar basalt in blocks.

In wintertime, when snow and ice make the trails on Old Rag too difficult and dangerous for most hikers, there is still a special breed of walker who enjoys the challenge this mountain has to offer. He or she comes equipped with proper clothing for exposure to cold and wind, and uses crampons when traveling over icy spots.

It is advisable to carry water when hiking up Old Rag. There is no water at Byrds Nest #1, picnicking only, which is situated in the saddle, about 0.4m. from the summit along the Saddle Trail. The other shelter, Old Rag Shelter, picnicking only, is much lower down on the Saddle Trail and water is available here. (*No camping is allowed on Old Rag above the 2500' elevation.*)

Access:

The Ridge Trail starts at the parking area on the Weakley Hollow Fire Rd. To reach the lower end of the Saddle Trail, one must walk the 2.5m. up the Weakley Hollow Fire Rd. to its junction with the Berry Hollow Fire Rd. and Old Rag Fire Rd. The automobile approach to the Weakley Hollow Parking Area is as follows: From Va. 231 south of Sperryville, turn west on Va. Sec. 602 at a point just south of the bridge over the Hughes River. Follow up the south side of the river, first on Rt. 602, then 707, then 600, for about 5 miles. The Weakley Hollow Rd. is the

CENTRAL SECTION

continuation of Rt. 600 within the Park. The parking lot is just inside the Park boundary. If it should be filled, there is some parking space available 0.3m. down Rt. 600, where the road makes a sharp turn; also there is an "overflow" parking area 0.5m. farther down.

Detailed trail data:

Circuit described in a clockwise direction, starting with the Ridge Trail.

0.0-7.1 From the Old Rag Parking Area on the Weakley Hollow Fire Rd. just inside the Park boundary, el. 1080', the Ridge Trail heads due south.

0.5-6.6 Spring is 100 ft. to right of trail, under walnut trees. This is the last sure water on the Ridge Trail.

1.3-5.8 Pass a wet weather spring, to right of trail, close under steep side of the ridge.

1.4-5.7 Reach crest of ridge in broad wooded saddle and turn sharply to the right.

1.6-5.5 Emerge from woods onto rocks.

2.7-4.4 End of the Ridge Trail. To right are the projecting rocks forming the summit of Old Rag, el. 3291'. The trail, now the Saddle Trail, descends south along the ridge crest.

2.8-4.3 Path leads right 300 ft. to site of former fire tower.

2.9-4.2 Spur trail leads right 300 ft. to cave formed by huge sloping rocks. Saddle Trail descends.

3.1-4.0 Reach the "Saddle." Here the shelter, Byrds Nest #1, no camping, is located. There are inside and outside fireplaces but no water. (Beyond the shelter the Ragged Run Rd. descends to the south. This road is *closed to hikers* outside the Park boundary.) Trail turns sharp right, leaving the ridge, and descends steadily by switchbacks along the northwest slopes of the mountain.

4.2-2.9 The Old Rag Picnic Shelter, no camping, is 100 ft. ahead here. Trail turns right onto blue-blazed dirt road and continues to descend.

4.6-2.5 Reach junction of the 3 fire roads, all yellow-blazed—Weakley Hollow, Berry Hollow, and Old Rag—at the site of the former Old Rag Post Office, turn right on Weakley Hollow Fire Rd. and descend. (From the fire road junction it is 5.0m. to the Skyline Drive, SDMP 43.0, via the Old Rag Fire Rd. and 1.6m.

left, via the Berry Hollow Fire Rd. to the foot of the Whiteoak Canyon Trail.)

7.1-0.0 Reach the Old Rag Parking Area and Va. Sec. 600 just beyond.

SKYLAND-BIG MEADOWS HORSE TRAIL

11.2 miles (18.0 kilometers)   yellow-blazed

From the stables at Skyland this trail leads across the Drive and over to the Old Rag Fire Rd. which it follows down to Comer's Deadening. Here it turns right and enters Whiteoak Canyon. It crosses Whiteoak Run just above the Upper Falls, then follows the Whiteoak Fire Rd. almost to its junction with the Skyline Drive, SDMP 45.0. From here it parallels the Drive until beyond the Upper Hawksbill Parking Area; it then descends along the southwest slope of Spitler Hill and circles the head of the Rose River Canyon. It again crosses the Drive just south of Fishers Gap and then parallels the Drive to reach the Big Meadows stables. The trail has posts marking the half-miles.

The section of horse trail between Whiteoak Canyon Tr. and Fishers Gap gets very little horse traffic so is pleasant walking. That part near the Rose River is quite scenic. Hikers should remember to yield the right-of-way to a horse party should they meet.

Detailed trail data:
Skyland to Big Meadows

0.0-11.2 Trail leads from Skyland stables, crossing the *AT*. It then passes through much mountain laurel as it angles toward the Skyline Drive.

0.2-11.0 Cross to the east side of the Skyline Drive. Trail now parallels the Drive.

0.6-10.6 Come into the Old Rag Fire Rd. and follow it to the left. (A parking area is 200 ft. to the right along the road. The Skyline Drive is 0.1m. farther.)

1.5-9.7 Horse trail turns sharply right away from the fire road at a signpost and heads toward Whiteoak Canyon. This area is known as Comer's Deadening. Horse trail now follows old road.

CENTRAL SECTION

2.7-8.5 Ford Whiteoak Run just above the Upper Falls. From here the horse trail follows the Whiteoak Fire Rd.

4.3-6.9 At a point on the Whiteoak Fire Rd. a little over 0.1m. from the Skyline Drive the horse trail turns left and parallels the Drive.

4.8-6.4 Intersection with Cedar Run Trail. (To the right, via the Cedar Run Trail, it is only a few feet to the Skyline Drive at Hawksbill Gap.)

6.2-5.0 Horse trail comes into old farm road at a point near the summit of Spitler Hill and follows the road to the left. (To the right the old road leads to the Skyline Drive coming in at a point just south of the Upper Hawksbill Parking Area, SDMP 46.7.) Ladies'-tresses, a type of orchid, may be found here, blooming in Sept. and Oct. For over a half mile the trail passes through old fields, now quite overgrown. Old road gradually narrows into trail.

8.0-3.2 Cross stream, a branch of the Rose River.

8.5-2.7 Cross a second branch of the Rose River.

9.1-2.1 The Dark Hollow Falls-Rose River Loop Trail enters from the left and follows the horse trail.

9.6-1.6 Cross the Rose River Fire Rd. at a point just east of Fishers Gap, SDMP 49.3. 0.1m. farther cross to the right (west) of the Skyline Drive. The horse trail swings out-of-sight of the Drive, then turns to parallel it.

11.0-0.2 Intersection with the Story of the Forest Nature Trail.

11.2-0.0 Big Meadows stables, SDMP 51.2. (See PATC Map No. 10: Big Meadows Inset.)

CRESCENT ROCK TRAIL

1.1 miles (1.8 kilometers)   blue-blazed

This short trail runs from the Skyline Drive, SDMP 44.4, across from the Crescent Rock Overlook (look for cement signpost just south of the north entrance) down to the Limberlost Trail, with a gentle downgrade all the way. A pleasant half-day circuit hike (4½m.) can be made by following this trail from the Overlook, turning right onto the Limberlost Trail and following it for 0.4m., then ascending the Whiteoak Canyon Trail to the Skyline Drive.

Cross the Drive and, a few yards up the road toward the Skyland stables, turn left onto the *AT* and follow it for two miles. There a short spur trail, marked by a cement post, leads to the north end of the Crescent Rock Overlook.

BETTYS ROCK TRAIL

0.3 miles (0.5 kilometers) blue-blazed

From the Crescent Rock Parking Overlook, SDMP 44.4, this short trail leads due north to a rocky outcrop known as Bettys Rock which affords excellent views west.

A short trail, 0.1m., leads downhill from the Bettys Rock Tr. (just north of the overlook) to the *AT*.

HAWKSBILL MTN. TRAIL

1.8 miles (2.9 kilometers) blue-blazed

NAKEDTOP TRAIL

0.7 miles (1.1 kilometers) blue-blazed

SERVICE RD. TO BYRDS NEST #2

0.9 miles (1.4 kilometers) not blazed

Hawksbill Mtn. is the highest mountain in the Shenandoah Park. Native spruce and balsam are found on its upper slopes. An observation platform at the summit, el. 4050', provides excellent views of Timber Hollow to the north and of Page Valley and the Massanuttens to the west. The hiker has the choice of four routes up the mountain. From its northern end at Hawksbill Gap, SDMP 45.6, a trail leads 0.8m. to the summit, then descends along the service road for about 0.4m. from where it forks left and descends 0.6m. farther to the Upper Hawksbill Parking Area, SDMP 46.7. A third route up Hawksbill is via the service road to the Byrds Nest #2. It leaves the Drive at SDMP 47.1, and reaches the shelter just below the summit in 0.9m. The fourth route is via the Nakedtop Trail. From the summit this trail leads down 0.7m. to the *AT*. A circuit route over Hawksbill could include the Hawksbill Tr. from

Hawksbill Gap to the summit, 0.8m., the Nakedtop Tr. down to the *AT,* 0.7m. and the *AT* back to Hawksbill Gap, 1.0m. See back of PATC Map No. 10.

Byrds Nest #2, an open-faced picnic shelter, is situated just below the summit of Hawksbill Mtn. No camping permitted. See Chap. 6: "Picnic Shelters, Huts and Cabins." Water is not available here but there is a spring 0.8m. downhill.

TRAILS IN THE BIG MEADOWS-CAMP HOOVER AREA

The Big Meadows Developed Area includes the Harry F. Byrd, Sr. Visitor Center, a wayside, lodge, cabins, restaurant, camp store, stables (wagon rides only), gift shop, picnic grounds and the largest campgrounds in the Park.

Big Meadows is located on a very broad, flat area of the Blue Ridge. Many geologists believe that this area is the remnant of an old, high peneplain. Because of its surprising flatness water does not run off easily and some of the area is quite boggy. There are several, uncommon in Virginia, plants growing here, Canadian burnet (Sanguisorba canadensis) for one. A network of trails and fire roads provides the camper with many miles of good walking. There are a number of circuit hikes possible in the area, some quite short, others which can provide a full day of hiking. Hikers using trails maintained primarily for horses should yield the right-of-way.

Camp Hoover, situated within the Park on the Rapidan River, was originally built for a presidential hide-away by Herbert Hoover while he was in office. Later he donated the camp to the U.S. Government for use by future presidents and their guests. The Park Service administers the property and welcomes visitors—hikers and horseback riders—on the grounds of the camp. Only three of the original buildings—the President's Cabin, the Prime Minister's Cabin and "The Creel" remain today. However, historical markers have been placed at the sites of the former buildings explaining how and by whom they were used.

Access to Camp Hoover from the east is via the Rapidan Fire Road and Va. Sec. 649. Refer to write-up for this road. To reach the camp from the Skyline Drive one can (1) follow the Rapidan Fire Rd. from Big Meadows, SDMP 51.3, (2) descend the Mill Prong Trail from Milam Gap, SDMP 52.8, or (3) follow the *AT* north from Bootens Gap, SDMP 55.1, to reach the Laurel Prong Trail and descend the latter.

RED GATE FIRE ROAD

4.8 miles (7.8 kilometers)   yellow-blazed

This road, gated at both ends, leads from the base of the mountains 4 mi. east of Stanley to the Skyline Drive at Fishers Gap, SDMP 49.3. (This road is the western portion of the old Gordonsville Pike. It continues on the east slope of the Blue Ridge as the Rose River Fire Road.) The Red Gate Fire Rd. climbs with a gentle grade and has many switchbacks to gain 1500 ft. of elevation. It offers a pleasant walk except that one does have to beware of cars as Park and concessionaire personnel use this road to reach Big Meadows.

To reach the lower end of the Red Gate Fire Rd. turn east in Stanley (from U.S. 340) on either Va. Sec. 624 or 689. Beyond the junction of these roads, follow Rt. 689 eastward for about 1 mile, then continue straight on Va. Sec. 611 where Rt. 689 turns sharply left. Continue on Rt. 611 to the Park boundary where road becomes the Red Gate Fire Rd. and is gated.

STORY OF THE FOREST NATURE TRAIL

1.8 miles (2.9 kilometers)   not blazed

See PATC Map No. 10, Big Meadows insert. The Story of the Forest Trail begins at the entrance road to the Byrd Visitor Center. It first heads east and crosses a lovely stone bridge. In 0.3m. a spur trail on the right leads down 300 ft. to the Skyline Drive at a point directly across from the Dark Hollow Falls Trail.

At 0.8m. the trail turns sharply left. (A trail straight ahead here leads to the campgrounds.) At 0.9m. reach the paved road that leads to the picnic and camping areas of Big Meadows. The nature trail turns left here and follows, for 0.9m., the paved path along the road and back to the Big Meadows Wayside (and Visitor Center).

CENTRAL SECTION

To reach the Amphitheatre Parking Area (and *AT)* from the nature trail turn right when reaching the road (at 0.9m.), follow the paved path as far as the campground registration office, walk along the road leading to the picnic area, keeping left at the road fork (wrong way for cars). Look for trail, just left of the parking area, that leads on to the *AT*.

LEWIS SPRING FALLS TRAIL

1.8 miles (2.9 kilometers)   blue-blazed

This trail leads from the *AT* at a point immediately below Big Meadows Lodge to Lewis Spring Falls and on to the *AT* at Lewis Spring. Used with the *AT* it offers a pleasant circuit trip of only 3.1m.

To reach the start of this trail find the path between the Amphitheatre Parking Area and the Big Meadows Lodge and follow it north about 0.1m. to the *AT* intersection marked by a signpost. The Lewis Spring Falls Trail will be directly across here. (To the left the *AT* leads "south". The southern end of the Lewis Spring Falls Trail is 0.9m. from here via the *AT*. To the right the *AT* leads "north" circling the Big Meadows Campground and reaching Fishers Gap in 1.6m.) Lewis Spring Falls Tr. descends. At 1.1m. a spur trail leads right steeply downhill for 0.2m. to the base of the falls. At 1.2m. a trail leads right 150 ft. to an overlook at the head of the falls. Trail now ascends steeply, reaching Lewis Spring Service Rd. at 1.7m. Reach the *AT* at 1.8m. (To complete the circuit hike, turn left on the *AT* and follow it back to Big Meadows.)

DARK HOLLOW FALLS-ROSE RIVER LOOP TRAIL

3.5 miles (5.6 kilometers)   first 2.6m. blue-blazed
                                                                last 0.9m. yellow-blazed

The Dark Hollow Falls Trail, 0.8m. in length, is the most popular one in the Park. It leads to a very lovely cascading waterfall on the Hogcamp Branch of the Rose River. For a very short trip park at the Dark Hollow Falls Parking Area on the Skyline Drive, SDMP 50.7. For a somewhat longer trip park at the Amphitheatre Parking Area of Big Meadows (follow road signs). On foot follow the exit road as far as the campground registration office. Then walk, going to the right, along the paved path which follows along the road. In 0.1m., at a cement post, turn left onto the Story of the Forest Nature Trail and continue on it for about 0.6m. Here at an intersection marked by a cement post continue straight ahead (the nature trail bears to the right here) and in 300 ft. reach Skyline Drive directly across from the Dark Hollow Falls Trail Parking Area.

For a more extended hike a circuit trip of about 6 miles can be made by starting at the Amphitheatre Parking Area, reaching the Dark Hollow Falls Tr. as described above, descending the Dark Hollow Falls Tr., then continuing along the Rose River Loop Trail (which is very scenic and passes a falls on the Rose River) to Fishers Gap, and finally returning to Big Meadows via the *AT*. (Refer to PATC Map No. 10 and to PATC publication: *Circuit Hikes in the Shenandoah National Park.*)

Detailed trail data:

Dark Hollow Falls Parking Area to Fishers Gap

0.0-3.5 Skyline Drive, SDMP 50.7, at north end of Dark Hollow Falls Parking Area. From here trail descends steadily with stream on its right.

0.6-2.9 Reach top of Dark Hollow Falls, a series of terraced cascades. From here trail descends very steeply.

0.8-2.7 Reach Rose River Fire Rd. It is a portion of the pre-Park Gordonsville Pike. (To the left, road leads 1.1m. to Fishers Gap.) Turn right onto the road and cross bridge over Hogcamp Branch. Fifty feet beyond the bridge, at trail sign, turn left off the road and follow the Rose River Loop Trail down the creek.

1.7-1.8 At junction marked by cement post turn sharply left and cross Hogcamp Branch. (Trail to right leads 0.3m. to the Rose River Fire Rd.) In 250 ft. cross a small stream. Fifty feet beyond, it passes the site of an old copper mine to the left of the trail. The trail soon approaches the main branch of the Rose River, turns left at a sign pointing to Rose River Falls and climbs along the west bank of the river.

2.3-1.2 Pass waterfall.

CENTRAL SECTION

2.6-0.9 Turn left, uphill, onto an old road, now the route of the Big Meadows-Skyland Horse Trail (yellow-blazed).

3.5-0.0 Turn right onto the Rose River Fire Rd. and in a few feet reach the Skyline Drive, SDMP 49.3, at Fishers Gap. (To complete the circuit hike cross the Drive and follow the Red Gate Fire Rd. a few feet to reach the *AT*. Turn left onto the *AT* and follow it 1.6m. back to Big Meadows. Turn left at cement post and reach Amphitheatre Parking Area in 0.1m. Return to Dark Hollow Falls Parking Area by following the exit road and Story of the Forest Nature Tr.)

ROSE RIVER FIRE ROAD

6.5 miles (10.5 kilometers)   yellow-blazed

From Fishers Gap, SDMP 49.3, this old road winds its way down to Va. Sec. 670 west of Syria. In pre-Park days it was known as the Gordonsville Pike and many hikers still refer to it by this name. (West of the Skyline Drive, the road continues as the Red Gate Fire Rd.)

The upper one mile can be used for circuit hikes either in combination with the Dark Hollow Falls Tr. and *AT* or with the Rose River Loop Trail. The lower portion is used for a circuit hike that involves ascending the Rose River either by scrambling over the rocks or following a "fisherman's trail" upcreek along the southwest bank, then following the Rose River Loop Trail left to the fire road, and finally descending the latter. Refer to PATC publication: *Circuit Hikes in the Shenandoah National Park*.

Access:

From Va. 231 at a point about 16 miles south of U.S. 522 near Sperryville and 5 m. north of Madison, turn west onto Va. Sec. 670. Follow Rt. 670 through Criglersville and Syria and continue on Rt. 670 to the Park boundary. Parking space near the end of Rt. 670 is very limited. From the boundary continue up road on foot, with river to right of the road in deep gorge. (At about the spot where the road bends to the left away from the river a path leads right, through an overgrown field, to the river and up it along the southwest bank. If you wish to find this "fishermen's" trail and have continued up the road too far you will find on the left of the road a yellow metal post marking the Upper Dark Hollow Tr.; if so, backtrack about 0.1m!)

Detailed trail data:

Fishers Gap to Va. Sec. 670

0.0-6.5 Skyline Drive at Fishers Gap, SDMP 49.3.

1.1-5.4 To the right the Dark Hollow Falls Tr., marked by post, leads uphill 0.8m. to Skyline Drive. Just beyond this trail junction road crosses Hogcamp Branch. Fifty feet farther a post marks the Rose River Loop Trail which leads left down Hogcamp Branch.

2.0-4.5 Stony Mtn. Tr. leads right for 1.1m. to Rapidan Fire Road.

2.5-4.0 To left a spur trail leads 0.3m. to Rose River Loop Trail.

5.2-1.3 Post on right marks Upper Dark Hollow Tr. (This trail leads 2.2m. to the Rapidan Rd. at Broyles Gap.)

6.5-0.0 Park boundary where road becomes Va. Sec. 670.

STONY MTN. TRAIL

1.1 mile (1.8 kilometers)   yellow-blazed

This trail may be weedy in summer. It follows an old road and is useful as it connects the Rose River Fire Road (Gordonsville Pike) and the Rapidan Fire Road. Its northern end is 2.0m down the Rose River Fire Rd. from the Skyline Drive. The southern end is 2.9m. down the Rapidan Fire Rd. from the Drive.

UPPER DARK HOLLOW TRAIL

2.2 miles (3.5 kilometers)   yellow-blazed

This trail route connects the Rose River Fire Rd. (Gordonsville Pike) and the Rapidan Fire Rd. Its lower end is about 1.3m. up the Rose River Fire Rd. from the Park boundary (at end of Va. Sec. 670). The trail route involves a climb of about 1250 ft. to reach its upper end on the Rapidan Fire Rd. at Broyles Gap. The lower portion of the trail passes through a beautiful hemlock forest. For the upper half of its route the trail utilizes an old roadbed so it offers easy walking. Hikers should find this trail useful as part of a circuit hike. Starting at the lower end of the Rose River Fire Rd., walk up the road for about 4m. to reach the Stony Mtn. Tr., then follow this trail about 1m. over to the Rapidan Fire Rd. Descend the Rapidan Rd. for about 1m. to Broyles Gap, then descend the Upper Dark Hollow Tr. back to the Rose River Fire Rd. and descend road to the car. (See PATC Map No. 10.) Total circuit is about 9m. in length.

TANNERS RIDGE HORSE TRAIL

2.5 miles (4.0 kilometers)   yellow-blazed

This is a loop trail that leads from the Big Meadows stables out along Tanners Ridge and back, crossing the *AT* twice.

TANNERS RIDGE ROAD

1.4 miles within the SNP (2.2 km.)   yellow-blazed

This road, gated at the Drive and at the Park boundary, leads west from the Skyline Drive, SDMP 51.6, for 1.4m. to the Park boundary where it becomes Va. Sec. 682 (about 6 miles from Stanley). There is a cemetery, still being used for burials, at the junction of this road with the *AT*. The *AT* junction is 0.3m. from the Drive.

RAPIDAN FIRE ROAD—VIRGINIA SECONDARY 649

9.8 miles (15.8 kilometers)   yellow-blazed

This fire road is gated at the Skyline Drive (at Big Meadows) and at the "first" Park boundary, just below the junction with the Camp Hoover Road. This upper portion of the road is used as a horse trail and also by hikers. It is useful as one segment of a circuit hike which also includes the Mill Prong Trail and *AT*. (See PATC publication: *Circuit Hikes in the Shenandoah National Park*.) The road continues east of the gate through a Virginia Wildlife Area and descends along the Rapidan River. It then reenters the SNP. After another mile along the river the road climbs to the top of the Chapman Mountain ridge before reaching the easternmost Park boundary. Although there is some traffic on this part of the road it is light and the road is not unpleasant for walking. There is a good swimming hole on the river at the junction of this road and the Graves Mill Fire Rd.

Access:

The upper end is on the Skyline Drive, SDMP 51.3, across from the Big Meadows Wayside where there is ample parking.

To reach the road from the east, turn west off Va. 231 onto Va. Sec. 670 at a point about 16 miles south of U.S. 522 near Sperryville and 5 miles north of Madison. Follow Rt. 670 for about 1m. beyond Criglersville. Here turn left onto Va. Sec. 649, crossing the Rose River and following up a side stream toward Chapman Mtn. Road is narrow but drivable over Chapman Mtn. and on beyond the junction with Va. Sec. 662 on the Rapidan River to just below the Camp Hoover Access Road where it reenters the SNP. Here it is gated.

Detailed trail data:

Skyline Drive to most eastward Park boundary. (All mileages given below are estimated.)

0.0-10.0 Junction with Skyline Drive, SDMP 51.3, across from Big Meadows Wayside.

1.2-8.8 To right of the road the Mill Prong Horse Spur Trail leads 1.8m. to Camp Hoover.

2.9-7.1 The Stony Mtn. Tr. leads left to Rose River Fire Rd.

3.8-6.2 Upper Dark Hollow Tr. leads left to Rose River Fire Rd.

5.4-4.6 At road junction fire road continues straight ahead. The road to the right leads up the Rapidan River for about 3/4 miles to Camp Hoover.

5.8-4.2 Reach Park boundary where road is gated and enter Virginia Wildlife Area where road becomes Va. Sec. 649 and is open to automobile traffic.

7.5-2.5 At road fork, Rt. 649 continues straight ahead descending along the Rapidan River. (Road to the right, the Fork Mtn. Rd., goes in and out of the SNP as it climbs to the radio tower on Fork Mtn. This road is gated.)

7.6-2.4 Reenter SNP.

CENTRAL SECTION

8.8-1.2 At road junction take left fork and climb, leaving the river. (Right fork is the Graves Mill Fire Rd. which follows on down the Rapidan River reaching the Park boundary in about 1.7m.)

9.4-0.6 At road junction on top of ridge (of Chapman Mtn.) continue straight ahead. (To right a Va. Forest Rd. leads out Blakey Ridge past the Utz Hightop Lookout Tower. Gated road to left is an access road to private land.)

10.0-0.0 Road leaves the Park. (From here it is 3.0m. to Va. Sec. 670, the road through Criglersville.)

MILL PRONG TRAIL

1.0 miles (1.6 kilometers)   blue-blazed

This trail leads from the *AT* in Milam Gap east to the Mill Prong Horse Spur Trail. The two trails can be used along with the Laurel Prong Trail and *AT* for a good circuit hike of 7.0m., or they can be used along with the Rapidan Fire Road, the Camp Hoover Rd., and the *AT* for another good circuit trip of 12m. (See PATC publication: *Circuit Hikes in the Shenandoah National Park.*)

Detailed trail data:
Milam Gap east

0.0-1.0 Junction with the *AT*, a few feet south of the Skyline Drive crossing at Milam Gap, SDMP 52.8. Trail descends gently through an old field and orchard, now overgrown.

0.6-0.4 Cross main branch of Mill Prong. Trail now descends through tall trees and fern-covered forest floor.

1.0-0.0 Cross another branch of Mill Prong and bear right, reaching junction with the Mill Prong Horse Spur Trail which comes in from the left. (Via the Mill Prong Horse Spur Tr. it is 1.0m. north to the Rapidan Fire Rd. and 1.2m. farther along the fire road to the Skyline Drive at Big Meadows Wayside.)

MILL PRONG HORSE SPUR TRAIL

1.8 miles (2.9 kilometers)   yellow-blazed

The upper end of this trail is on the Rapidan Fire Road at a point 1.2m. from the Skyline Drive at Big Meadows. The lower end is at Camp Hoover just west of the road bridge over Mill Prong. It is about 1.2m. from the Rapidan Fire Rd. to the junction with the blue-blazed Mill Prong Tr. and another 0.8 m. on to Camp Hoover.

Hikers may use this trail, along with the Mill Prong Trail and the *AT*, for a shorter circuit hike to Camp Hoover (about 8m.) than the Rapidan Fire Rd.—Camp Hoover Rd.—Mill Prong Tr.—*AT* circuit. (See PATC Map No. 10 and PATC publication: *Circuit Hikes in the Shenandoah National Park*.)

Detailed trail data:

Rapidan Fire Rd. to Camp Hoover

0.0-1.8 From the Rapidan Fire Rd., at a point 1.2m. from the Skyline Drive at Big Meadows, the horse trail heads southward.

1.0-0.8 Blue-blazed Mill Prong Tr. leads right for 1.0m. to the *AT* in Milam Gap. Trail now descends along the creek.

1.5-0.3 Cross to right of creek just below Big Rock Falls. Crossing is easy to miss.

1.8-0.0 Junction with the Camp Hoover Rd. at a point on the road 100 ft. west of the bridge over Mill Prong.

LAUREL PRONG TRAIL

2.8 miles (4.5 kilometers)   blue-blazed

This trail starts from the *AT* near Bootens Gap, descends very gently along the south slope of Hazeltop Mtn. to Laurel Gap, then descends more steeply through an area of much mountain laurel (kalmia). For the final mile it leads through the valley of Laurel Prong. To the right of the trail, in several locations along the creek, one can find the great laurel or rosebay rhododendron which blooms here in late June or early July. Near its end at Camp Hoover the trail passes through much large hemlock. In some places a carpet of false lily of the valley, blooming in late May, carpets the ground; in other places running cedar, a type of club moss, acts as a ground cover.

Access:

From Bootens Gap, SDMP 55.1, follow the *AT* north for 0.6m. A cement post marks the Laurel Prong trailhead.

CENTRAL SECTION

To reach the lower end of the trail, follow directions for getting to Camp Hoover from the east. The Laurel Prong trailhead is near the end of the access road to Camp Hoover, about 300 ft. west of the bridge over Mill Prong.

Detailed trail data:
   AT to Camp Hoover
   0.0-2.8 Junction with the *AT* at a point 0.6m. north of Bootens Gap.
   1.0-1.8 Reach Laurel Gap. Cement post marks start of the Cat Knob Tr., blue-blazed, which leads right, uphill, for 0.5m. to its upper end on the Jones Mtn. Tr. Laurel Prong Tr. turns left here and continues to descend.
   2.2-0.6 Cement post marks the Fork Mtn. Trail, yellow-blazed, which leads right for about 1 1/2 miles to "The Sag" and the Fork Mtn. Fire Rd. (The upper end of the Fork Mtn. Tr. also connects with the Staunton River Tr. and the Jones Mtn. Tr., both blue-blazed.)
   2.8-0.0 Reach Camp Hoover. To reach Mill Prong Horse Spur Trail follow access road left for 250 ft.

CAT KNOB TRAIL

0.5 miles (0.8 kilometers)   blue-blazed

This is a short trail which connects the Laurel Prong and Jones Mtn. Trails. The shortest route to Jones Mtn. Cabin from Skyline Drive, 5.7m., would use this "short cut", along with the *AT*, Laurel Prong Tr., Jones Mtn. Tr., and Nicholson Moonshine Tr. (Jones Mtn. Cabin Tr.).

GRAVES MILL FIRE ROAD

The Graves Mill Fire Road is the continuation of Va. Sec. 662 within the Park.

2.2 miles (3.1 kilometers)   yellow-blazed

Enter the SNP about 1.3m. north of Graves Mill. (Graves Mill is about 5 1/2m. up Va. Sec. 662 from Wolftown on Va. 230.) Within the Park the road continues up the Rapidan River to its junction with the Rapidan Fire Rd. (continuation of Va. Sec. 649 within the Park). It is open to automobile traffic its entire length but is very rough; it serves as an access road to the Camp Hoover area and to the Staunton River Trail. The Rapidan River along this road offers a number of spots suitable for swimming.

FORK MTN. ROAD

approx. 4 1/2 miles (7.2 kilometers)　　　　　　　　yellow-blazed

This road is gated. It leads from the Rapidan Fire Rd. about 2m. southeast of Camp Hoover up the eastern and southern slopes of Fork Mtn., winding in and out of the SNP. It reaches "The Sag", the divide between the Staunton River drainage area and that of Laurel Prong, then climbs to the tower on the top of Fork Mtn., el. 3840'. Where the road crosses the upper reaches of the Staunton River the Staunton River Tr. enters from the left. At "The Sag" the Fork Mtn. Tr. leads west 1.3m. to Laurel Prong Tr. and the Jones Mtn. Tr. leads south to Cat Knob and then descends the Jones Mtn. ridge to end of the Staunton River Tr.

STAUNTON RIVER TRAIL

approx. 4.3 miles (6.9 kilometers)　　　　　　　　　blue-blazed

This trail follows up the Staunton River from Va. Sec. 662 at the junction of the Staunton and Rapidan Rivers all the way to its source and continues on to "The Sag" where it connects with the upper ends of the Jones Mtn. Tr., blue-blazed, and the Fork Mtn. Tr., yellow-blazed. The last 0.8m. of the trail is along the Fork Mtn. Fire Rd. which continues beyond "The Sag" to the summit of Fork Mtn.

Jones Mtn. Cabin users can make a nice circuit hike of about 7 1/2 miles by ascending the Jones Mtn. Tr. and returning via the Staunton River Tr. (and including the McDaniel Hollow Tr. if so desired.)

Access:

To reach the lower end of this trail follow Va. 230 west from U.S. 29 south of Madison for 4 miles to Wolftown (or follow Va.

CENTRAL SECTION

230 northeast from U.S. 33 in Stanardsville). Turn north onto Va. Sec. 662 and continue on paved road as far as Graves Mill, 5.5m. At road junction, take the right fork, still Rt. 662, which crosses Kinsey Run and follows up the Rapidan River soon entering the SNP as the Graves Mill Fire Rd. At 2.0m. beyond Graves Mill reach junction of the Staunton and Rapidan Rivers. There is room for a few cars on the fire road and also a few feet up the Staunton River Tr. One small parking area is reserved for cabin users. Do not block either road.

Detailed trail data:

0.0-4.3 Junction with Va. Sec. 662 at the junction of the Staunton and Rapidan Rivers. The trail follows an old road along the southwest side of the Staunton River.

2.0-2.3 Junction with the Jones Mtn. Tr. which leads left, uphill. (Jones Mtn. Tr. leads 4.8m. passing Bear Church Rock, then along the ridge of Jones Mtn. to Cat Knob and then down its upper end at "The Sag." Jones Mtn. Cabin is reached by following this trail for 0.8m. from the Staunton River Tr. junction, then following the side trail 0.2m.)

2.4-1.9 Junction with the McDaniel Hollow Tr., blue-blazed, which leads southeast to join the Jones Mtn. Tr. in 0.5m.

3.5-0.8 Turn left onto the Fork Mtn. Fire Rd. and continue to climb.

4.3-0.0 Reach "The Sag." Here the Staunton River Tr., the Fork Mtn. Tr. and the upper end of the Jones Mtn. Tr. meet. (The Fork Mtn. Fire Rd. continues to the summit of Fork Mtn.)

FORK MTN. TRAIL

approx. 1.4 miles (2.2 kilometers)　　　　　　　　　　yellow-blazed

This very lovely trail has its lower end on the Laurel Prong Tr. 0.6m. from Camp Hoover. The Fork Mtn. Tr. crosses Laurel Prong in an area of much rosebay rhododendron, R. maximum, and hemlock. As it gradually climbs Fork Mtn. the rhododendron is replaced by mountain laurel. The route of the trail follows an old farm road as it switchbacks up the mountain to reach a junction with the Fork Mtn. Fire Rd. at "The Sag." At this junction it

JONES MOUNTAIN TRAIL

approx. 4.8 miles (7.7 kilometers)　　　　　　　　　　blue-blazed

The lower end of this blue-blazed trail is on the Staunton River Trail two miles from its junction with Graves Mill Fire Rd., the extension of Va. Sec. 662 within the Park. The trail's upper end is at "The Sag" on Fork Mtn. Access to Jones Mtn. Cabin, a mountain cabin restored by the PATC and available for use by campers, is via this trail. Reservations for the use of the cabin must be made at PATC Headquarters. See Chap. 6: "Picnic Shelters, Huts and Cabins." The trail passes over Bear Church Rock which offers an excellent view of the Staunton River Valley and eastward.

Detailed trail data:

Staunton River Tr. to "The Sag"

0.0-4.8 Junction with the Staunton River Trail at a point 2.0m. west of Va. Sec. 662. (Staunton River Tr. follows up the river and reaches "The Sag" in 2.3m. from this junction.)

0.5-4.3 Junction with the blue-blazed McDaniel Hollow Trail, which leads right for 0.5m. to end of the Staunton River Trail.

0.7-4.1 Jones Mtn. Cabin Trail leads left (east) for 0.2m. to the cabin.

1.2-3.6 Reach Bear Church Rock which offers an excellent view to the north and east.

1.3-3.5 Reach highest point. The trail now follows the ridge of Jones Mtn.

2.2-2.6 Where the ridge from Bear Church Rock and Bluff Mtn. join, the trail turns northwestward.

3.4-1.4 Reach a slight sag between Jones Mtn. and Cat Knob.

4.0-0.8 Reach the summit of Cat Knob. Trail swings sharply to the northeast here. (Cat Knob Trail leads left, ending on the Laurel Prong Tr. in 0.5m.)

4.8-0.0 Reach "The Sag" and the junction with the Fork Mtn. Fire Rd. and the upper ends of the Fork Mtn. Tr. and the Staunton

CENTRAL SECTION

River Tr., both blue-blazed. (It is 2.3m. down the Staunton River Tr. to the lower end of the Jones Mtn. Tr., thus offering a 7 1/2 mile circuit hike to users of Jones Mtn. Cabin.)

McDANIEL HOLLOW TRAIL

approx. 0.5 miles (0.8 kilometers)　　　　　　　　　blue-blazed

This short blue-blazed trail has one end on the Jones Mtn. Tr., its other end on the Staunton River Tr. It follows the route of an old mountain road across McDaniel Hollow and affords a short cut for hikers making a circuit using the Staunton River and Jones Mtn. Trails.

NICHOLSON MOONSHINE TRAIL

1.3 miles (2.0 kilometers)

The northern end of this trail is on the Jones Mtn. Tr. 0.8m. up that trail from the Staunton River Tr. It passes by the Jones Mtn. Cabin (for reservations contact PATC Headquarters; see Chap. 6: "Picnic Shelters, Huts and Cabins") in 0.3m., continues past the spring and slabs the mountainside as far as Wilson Run. (As this guide is being revised, the trail has not been blazed beyond the cabin but is graded and cleared.)

POWELL MTN. TRAIL

3.0 miles (4.8 kilometers)　　　　　　　　　　　　blue-blazed

The trail leads from the Skyline Drive at the Hazeltop Ridge Overlook, SDMP 54.4, to the summit of Powell Mtn. in 1.2m. It then descends westward to the Park boundary and on to Va. Sec. 759. It can be used along with the upper stretch of Rt. 759, the Meadow School Fire Rd. and the *AT* for a circuit trip of under 10 miles. (See PATC Map No. 10.)

WEST NAKED CREEK FIRE RD.

1.8 miles (2.9 kilometers)　　　　　　　　　　　yellow-blazed

This fire road cuts across a long westward-reaching side arm of the Park. At present it connects with no maintained trails so it is of use only to bushwhackers. If and when a trail is constructed along East Naked Creek within the Park it might be extended as far as this fire road, making the road of more interest to hikers. (See PATC Map No. 10.)

MEADOW SCHOOL FIRE RD.

approx. 1.5 miles (2.4 kilometers)　　　　　　　　　yellow-blazed

This road, gated at the Skyline Drive and at the Park boundary, descends the west slope of the Blue Ridge. Its upper end is on the Skyline Drive, SDMP 56.8, at a point directly opposite the Slaughter Tr. which leads past Bearfence Mtn. Hut. Outside the Park the Meadow School Fire Rd. becomes Va. Sec. 759. (From the lower end of the fire road it is about 10m., via Rt. 759, to Elkton. Fire Road not shown on 12th edition of PATC Map No. 10.)

LEWIS MTN. EAST TRAIL

1.0 mile (1.6 kilometers)　　　　　　　　　　　　blue-blazed

One end of this trail is on the *AT* at the south edge of the Lewis Mtn. Campground. The first 1.0m., over the highest peak of the mountain, can be followed with no difficulty but beyond here the trail is impossible to follow when we last checked.

CONWAY RIVER FIRE RD.

1.4 miles within the Park (2.3 kilometers)　　　　　yellow-blazed

This road, gated at the top and at the Park boundary, leads from the Skyline Drive, SDMP 55.1, to the edge of the Park, about 1.4m., then continues through land set aside as a Virginia Wildlife Area for another 2-3/4m.; then, as Va. Sec. 615, it continues on down to the valley as far as Graves Mill on the Rapidan River.

BEARFENCE MTN. LOOPS

0.3 miles (.5 kilometers) each loop　　　　　　　　blue-blazed

A very short but very scenic trail leads from the *AT* up over the

CENTRAL SECTION

rocky ridgetop of Bearfence Mtn., then back down to the *AT*. In addition, a very rough trail—more a rock scramble than a real trail—continues north along the ridgetop for another 0.2m, then swings downhill, crossing the *AT* and continuing on for another 0.1m. to the Bearfence Mtn. Parking Area on the Skyline Drive, SDMP 56.4. The Bearfence Mtn. loops and *AT* together make a rough figure eight. The Park Service conducts nature hikes here during the summer. The southernmost junction of the loop trails with the *AT* is 0.6m. north of the access road to Bearfence Mtn. Hut via the *AT*. The northernmost junction is 0.4m. farther north along the *AT*.

SLAUGHTER TRAIL

4.0 miles (6.4 kilometers)   yellow-blazed

This former fire road's upper end is on the Skyline Drive, SDMP 56.8, and is just across the drive from the Meadow School Fire Rd., also yellow-blazed. Its lower end is near the Conway River on Va. Sec. 667 at a point roughly 7 1/2 miles north of Va. 230 (and an additional 3m. from Stanardsville). From the Drive the trail first follows the Service Rd. to Bearfence Mtn. Hut for 0.1m., crossing the *AT* a few feet from the Drive.

The first 1.5m. is pleasant walking and should be particularly lovely in early June as there is much mountain laurel along the trail as it descends along the Devils Ditch. The Park Service hopes to construct a trail connecting Slaughter Tr. with the Lewis Mtn. East Tr. A long circuit hike can be made now by descending the Pocosin Fire Rd. and Pocosin Hollow Tr., continuing outside the Park to Va. Sec. 667, then following up Rt. 667 and Slaughter Tr., and finally following the *AT* south to Pocosin Fire Rd.; total distance about 13 miles.

POCOSIN FIRE RD.

2.5 miles (4.0 kilometers)   yellow-blazed

From the Skyline Drive, SDMP 59.5, this road leads southeastward passing Pocosin Cabin, a locked structure available for use of hikers and campers. (Reservations must be made in advance at PATC Headquarters. See Chap 6: "Picnic Shelters, Huts, and Cabins".) The road can be used along with the Pocosin Horse Trail, South River Fire Rd. and *AT* for an excellent circuit hike of about 7 1/2m. A somewhat longer circuit hike would also include the South River Falls Trail. The fire road becomes Va. Sec. 637 outside the Park. It is gated at the Skyline Drive and at the Park boundary.

Detailed trail data:
0.0-2.5 Skyline Drive, SDMP 59.5.
0.2-2.3 Intersection with the *AT*. (Via the *AT* it is 2.8m. south to the South River Fire Rd. and 0.5m. farther to the South River Falls Trail.)
0.3-2.2 Pocosin Cabin to right of the road.
1.1-1.4 From the road the Pocosin Horse Trail leads 1.3m. to the South River Fire Rd. (Via the South River Fire Rd. it is 1.2m. to the junction with the South River Falls Tr. and 0.8m. farther to the *AT.)* Just beyond this junction and to the right of the road are the interesting ruins of the former Upper Pocosin Mission.
1.3-1.2 To the left, the Pocosin Hollow Tr. leads north.
2.5-0.0 Park boundary. Road continues outside the Park. It becomes Va. Sec. 637 farther east.

POCOSIN TRAIL

1.3 miles (2.1 kilometers)   yellow-blazed

This trail connects the Pocosin Fire Road and the South River Fire Rd. and can be used with them for a good hike. At the junction of the trail with the Pocosin Fire Rd. one can examine the ruins of the old Upper Pocosin Mission. On the trail about 0.1m. from its end on the South River Fire Rd. a side road leads east passing the interesting, periwinkle-covered South River Cemetery in 0.1m.

POCOSIN HOLLOW TRAIL

2.8 miles (4.5 kilometers)   blue-blazed

Pocosin Hollow, like Nicholson Hollow and the "Hazel Country'' farther north, was once well-populated. When bushwhacking one sees remnants of old farm roads, rock walls and chestnut log fences, old homesites and at least one quite large cemetery with fieldstone grave markers.

The Pocosin Hollow Tr. has its upper end on the Pocosin Fire Rd., 1.3m. from Skyline Drive, SDMP 59.5. The trail heads north, then swings eastward descending along the run. (Most of the old homesites are up the hollow from where the trail reaches the run.) At the Park boundary the trail ends on a private road (not posted) which leads 0.7m. to Va. Sec. 667. (This point is about 6 miles from Va. 230 and an additional 3 miles from Stanardsville.) From the road junction it is 1.5m. up Rt. 667 (and the Conway River) to the lower end of the Slaughter Tr. and 5m. farther following up the river and, once in the Park, the Conway River Fire Rd., to Bootens Gap.

SOUTH RIVER FALLS TRAIL

1.9 miles (3.1 kilometers)   blue-blazed

This scenic trail leads from the South River Picnic Grounds, SDMP 62.8, down into the deep wooded gorge of the South River. It continues as far as the foot of the very lovely South River Falls. From top to bottom the trail loses 1000 ft. of elevation. The cascading falls are about 70 ft. high.

Detailed trail data:

0.0 Trailhead is on the road that loops through the South River Picnic Grounds at a point where the road is farthest to the east.

0.1 Intersection with the *AT*. (Via the *AT* it is 3.0m. south to Swift Run Gap and 3.3m. north to Pocosin Cabin.)

1.0 Pass observation point near the top of the falls.

1.2 At junction with an old road turn right, downhill (to the left, the old road leads to the South River Fire Rd.).

1.8 Reach the South River about 500 ft. below the falls. Go upstream on foot-trail.

1.9 Base of falls. For a circuit hike and an easier return to the picnic grounds, backtrack for the first 0.7m. Where the South River Falls Tr. turns left off the old road, continue straight for another 0.4m. to reach the South River Fire Rd. Follow the fire road uphill about 0.8m. to the *AT* intersection. Turn left onto the *AT* and follow it 0.5m. to the South River Falls Trail.

SOUTH RIVER FIRE ROAD

2.3m. described (3.7 kilometers)   yellow-blazed

This road leads east from the Skyline Drive, SDMP 62.7, just north of the South River Overlook. It can be used as a link in several possible circuit trips in combination with the South River Falls Trail, the *AT*, the Pocosin Horse Trail, and the Pocosin Fire Rd. To the east the road eventually becomes Va. Sec. 642 which comes into paved Va. Sec. 637 about 5m. north of Stanardsville. The road is gated at the Drive and at the Park boundary.

Detailed trail data:
Skyline Drive eastward
  0.0 Skyline Drive, SDMP 62.7, just north of the South River Overlook.
  0.3 Intersection with the *AT*. (From here via the *AT* it is 0.5m. south to the South River Falls Trail and 2.8m. north to Pocosin Cabin.)
  1.1 Junction with an old road, a branch of the South River Falls Trail.
  1.5 Cross gate.
  2.0 An old road leads uphill on the left.
  2.3 Junction with the Pocosin Horse Trail. (Horse trail leads left for 1.3m. to the Pocosin Fire Rd. The horse trail, a road here, is gated.) From this junction the fire road continues on down into the valley, becoming Va. Sec. 642.

SADDLEBACK MTN. TRAIL

1.4 miles (2.3 kilometers)   blue-blazed

This trail runs from the *AT* to the *AT* passing the South River Maintenance Building (not available for camping). To reach the northern trailhead park in the South River Picnic Grounds and follow the South River Falls Tr. 0.1m. to the *AT*, then follow the

CENTRAL SECTION

AT south (to the right) for 0.5m. The southern trailhead is 1.1m. farther south along the *AT*. Total distance for the circuit hike is only 3 1/2 miles and there are no hard climbs so it's an ideal walk for families with small children.

BIG BEND FIRE ROAD (abandoned)

4.2 miles (6.1 kilometers)   no longer blazed

The roadway may soon be too overgrown for pleasant walking. Until this happens the former road is ideal for the hiker who wants to walk with no climbing, as there is no more than 500 ft. change in elevation in its entire length. It leads north from U.S. 33 at a point 1.3m. east of Swift Run Gap. It connects with no other trail.

LEWIS MOUNTAIN WEST TRAIL

approx. 1.5 miles (2.4 km.) to Park boundary   blue-blazed

The trail starts from the Drive at a point just across from the Lewis Mtn. Campground entrance, SDMP 47.5. Outside the Park the trail passes through private property which may be posted. For this reason the Park Service, some time in the future, may relocate the lower section of trail so that the lower end will be on the Meadow School Fire Rd.

DRY RUN FALLS FIRE ROAD

2.8 miles (4.5 kilometers)   yellow-blazed

This fire road, gated at Skyline Drive and near the Park boundary, leads from the Drive, SDMP 62.6, down the west side of the Blue Ridge. The former trail to Cedar Falls, now completely overgrown, started from this road. Farther down the road, a faint trace of an old road leads left to Dry Run a few hundred feet upcreek from Dry Run Falls. These falls are well worth seeing after a period of wet weather.

The lower end of the fire road is on Va. Sec. 625. From this point it is 3.1 m. to Va. Sec. 759. From the junction with Rt. 759 it is 2.6m. via Rt. 759 to U.S. 340 in Elkton. (To the right it is 1.1m. to Hensley Church.)

SOUTHERN SECTION

HIGHTOP HUT RD.

0.7 miles (1.1 kilometers) blue-blazed

This road leads from the Smith Roach Gap Fire Road, at a point on the fire road about ¾m. from the Skyline Drive, SDMP 68.6, and continues to the Hightop Hut, crossing the *AT* 0.2m. before reaching it. For a short circuit hike one can follow the *AT* from Smith Roach Gap to the summit of Hightop, then descend by backtracking as far as the Hightop Hut, following the latter to the Smith Roach Gap Fire Rd. and following the fire road back to the Smith Roach Gap.

SMITH ROACH GAP FIRE ROAD/HORSE TRAIL

1.0 miles (1.6 kilometers) within the Park yellow-blazed

This road leads southeastward from the Skyline Drive at Smith Roach Gap, SDMP 68.6, to the Park boundary. The access road to Hightop Hut leads left from the fire road at a point on the latter about ¾m. from the Drive. Beyond this point the road is blocked to vehicular traffic as well as at the Park boundary. A short way beyond the Park boundary the road divides. The left fork, as Va. Sec. 626, descends gradually, skirting the head of Whiteoak Spring Branch, then descending a ridge extending from Hightop Mtn., and finally coming into Va. Sec. 630 at a point very near Va. Sec. 810. The right fork leads south over private land, following a long ridge toward Slaters Mountain, eventually coming into Va. Sec. 631. Both road branches are of interest to hikers.

SIMMONS GAP FIRE ROAD

1.0 miles (1.6 km.) east of Skyline Drive and 1.5 miles (2.4 km.) west of Skyline Drive within the Park yellow-blazed

This road, which crosses the Skyline Drive at Simmons Gap, SDMP 73.2, leads from the Park boundary in Beldor Hollow, as a continuation of Va. Sec. 628, to the eastern boundary of the Park

SOUTHERN SECTION

where it becomes Va. Sec. 628 again. The road is gated at both Park boundaries and on both sides of the Drive.

ROCKY MOUNT TRAIL

5.4 miles (8.7 kilometers) blue-blazed

In the southern section of the Park there is a Rocky Mount, a Rocky Mountain and a Rockytop. Rocky Mount is the most northern of these. The Rocky Mount Trail starts at the Skyline Drive, SDMP 76.1, and is marked by a cement signpost. It leads along a northward-bearing side ridge reaching the peak, Rocky Mount, el. 2741', in 3.4m. From the peak it descends steeply to Gap Run.

There are several interesting circuit hikes which include this trail. One of these involves descending the Rocky Mount Trail, turning right, following the Gap Run Trail to its upper end on the Rocky Mount Trail and returning to the start via the latter trail; total distance about 10 miles.

Detailed trail data:

Skyline Drive to Gap Run

0.0-5.4 Skyline Drive, SDMP 76.1. The Rocky Mount Tr. follows along a ridge which extends northward. Many good views are offered.

2.2-3.2 Reach trail junction. (To the right the blue-blazed Gap Run Trail leads down along Gap Run to rejoin the Rocky Mount Trail.)

3.4-2.0 Reach the summit of Rocky Mount, el. 2741 '. From here the trail descends rather steeply. In about a mile the trail turns right off the ridge, descends to a creek, and follows down the creek.

5.4-0.0 End of Rocky Mount Trail. The Gap Run Trail (blue-blazed) leads right, rejoining the Rocky Mount Tr. in 2.3m.

GAP RUN TRAIL

2.3 miles (3.7 kilometers) blue-blazed

This blue-blazed trail starts from the Rocky Mount Trail at a point 2.2m. from the Skyline Drive and leads down along Gap

Run to rejoin the Rocky Mount Tr. at its lower end in the gap. The Gap Run Trail is often used along with the Rocky Mount Trail for a circuit hike.

ONEMILE RUN TRAIL

4.5 miles (7.2 kilometers)   blue-blazed

This trail leads north from the Skyline Drive and follows, for a mile, the narrow Twomile Ridge which separates Twomile Run and Onemile Run. It then turns left off the ridge and descends to Onemile Run, continuing down the run for nearly two miles. Then it swings north and crosses over to Twomile Run and ends on a private road just north of that run.

Access:

To reach the start of this trail, park at the Twomile Run Overlook, SDMP 76.2, and walk south along the Drive for about 0.1m. Trailhead is marked. (The *AT* comes within 100 ft. of the east side of the Drive 100 ft. south of here. Look for unmarked path.)

Because there is at present a problem with public access across the private land the trail crosses to reach its lower trailhead, it is advisable to use only the upper one. Remember that posted trail closures must be respected.

Detailed trail data:

0.0 From Skyline Drive, SDMP 76.3, the trail heads northwestward along Twomile Ridge.

1.0 Here, in a sag, the trail leaves the ridge and descends westward. (The former Twomile Ridge Tr. which continued out the ridge is no longer maintained. There is an excellent viewpoint about 1.2m. out Twomile Ridge from the sag.)

1.4 Reach Onemile Run and descend along the run.

2.9 Trail leaves Onemile Run and heads northward.

3.7 Reach Park boundary. Although blazes continue outside the Park, some of the land through which the trail passes is now posted denying public access, so it is advisable to turn back here. Posted closures must be respected.

SOUTHERN SECTION 233

IVY CREEK MAINTENANCE BLDG. ROAD

0.4 miles (0.6 kilometers)   not blazed

This short road, which runs from the Skyline Drive, SDMP 79.4, to the Ivy Creek Maintenance Bldg. (no camping) can be used by hikers as part of short circuit hike which would include a climb up to the Loft Mtn. ridge via the Deadening Nature Trail, SDMP 79.5, then the stretch of *AT* between the Nature Trail and the Ivy Creek Maintenance Bldg., and the return to the Skyline Drive via the service road and, finally, a 0.1m. walk along the Drive for a total circuit distance of 2.1m.

DEADENING NATURE TRAIL

1.3 mile circuit (2.1 kilometers)   not blazed

This is a short but very interesting Park Service selfguiding trail. (See Loft Mtn. Developed Area map inset, back of PATC Map No. 11.) It involves a fairly steep climb from the Skyline Drive to the *AT* on Loft Mtn. and an equally steep descent. The trail starts on the east side of the Drive, right at the entrance to the Loft Mtn. Developed Area, SDMP 79.5. It climbs 0.6m. to the *AT,* turns left and follows the *AT* for 0.1m., then descends 0.6m. to its starting point.

DOYLES RIVER TRAIL

4.7 miles (7.5 kilometers)   blue-blazed

This is a lovely trail. There are beautiful waterfalls on both the Doyles River and Jones Run. Enormous trees growing near the creeks add interest. The trail, combined with a short section of the *AT,* forms an 8 mile loop ideal for a circuit hike.

This graded trail was constructed by the CCC in 1936-37. It involves a steep descent along one water course and a steep climb along the other. The northern terminus is at the Doyles River Cabin Parking Area on the Skyline Drive, SDMP 81.1, el. 2800'.; the southern terminus, also on the Drive, is at the Jones Run Parking Area, SDMP 83.8, el. 2790'. The elevation of the trail at the junction of Doyles River and Jones Run is only 1500 ft. The

SIDE TRAILS

Doyles River Trail and the *AT* intersect just below the Doyles River Parking Area at a point on the *AT* 2.2m. north of Browns Gap and again just below the Jones Run Parking Area at a point on the *AT* 1.2m. south of Browns Gap. (Distance along the *AT* between the trail intersections is 3.4m.)

The Doyles River Cabin, a locked structure, is located near the Doyles River Trail, 0.4m. from its northern terminus. For use of this cabin, reservations must be obtained in advance from PATC Headquarters. (See Chap. 6: "Picnic Shelters, Huts and Cabins.")

The old Browns Gap Fire Road leads down the mountain from Browns Gap to Browns Cove, intersecting the Doyles River Trail a short distance above the upper falls on the Doyles River. A shorter loop hike, 6½ miles in length, can be made by descending Jones Run along the Doyles River Trail, ascending Doyles River past the upper falls, then following the Browns Gap Fire Rd. to the *AT*, and finally proceeding south along the *AT* to the Doyles River Trail intersection.

Detailed trail data:

South (where there is ample parking space) to north

0.0-4.7 Southern terminus, Jones Run Parking Area, Skyline Drive, SDMP 83.8, el. 2700'. Trail crosses the *AT* in 100 ft., then continues eastward, descending.

0.6-4.1 Trail crosses Jones Run.

1.5-3.2 Trail returns to the run and follows down along its south bank.

1.6-3.1 Reach base of a sloping falls.

1.7-3.0 Reach top of the Upper Falls. A short side trail affords good view of the falls.

1.9-2.7 Reach top of Lower Falls.

2.5-2.2 Reach "half-way" point, the junction of Jones Run and Doyles River. Trail ascends from here.

3.2-1.5 Reach top of the Lower Falls of Doyles River, a two-step cascade between high rock cliffs.

3.5-1.2 Reach top of the Upper Falls. This is a three-step cascade in a lovely canyon.

3.8-0.9 Cross Browns Gap Fire Rd. (Road leads west uphill for 1.7m. to intersect the *AT* at Browns Gap. To the east the road

SOUTHERN SECTION

leads down into Browns Cove becoming Va. Sec. 810 at a point about 18m. from Stanardsville and 11m. from Crozet.)

4.4-0.3 Pass spring on right of trail. Here a spur trail on the right leads 0.1m. steeply up to Doyles River Cabin.

4.7-0.0 Cross the *AT*. (Via the *AT* from this junction it is 10.0m. north to Simmons Gap, 2.2m. south to Browns Gap, and 3.4m. to the southern terminus of the Doyles River Trail.) In 200 ft. reach Skyline Drive at Doyles River Cabin Parking Area, SDMP 81.1, el. 2800'.

BROWNS GAP FIRE RD.

3.5 miles within the Park (5.2 kilometers) yellow-blazed

This old road, the eastern extension of the Madison Run Rd., leads from the Skyline Drive at Browns Gap, SDMP 82.9, down the east slopes of the Blue Ridge to Browns Cove, crossing the Doyles River Trail and the Doyles River in 1.8m. The old road continues beyond the Park boundary for another 1.0m. where it becomes Va. Sec. 629. The start of Rt. 629 is at a point 0.8m. above the highway bridge over the Doyles River and 1.2m. from Va. Sec. 810. One should park along or near Rt. 810 as Rt. 629 is only a one-track road above the bridge and there is almost no place to pull off the road.

The Browns Gap Rd. was used by Stonewall Jackson and his men during the Civil War. About 0.4m. down from the Skyline Drive, to the left of the road, a short footpath leads to the grave of William H. Howard, Co. F, 44 Va. Inf., C.S.A. Farther down the road but above the Doyles River is a tulip tree of tremendous girth. The stretch of the old road between the Doyles River Tr. intersection and the Park boundary is quite lovely. There are many large trees including hemlock, and the road itself clings along the edge of a steep hillside with the river far below.

BIG RUN AREA

Big Run and its tributaries comprise the largest watershed in the Park. This area is contained in the largest of the Park's wilderness areas and is separated from the one just south of it only by the Madison Run Fire Rd. The ten trails included in the Big Run Area are for the most part rugged but scenic. There are many circuit hikes that can be made; some are quite long so are ideal for backpackers.

A serious fire, the worst the Shenandoah Park has experienced since the 1930's, burned over 4300 acres of the watershed in May, 1986. It will undoubtedly be some time before the area regains much of its vegetation and wildlife.

BIG RUN PORTAL TRAIL

4.4 miles (7.1 kilometers)   yellow-blazed

This is the valley route through the canyon of Big Run, which flows from south to north. The grade of the trail is very gentle all the way from the Park boundary to its upper end on the Big Run Loop Trail. It is a very pleasant walk and makes one leg of a circuit hike with the other leg being either the Rockytop Trail or the Rocky Mtn.-Brown Mtn. Trail. The cliffs, talus slopes and gorge at "The Portal" just below the Big Run Portal Trail's bridge over Big Run are very spectacular.

Access:

The upper end can be reached from the Big Run Loop Trail, following it "south" from Big Run Parking Overlook, SDMP 81.2, for 2.2m. to its lowest elevation or following the Big Run Loop Trail north from its intersection with the *AT* at a point 0.6m. north of Browns Gap, SDMP 82.9. Access across private land at the Park boundary is by goodwill of the landowner. Posted closures must be respected.

Detailed trail data:

Park boundary to Big Run Loop Tr.

0.0-4.4 Gate on road at Park boundary.

0.2-4.2 Junction with Rockytop Trail which enters from the right. (To the left here one can bushwhack down to Big Run at "The Portal".) Trail descends from here to reach the run.

0.7-3.7 Cross bridge over Big Run. Rocky Mountain-Brown Mtn. Trail comes in on left at far end of bridge. Trailhead is marked by cement post. Continue up the run. There are nine fords

SOUTHERN SECTION

on the trail, seven of Big Run, the other two of side streams. When the run is full the fording may be difficult.

1.7-2.7 There is a deep pool here. To the left the area is flat and shrubby where once there was a field. Slightly above the pool are the third and fourth fords.

2.1-2.3 At a fork, continue ahead crossing Rocky Mtn. Run, a side stream, immediately after. (Left fork is the Rocky Mtn. Run Tr. which connects with the Rocky Mtn.-Brown Mtn. Tr. in 2.7m.) 250 yds. farther the Patterson Ridge Tr. enters road from the left.

3.0-1.4 Trail crosses to west bank here, recrosses in 0.3m. and again in another 0.2m.

3.7-0.7 The ninth ford, this time of a side creek entering from the right.

4.4-0.0 Trail ends at junction with Big Run Loop Trail.

ROCKY MTN. RUN TRAIL

2.7 miles (4.3 kilometers)   blue-blazed

This trail runs from the Big Run Portal Tr. up to the Rocky Mtn.-Brown Mtn. Trail and is used with them for a circuit hike.

PATTERSON RIDGE TRAIL

3.1 miles (5.0 kilometers)   yellow-blazed

This trail leads from the Skyline Drive, SDMP 79.4, at a point opposite the service road leading to Ivy Creek Maintenance Bldg., descending westward along Patterson Ridge. It comes into the Big Run Portal Tr. at a point 0.1m. above the lower end of the Rocky Mtn. Run Tr. and 1.5m. above the lower end of the Rocky Mtn.-Brown Mtn. Trail. It can be used for circuit hikes.

BIG RUN LOOP TRAIL

4.2 miles (6.7 kilometers)   blue and yellow-blazed

This trail affords access to the upper end of Big Run. The Big Run Loop Tr. together with the Big Run Portal Tr. affords access to the lower ends of the Rockytop Tr. and the Rocky Mtn.-Brown

Mtn. Tr. as well as the Rocky Mtn. Run Tr. and the Patterson Ridge Tr. The Big Run Loop Tr., at its southern end, links the *AT* with the Rockytop Tr.

An excellent short circuit hike of 5.8m. can be made by using the *AT* in one direction and the Big Run Loop Tr. in the other.

Access:

The northern end of this trail is at the Big Run Parking Overlook on the Skyline Drive, SDMP 81.2. (250 ft. north and across the Drive from here is the northern end of the Doyles River Tr. which crosses the *AT* within 200 ft.)

The southern end of this trail is on the *AT* at a point 0.6m. north of Browns Gap, SDMP 82.9m.

Detailed trail data:

North to South

0.0-4.2 Big Run Parking Overlook. Trail, here blue-blazed, descends steeply by switchback.

0.7-3.5 From here the trail follows the crest of a ridge between branches of Big Run, then swings left down into the main hollow.

2.2-2.0 Junction with the Big Run Portal Tr. (yellow-blazed). Turn left. This 1.3m. section is dual-blazed blue and yellow. The trail ascends steadily following above a branch of Big Run.

3.0-1.2 Turn sharply right, away from the ravine.

3.5-0.7 At trail junction in sag the Big Run Loop Tr. (blue-blazed) turns left. The Rockytop Tr. goes right (blue-blazed) and leads along the ridge 5.7m. to the Big Run Portal Tr. The Madison Run Spur Trail (yellow-blazed) goes straight ahead to descend in 0.3m. to the Madison Run Road entering it at a point on that road 0.8m. from Browns Gap.

4.2-0.0 Junction with the *AT* at a point on the latter 0.6m. north from Browns Gap, SDMP 82.9, and 0.3m. south of the Skyline Drive crossing at SDMP 82.2.

MADISON RUN SPUR TRAIL

0.3 miles (0.5 kilometers)   yellow-blazed

This short trail runs from the junction of the Rockytop Trail with the Big Run Loop Tr. down to Madison Run Fire Rd. entering it at a point 0.8m. west of the Skyline Drive at Browns Gap.

SOUTHERN SECTION

ROCKY MOUNTAIN-BROWN MOUNTAIN TRAIL

5.3 miles (8.5 kilometers) blue-blazed

Rocky Mtn. and Brown Mtn. comprise the ridge extending west from the main Blue Ridge along the north side of Big Run. To the north of this ridge is the lower Twomile Ridge with Rocky Mount in the background. To the south is the high imposing ridge along which the Rockytop Trail runs.

From the Brown Mtn. Parking Overlook on the Skyline Drive, SDMP 76.9, this blue-blazed trail leads west along the ridge, first crossing the twin summits of Rocky Mountain, then over Brown Mtn. before dropping steeply to the Big Run Portal Tr. A popular loop hike is made by descending this trail and ascending the Big Run Portal Tr. then turning left onto the Big Run Loop Tr. to the Big Run Overlook (total distance 11m.). To make a complete circuit continue by walking north a few feet, cross the drive and descend to the *AT*. Turn left, north, follow the *AT* to the Ivy Creek Overlook, then walk north along the Drive the remaining distance to Brown Mtn. Overlook. Complete circuit distance is about 18m.

A shorter circuit hike can be made by descending the Rocky-Mtn.-Brown Mtn. Tr, following up the Big Run Portal Tr. for 1.3m., then turning onto the Rocky Mtn. Run Tr. and climbing along this trail for 2.7m. to its junction with the Rocky Mtn.-Brown Mtn. Tr. Turn right to reach return to Brown Mtn. Overlook. Circuit distance 9.3m.

Access to the lower end of the Rocky Mtn.-Brown Mtn. Tr. is via the Big Run Portal Tr.

Detailed trail data:

Skyline Drive to Big Run Portal Trail

0.0-5.3 Brown Mtn. Overlook, Skyline Drive, SDMP 76.9.

0.7-4.6 On left the Rocky Mtn. Run Trail (blue-blazed) leads down to the Big Run Portal Tr.

1.6-3.7 Reach crest of the peak of Rocky Mtn., el. 2800'. Here are striking views of the Massanutten range. The footing is rough beyond this point.

2.2-3.1 Pass to the right of the second peak of Rocky Mtn., el. 2864'. Along the trail from here to the summit of Brown Mtn.

there is much turkeybeard (Xerophyllum asphodeloides), a grass-like member of the lily family blooming in early June. Turkeybeard is a close relative of western beargrass.

3.1-2.2 Reach summit of Brown Mtn., el. 2560'. The Brown Mtn. ridge, like Rockytop to the southwest, consists of a sandstone streaked with fossil wormholes. The trail now descends along a ridge crest with magnificent views of Rockytop, the Shenandoah Valley and the south end of the Massanutten Range. It then descends steeply toward Big Run.

5.3-0.0 Junction with Big Run Portal Tr. at east end of the bridge over Big Run. "The Portal" of Big Run is a short distance down creek from here. To the left, upstream, it is 1.4m. to the lower end of the Rocky Mtn. Run Tr. and 3.7m. to the Big Run Loop Tr. To the right on the Big Run Portal Trail it is 0.5m. to the lower end of the Rockytop Tr. and 0.2m. farther to the gate at the Park boundary. Access across private land at the Park boundary is by goodwill of the landowner. Posted closures must be respected.

ROCKYTOP TRAIL

5.7 miles (9.2 kilometers) blue-blazed

This trail extends along the crest of the ridge which forms the sheer southwest wall of Big Run Canyon. It takes its name from its outstanding feature, Rockytop. (Hikers prefer to call the more northern peak, el. 2856', the "real" Rockytop, rather than the one marked on U.S. topographic maps.) Where the trail skirts the western face of this highest peak it offers a superb view of the peaks to the southwest and of the Shenandoah Valley. In addition, the rocks of this part of the ridge are quite fascinating. An examination of them will show they contain long slender cylindrical markings, perhaps an eighth inch in diameter. It is believed that these are fossils of wormholes now 500 million years old! (See Chap. 3: "Geology of the SNP.") For the wildflower enthusiast the Rockytop Trail also offers an abundance of the turkeybeard, our eastern version of the West's beargrass. You'll find it in bloom in early June.

This trail has a rather narrow footway and is rough underfoot.

SOUTHERN SECTION 241

However, its advantages far outweigh its disadvantages. It offers excellent views, access to the Austin Mtn. Tr. and the Lewis Peak Tr. and can be used with either the Lewis Peak Trail or the Big Run Portal Tr. for a circuit hike.

Access:

The upper end of the Rockytop Trail is on the Big Run Loop Tr. To reach it from the Skyline Drive follow the *AT* north from Browns Gap, SDMP 82.9, for 0.6m., turn left onto the Big Run Loop Tr. and follow it for 0.7m. Rockytop-Big Run Loop Trail junction is marked by a cement post.

The lower end of the Rockytop Trail is on the Big Run Portal Tr., 0.2m. east of the gate at the Park boundary. Access across private land at the Park boundary is by goodwill of the landowner. Posted closures must be respected.

Detailed trail data:

Big Run Loop Tr. to Big Run Portal Tr.

0.0-5.7 From junction with the Big Run Loop Tr., marked by cement post, Rockytop Tr. ascends.

0.4-5.3 Take right fork here. (Left fork is Austin Mtn. Tr. which leads 3.2m. down Austin Mtn. ridge and comes into Madison Run Rd. near the Park boundary.) Trail now skirts the right side of the ridge for 0.6m., then swings over to the left side, crossing a talus slope with views of Austin and Lewis Mtns.

2.2-3.5 Junction with Lewis Peak Trail, blue-blazed, is marked by cement post. Rockytop Tr. is right fork.

3.0-2.7 Reach sag at base of the hikers' "Rockytop", the highest peak of the ridge, and ascend along its left side.

3.5-2.2 Cross talus slope with outstanding views of Austin Mtn., Lewis Mtn. and Lewis Peak to the southwest and the Shenandoah Valley and Massanutten range farther north. Many of the rocks here and on the smaller rock slopes beyond this point are full of the "wormhole" fossils giving the rocks a striated appearance.

3.6-2.1 Bear right and ascend by switchbacks over the crest of a ridge bearing northwest here and descend along the northbearing ridge. (Hangman Run splits the main ridge here.)

5.7-0.0 Reach Big Run Portal Tr. Junction is marked with cement signpost. To left on the Big Run Portal Tr. it is 0.2m. to the Park boundary where it is gated. (Access across private land at the Park boundary is by goodwill of the landowner. Posted closures must be respected.) To the right, in 0.5m., it reaches the junction with the Rocky Mtn.-Brown Mtn. Tr., then continues to its upper end on the Big Run Loop Tr., 4.2m. (From the latter junction it is 1.3m. via the Big Run Loop Tr. back to its intersection with the Rockytop Trail. Round trip from Browns Gap is 13.4m.)

AUSTIN MTN. TRAIL

3.2 miles (5.1 kilometers)   blue-blazed

This trail runs from the Rockytop Trail across Austin Mtn. and on down to Madison Run Fire Rd. The Austin Mtn. Tr. is the more southern of the parallel routes that lead westward from the high ridge of the Rockytop Tr. to outlying conical peaks. The upper (eastern) end of the Austin Mtn. Tr. begins on the Rockytop Trail near the upper end of the latter. It follows a side ridge between Deep Run and Madison Run to just short of the top of Austin Mtn. The trail slabs the south side of the mountain, then descends steeply to Madison Run Fire Rd. Sections of this trail are rocky, steep and poorly graded. Heavy-duty foot gear is recommended.

Access:

To reach the upper end of this trail follow the *AT* for 0.6m. north from Browns Gap, SDMP 82.9. Turn left onto the Big Run Loop Trail and follow it for 0.7m. to its junction with the Rockytop Trail. Then follow the Rockytop Trail (straight ahead at the junction) for 0.4m. to the Austin Mtn. Tr. trailhead.

The lower end of the Austin Mtn. Tr. is on Madison Run Fire Rd. at a point on the road 4.4m. from the Skyline Drive at Browns Gap, SDMP 82.9. To reach the trail from U.S. 340 follow Va. Sec. 663 from Grottoes (or Va. Sec. 659 from just north of Grottoes) and continue on Rt. 663 beyond the junction with Rt. 659 passing Va. Sec. 708 on the left and parking at the junction of a second road, also entering from the left. From here (about 2.5m. from U.S. 340) continue up Rt. 663 on foot another 0.2m. to where road is gated, then continue up the fire road for 0.7m. to trailhead marked by cement post.

Detailed trail data:
Rockytop Tr. to Madison Run Rd.

0.0-3.2 Junction with Rockytop Trail.

2.1-1.1 Here the trail descends steeply across rock slopes and under cliffs.

2.7-0.5 Sharp turn in the trail. Steep descent continues.

3.2-0.0 Reach Madison Run Rd. To the left, via the road, it is 4.4m. to the Skyline Drive at Browns Gap. To the right it is 0.6m. to the lower end of the Furnace Mtn. Tr. and 0.1m. farther to where the road is gated and becomes Va. Sec. 663. Circuit hike from Browns Gap using the *AT*, Big Run Loop Tr., Rockytop Tr., Austin Mtn. Tr. and Madison Run Fire Rd. is about 9½m.

LEWIS PEAK TRAIL

2.6 miles (4.2 kilometers)   blue-blazed

This blue-blazed trail is the more northern of the parallel routes leading west from the Rockytop Trail. It continues beyond Lewis Peak, descending to the Park boundary and on a short distance farther to a dirt road in the valley. Lewis Peak itself is reached by a 0.3m. side trail. From the peak there is a panoramic view of the Shenandoah Valley and the Massanutten range to the northwest and west and the surrounding peaks of the Blue Ridge on the north, east, and south.

Access:

The upper end is reached via the Rockytop trail. The trailhead is 2.3m. from the Rockytop Tr.-Big Run Loop Tr. junction and 3.4m. from the Rockytop Tr.-Big Run Portal Tr. junction. To reach the lower end of the Lewis Peak Tr. turn east off U.S. 340 onto Va. Sec. 708 at a point about 4 miles NE of Grottoes. In 1½ miles or less turn left onto a private road leading north. This road is gated in about 0.5m. Lewis Peak trailhead is 0.2m. farther along the road. In parking be careful not to block the road or any driveway. Access across private land at the Park boundary is by goodwill of the landowners. Posted closures must be respected.

Detailed trail data:
Rockytop Tr. to Shenandoah Valley

0.0-2.6 Junction with the Rockytop Trail. (From this point, via the Rockytop Tr., it is 1.9m. to the junction with the Austin Mtn. Tr. and 2.3m. to its upper end on Big Run Loop Tr. To the north via the Rockytop Trail it is 3.4m. to the Big Run Portal Tr. and, via the latter, another 0.2m. to the Park boundary.) From the junction, Lewis Peak Tr. follows the crest of a ridge extending west between the two branches of Lewis Run.

0.7-1.9 Reach sag.

0.9-1.7 At junction main trail goes left. (Right fork is a 0.3m. spur trail leading to the summit of Lewis Peak, el. 2760'. From Lewis Peak there is a panoramic view of the Shenandoah Valley, the Massanutten range and the surrounding peaks of the Blue Ridge.) Main trail now descends toward the west and northwest along a ridge paralleling Upper Lewis Run.

2.4-0.2 Cross Upper Lewis Run. Fifty feet beyond turn right onto well-worn road, passing by a cabin.

2.6-0.0 Come into (private) road where trail ends. Access across private land at the Park boundary is by goodwill of the landowners. Posted closures must be respected.

MADISON RUN FIRE ROAD

5.1 miles (8.2 kilometers)   yellow-blazed

This road, gated at each end, runs from Browns Gap down the west side of the Blue Ridge, becoming Va. Sec. 663 outside the Park. It can be used with either Austin Mtn. Tr. or Furnace Mtn. Tr. for a circuit hike. The upper end of this road starts at Browns Gap, SDMP 82.9, el. 2599'. The lower end of this road can be reached by following Rt. 663 east to where it becomes the fire road, a distance of about 2¾m. from U.S. 340 in Grottoes. Elevation at the Park boundary is 1360'. Madison Run Spur Tr., 0.3m, connects the fire road with the Big Run Loop Tr.

STULL RUN FIRE ROAD-CRIMORA FIRE ROAD
LEWIS RUN FIRE ROAD

yellow-blazed within Park

Starting at a point near the junction of Rts. 663 and 629 east of

SOUTHERN SECTION

Grottoes, the Stull Run Fire Rd. leads south. In about 2 miles it runs out of the Park and continues as a private road. A bit farther south a short section of the road, where it follows Stull Run, lies within the Park but this portion is being abandoned and closed to vehicles. No trails connect with the fire road but it offers bushwhackers access to the Wilderness Area that includes Abbott Ridge and Hall Mountain.

The Crimora Fire Rd. runs from Va. Sec. 614 near Paine Run south to Va. Sec. 612 east of Crimora. Only a very small amount-two short segments-of this road lies within the Park, but the southern stretch of the road from Rt. 612 north serves as access to the Riprap Trail.

The Lewis Run Fire Rd. leads southwest from Park property where it touches U.S. 340, about 6 miles north of Grottoes, and continues outside the Park through private lands to end on Va. Sec. 708. The lower end of the Lewis Peak Trail is on the private portion. Access across private land at the Park boundary is by goodwill of the landowners. Posted closures must be respected.

TRAYFOOT MOUNTAIN TRAIL

5.4 miles (8.7 kilometers)   blue-blazed

This trail leads from the Skyline Drive to the top of Trayfoot Mountain, el. 3374', then descends along a narrow ridge leading southwest and forming the divide between Paine Run and Stull Run. Along the route are some rock formations offering outstanding views. The trail's lower end on the Paine Run Tr. is at an elevation of only 1440'. Together the trails offer a good loop hike of about 9m. (A complete circuit would include the stretch of *AT* between Blackrock Gap and the Trayfoot Mtn. Tr. for a total distance of about 10m.)

The Trayfoot Mtn. Tr. offers the shortest route (about 0.5m.) to Blackrock from the Drive. There is parking space for several cars on the trail a few hundred feet from the Drive. The Furnace Mtn. Tr. has its upper end on the Trayfoot Mtn. Tr.

Access:

Upper end is on the Skyline Drive, SDMP 84.7, about 2m. south of Browns Gap. To reach the lower terminus turn east from

U.S. 340 about 4½m. south of Grottoes onto Va. Sec. 614 at a point just south of the highway bridge over Paine Run. Follow Rt. 614 and continue beyond state maintenance. Continue past an open gate a short distance and park, to the right of the road, on Park property at a small turnaround and parking area. (Note: Old Crimora Fire Rd. leads south here. Do not block it.) Continue up private road on foot to Paine Run. The Paine Run Tr., blocked to vehicles at its lower end by large rocks, is just north of the run. Follow it up the run for 0.3m. to the start of the Trayfoot Mtn. Tr. Access across private lands at the Park boundary is by the goodwill of the landowners. Please help them keep both road and parking area free of trash. Remember that posted closures must be respected.

Detailed trail data:
Skyline Drive to Paine Run Tr.

0.0-5.4 Trailhead on Skyline Drive, SDMP 84.7. Trail leads west, soon almost touching but not crossing, the *AT*. The trails run parallel for about 0.1m. Then the Trayfoot Mtn. Tr. passes to the south of Blackrock whereas the *AT* circles through the Blackrock area.

0.4-5.0 Intersection with the *AT*, just south of Blackrock.

0.5-4.9 An old road to the left here leads down a southwestward extending ridge paralleling the *AT*. (Road serves as the service road to Blackrock Hut.) Trayfoot Mtn. Tr. continues straight ahead and enters the largest Wilderness Area in the Park.

0.9-4.5 Where trail reaches the ridge crest a spur trail, blue-blazed, leads right and back along the ridge crest for 0.1m. to the *AT* at Blackrock.

1.4-4.0 Where trail turns sharply to the left climbing Trayfoot Mtn., the Furnace Mtn. Tr., blue-blazed, leads north (straight ahead), reaching the Madison Run Fire Rd. in 3.4m.

1.6-3.8 Just short of the summit of Trayfoot Mtn. the trail leaves the old fire road route and bears right, heading southwest along the crest of the long Trayfoot Mtn. ridge. Descend gradually, crossing numerous knobs. There are numerous views on both sides of the trail.

4.8-0.6 Turn sharply left (east). Excellent view of Buzzard Rock Peak across Paine Run from here.

SOUTHERN SECTION

5.1-0.3 Turn sharply right.
5.4-0.0 Junction with yellow-blazed Paine Run Tr. To left the latter, in a few feet, crosses the creek coming out of Lefthand Hollow. It continues for 3.4m. to the Skyline Drive at Blackrock Gap. To the right this trail reaches the Park boundary in 0.3m. and comes into private road leading left. The road becomes, in 0.8m., Va. Sec. 614. It is about 2m. farther to U.S. 340.

BLACKROCK SPUR TRAIL

0.1 mile (0.2 kilometers)   blue-blazed

From the *AT* at Blackrock this trail follows the ridge crest toward Trayfoot Mtn. coming into the Trayfoot Mtn. Tr. where the latter reaches the ridge crest. This is a very short, but useful, connector trail.

FURNACE MOUNTAIN TRAIL

3.4 miles (5.5 kilometers)   blue-blazed

This trail, which has its upper end on the Trayfoot Mtn. Tr., leads down the long northwest-bearing ridge of Trayfoot Mtn. toward the peak of Furnace Mtn. From a sag at the base of this peak the main trail descends along the west slopes of the mountain while a spur trail leads right 0.5m. over the summit to an excellent viewpoint. Almost the entire trail lies within a Wilderness Area and is in one of the remoter sections of Shenandoah Park. The lower end of the trail is on the Madison Run Fire Road, a tenth of a mile east of the Park boundary (and gate).

Access:
To reach the lower end of the trail follow Va. Sec. 663 east from U.S. 340 in Grottoes (or follow Va. Sec. 659 from a point on U.S. 340 north of Grottoes to Rt. 663, then continue left on Rt. 663) and continue up road to Park boundary where road is gated. Continue up road (Madison Run Fire Road) on foot. Lower end of Furnace Mtn. Trail is 0.1m. up the road, on the south side. It is marked by a cement post. It crosses Madison Run, then heads *downstream* for a hundred feet or so before starting to climb.

To reach the upper end of this trail follow the Trayfoot Mtn. Tr. from the Drive, SDMP 84.7, for 1.4m. to where the latter trail makes a sharp bend to the left before ascending toward the summit of Trayfoot Mtn. The trailhead is right at the bend, to the right of the road. One may also reach the trailhead by following the *AT* 1.1m. from where it crosses the Skyline Drive, SDMP 84.3, to Blackrock. From here take the blue-blazed trail leading out along the ridge and follow it 0.1m. to where it joins the Trayfoot Mtn. Tr. Continue out the ridge for 0.6m. to the sharp bend described above.

Detailed trail data:
Trayfoot Mtn. Tr. to Madison Run Fire Rd.

0.0-3.4 Junction with the Trayfoot Mtn. Tr. Trail follows ridge leading north-northwest.

0.7-2.7 Here the trail turns sharply right. Caution is needed because former trails, one to Hall Mtn. and one that leads out Abbott Ridge, may still be visible.

1.8-1.6 Take left fork at trail junction. (Trail to the right leads for 0.5m. to beyond the summit of Furnace Mtn.; it ends on a ledge with an excellent view over Madison Run.)

3.4-0.0 Reach Madison Run Fire Rd. (Lower end of Austin Mtn. Tr. is 0.6m. to the right, up the fire road. To the left in 0.1m. the road is gated at the Park boundary. From the gate where it becomes Va. Sec. 663 it is about 2.5m. to U.S. 340 in Grottoes.)

PAINE RUN TRAIL

3.7 miles (6.0 kilometers)　　　　　　　　　　　　yellow-blazed

This trail, formerly a fire road, leads west from the Skyline Drive at Blackrock Gap, SDMP 87.4. In about one mile it passes near the Blackrock Springs, the site of a former hotel. Below the springs the trail descends along Paine Run, finally passing through a narrow gorge between the SE end of the Trayfoot Mtn. Ridge and a sharp peak, Buzzard Rock. The trail, now permanently closed to vehicles at its lower end, comes into a privately owned road which leads due west for 0.8m. before becoming Va. Sec. 614.

SOUTHERN SECTION

To reach this road from U.S. 340, turn east on Va. Sec. 614 at a point just south of the highway bridge over Paine Run. Continue beyond the state maintenance to parking area. Continue along the private road on foot to reach Paine Run. Find the Paine Run Tr., blocked to motor vehicles by boulders, on the north side of the creek.

At a point about 0.3m. up from the lower end of the Paine Run Tr. the Trayfoot Mtn. Tr. heads north and then east for 5.4m. to end on the Skyline Drive. A 9½m. circuit hike can be made from Blackrock Gap by following *AT* north to Blackrock, next the Blackrock Spur Tr. that leads along the ridge from Blackrock to the Trayfoot Mtn. Tr., then follow the Trayfoot Mtn. Tr. west and south down to Paine Run Tr. and ascend the latter back to Blackrock Gap.

RIPRAP TRAIL

4.5 miles (7.2 kilometers)   blue-blazed

This is a very picturesque route. From its northern trailhead on the *AT* it swings west and climbs along Calvary Rocks where excellent views are to be had, then continues on by Chimney Rock with more views. It descends Cold Spring Hollow and on down Riprap Hollow. This is one of the few areas of the Park where one can find the Catawba rhododendron (blooming in late May), a very common shrub farther south. The lower end of the trail is on the Crimora Fire Rd., just at the Park boundary. The lower end of the Wildcat Ridge Tr. is on this trail. A popular circuit hike, 9½m., makes use of the Wildcat Ridge Tr., most of the Riprap Tr. and the section of *AT* between them.

In addition to rhododendron and mountain laurel one may find fly poison and turkeybeard, starflower and wild bleeding heart in bloom around the end of May.

Access:

To reach the northern end of the Riprap Tr., park at the Riprap Trail Parking Area, SDMP 90.0, take the short spur trail to the *AT* and turn right. Follow the *AT* north for 0.4m. to the start of the Riprap Tr.

To approach the southern terminus turn east from U.S. 340 onto Va. Sec. 612 at Crimora and drive about 1.7m., nearly to the end of state maintenance, then follow the Crimora Fire Rd. left for about 1 mile. Large boulders at the trailhead block the trail to vehicles.

Detailed trail data:
North to south

0.0-4.5 Junction with *AT* at a point on the *AT* 0.4m. north of the short spur trail leading to Riprap Tr. Parking Area, SDMP 90.0 (and 2.9m. south of Blackrock Gap via the *AT*).

1.0-3.5 Spur trail leads right for 15 ft. to cliffs near Calvary Rocks.

1.2-3.3 Trail turns sharply left here. A spur trail leads right for 75 ft. to edge of cliffs, Chimney Rock, with fine views north.

1.8-2.7 Turn sharply left from the ridge down into Cold Spring Hollow.

2.8-1.7 Trail descends steeply through a rocky chasm. Route here is very spectacular.

3.0-1.5 Cross to east of stream.

3.1-1.4 Recross stream. There is a deep pool at the base of a sloping falls here which makes an excellent swimming hole. A considerable amount of pink Catawba rhododendron grows near the run.

3.6-0.9 Junction with the Wildcat Ridge Tr. which goes east (left) climbing for 2.7m. to end on the Skyline Drive, SDMP 92.1.

4.5-0.0 Reach Crimora Fire Rd. at Park boundary. A foot trail leads southeast here up Dorsey Hanger Hollow to lovely Crimora Lake. A mining road on the south side of the lake connects this lake with the mine lakes to the south and to the Turk Gap Tr.

WILDCAT RIDGE TRAIL

2.7 miles (4.4 kilometers)　　　　　　　　　　　　　　blue-blazed

This lovely trail starts at the Wildcat Ridge Parking Area on Skyline Drive, SDMP 92.1. It crosses the *AT* in 0.1m., continues west following the Wildcat Ridge, then descends into Riprap Hollow to end on the Riprap Tr. It is used along with the Riprap

SOUTHERN SECTION

Tr. and *AT* for an exceptionally beautiful circuit of about 9½ miles.

Detailed trail data:
Skyline Drive to Riprap Trail

0.0-2.7 Junction with the Skyline Drive at Wildcat Ridge Parking Area, SDMP 92.1.

0.1-2.6 Intersection with *AT*. (To right, via the *AT*, it is 2.8m. to the Riprap Trail Parking Area and 3.1m. to the northern end of the Riprap Tr. To the left it is 0.3m. to the next *AT* crossing of the Drive and 2.3m. to Turk Gap.) From here the trail descends gradually along Wildcat Ridge.

1.0-1.7 Cross over knob, el. 2514', then continue descent along the ridge. There are occasional good views south. In winter one may be able to glimpse Crimora Lake in Dorsey Hangar Hollow below the trail.

1.5-1.2 Come into a sag.

1.8-0.9 In another sag the trail turns sharply to the right, leaves the ridge crest and descends steeply.

2.1-0.6 Cross a run, then turn sharply left descending along it and recrossing it farther down.

2.6-0.1 To right, across the run, is a conspicuous cave at base of cliffs. A short spur trail leads to the cave.

2.7-0.0 Junction with Riprap Tr. (To left via the Riprap Tr. it is 0.9m. to the Park boundary and Crimora Fire Rd. To right it is 3.6m. to the *AT*.)

TURK GAP TRAIL

1.6 miles (2.6 kilometers) yellow-blazed

The former fire road is permanently blocked to vehicles at each end. From Turk Gap, SDMP 94.1, it leads down the west side of the Blue Ridge reaching the Park boundary just above the muddy ponds of the old Crimora mine. (The Crimora Manganese Mine was one of the largest manganese mining operations in the Blue Ridge. The operations commenced in 1867 and extended, through various mining methods, periodically to 1947; operations were resumed in 1949, but the mines are now closed. The manganese was mined out of clay deposits in a syncline of Cambrian quartzite. Visitors will find this area more interesting if they have read the detailed history of the mines, "The Crimora Manganese Mine" by Samuel V. Moore, in the October 1947 PATC bulletin.)

To use Turk Gap Trail for a loop or circuit hike, descend this trail and continue down to the ponds. Here one can follow an old mine road north to lovely Crimora Lake in Dorsey Hanger Hollow. (Crimora Lake, an artificial lake, formerly furnished water power for mining operations.) From Crimora Lake follow the foot trail that follows the outlet stream from below the dam. This trail ends on the Riprap Tr. near its lower end and just inside the Park boundary. Follow the Riprap Tr. north and east all the way to Skyline Drive for the loop trip of about 7½ miles, or turn right onto the *AT* 0.1m. before reaching the Drive and continue along the *AT* back to Turk Gap, a circuit of about 9½ miles.

TURK MOUNTAIN TRAIL

0.9 miles (1.5 kilometers)   blue-blazed

This short trail is highly recommended. It starts from the *AT* at a point 0.2m. south of Turk Gap and heads west following a ridge. In about 0.4m., where the Sawmill Ridge goes off to the left, the Turk Mtn. Tr. continues straight ahead and begins to climb up Turk Mtn., el. 2981'. The view from the summit is outstanding. As on several of the other peaks of the Park which are west of the main Blue Ridge crest, the rock is a type of sandstone full of fossil wormholes, giving it a distinctive striated appearance. In early June turkeybeard, a member of the lily family, can be found growing here.

MOORMANS RIVER FIRE ROAD

9.5 miles (15.3 kilometers)   yellow-blazed

This was the original route of the Appalachian Trail between Blackrock Gap and Jarman Gap. From Blackrock Gap the road leads southeast, then south, following down the North Fork of the Moormans River to Va. Sec. 614. From here the fire road fords the North Fork at a point a short distance above the Charlottesville

SOUTHERN SECTION

Reservoir. It then climbs southwestward to Jarman Gap following up the South Fork of the Moormans River. The fire road is gated at both ends and at the Park boundaries.

A rather long circuit hike, 21m., can be made by following the fire road in one direction and the *AT* in the other. For shorter circuits a portion of the fire road can be used along with the Turk Branch Trail and *AT*. From Blackrock Gap a circuit using the fire road, the trail and the *AT* is about 18m. long; from Jarman Gap a circuit using the southern portion of the fire road, the trail and the *AT* is only 8m. in length.

To reach the fire road from the valley follow Va. Sec. 810 from Crozet to White Hall (about 4½m.). Then follow Va. Sec. 614 west for 5¾m. to its end just beyond the Charlottesville Reservoir. The junction with the fire road is here.

Detailed trail data:
North to south

0.0-9.5 From the Skyline Drive at Blackrock Gap, SDMP 87.4, el.2321', the road leads southeast, immediately crossing the *AT*.

1.4-8.1 Take right fork and cross stream. (Old road to the left leads up the valley through overgrown fields to Via Gap.) Continue downstream, heading almost due south.

1.6-7.9 To the left an old road leads uphill to Pasture Fence Mtn.

3.7-5.8 To the right a side trail leads 0.1m. up Big Branch to a series of cascades, the highest of which has a free fall of about 50 ft.

5.5-4.0 Cross Va. Sec. 614 at the end of that road. (Rt. 614 leads 5¾m. to White Hall on Va. Sec. 810.) In 0.1m. ford the North Fork of the Moormans River. The ford, el. 1000', is a few hundred feet below the former highway bridge, the foundations of which are still visible, and a few hundred feet upriver from the Charlottesville Reservoir. The fire road continues south to reach the South Fork of the Moormans River, then climbs along it, crossing the stream a number of times.

7.6-1.9 To the right the Turk Branch Tr. leads up the mountain 2.1m. to the Skyline Drive, joining it at Turk Gap, SDMP 94.1.

9.3-0.2 Intersection with the *AT* at a point on the *AT* 0.2m. north of the Bucks Elbow Mt. Fire Rd.

9.5-0.0 Junction with Skyline Drive and Bucks Elbow Mtn. Fire Rd. at Jarman Gap, SDMP 96.7, el. 2173'. (The *AT* is 0.1m east here via the Bucks Elbow Mtn. Fire Rd.)

TURK BRANCH TRAIL

2.1 miles (3.4 kilometers)   yellow-blazed

This is a pretty trail and not a difficult one to follow. From the Skyline Drive and *AT* at Turk Gap, SDMP 94.1, el. 2600', the trail follows an old road down the east side of the Blue Ridge. Its lower end is on the Moormans River Fire Road, el. 1440' at a point on the fire road 1.9m. north of Jarman Gap. By descending the Turk Branch Tr. to the fire road, following up the fire road (south) to the *AT* just below Jarman Gap, and then taking the *AT* north to Turk Gap, a circuit hike of about 7½m. can be made. (Starting the circuit at Jarman Gap the hike would be a quarter mile longer as one would first have to hike down the Moormans River Fire Rd. to its intersection with the *AT;* then, after the circuit, retrace that distance along the fire road back to the Drive.) A much longer circuit can be made by descending the Turk Branch Tr., then following the fire road north to Blackrock Gap, and returning to Turk Gap via the *AT* (circuit about 18m.).

BUCKS ELBOW MTN. FIRE ROAD

0.6 miles (10 kilometers) within the Park   not blazed

From the Skyline Drive and its junction with the Moormans River Fire Road at Jarman Gap, SDMP 96.7, the Bucks Elbow Mtn. Fire Rd. leads east, uphill, winding its way up to the top of Bucks Elbow Mtn. (outside the Park) to an FAA installation. The road is gated near Skyline Drive. The road intersects the *AT* at a point 0.1m. from the Drive.

On the west side of the Drive the Jarman Gap Fire Road has been totally abandoned.

SOUTHERN SECTION

GAS LINE ROAD

2.0 miles (3.2 kilometers) yellow-blazed

From the Skyline Drive, SDMP 96.2, the Gas Line Road leads down the west slopes of the Blue Ridge to the Park boundary. It was constructed to give access to the gas pipeline and is of little interest to hikers at present. Like the fire roads it is gated at the Skyline Drive.

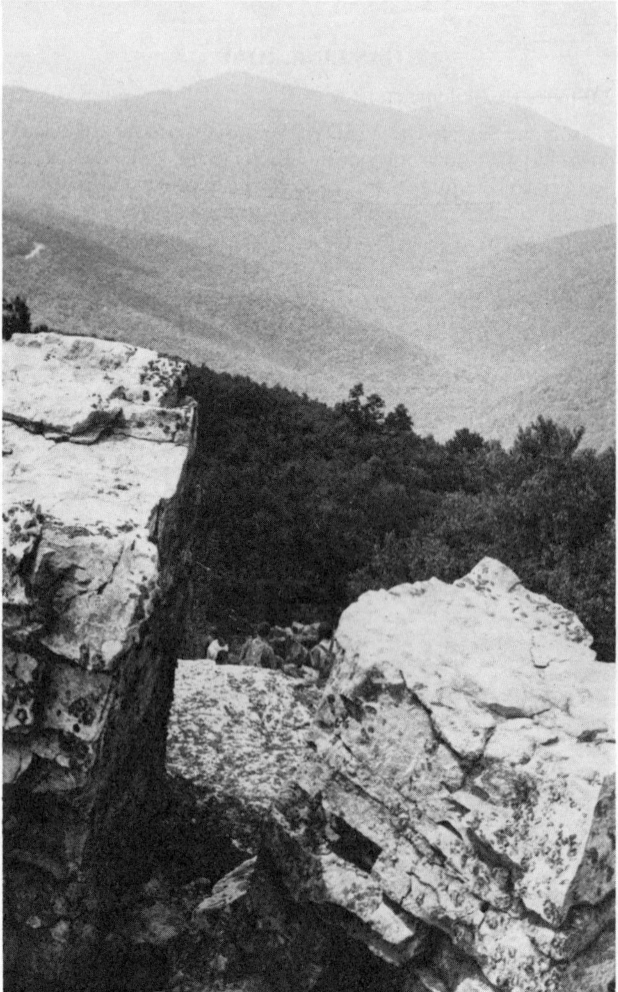

Chapter 6

PICNIC SHELTERS, HUTS AND CABINS

Picnic Shelters

Of the open-faced shelters in the Shenandoah Park five, the Old Rag Shelter and the four Byrds Nests, may be used for picnicking only. Water is available during the warmer months at all but Byrds Nest #1, situated on a shoulder of Old Rag Mountain and Byrds Nest #2 on the summit of Hawksbill Mtn. Byrds Nest #3 is located on the *AT* between Marys Rock and Pinnacle Overlook; Byrds Nest #4 is near the *AT* (0.3m.) a short distance north of Beahms Gap.

Huts

Huts are the open-faced shelters in the Park which may be used for camping by *AT* backpackers. Park camping permits are required here as for other backcountry camping. There are seven huts in the Park—Gravel Springs and Pass Mtn. Huts in the North Section, Rock Spring and Bearfence Mtn. Huts in the Central Section and Hightop, Pinefield, and Blackrock Huts in the Southern Section. During the summer the Potomac Appalachian Trail Club (PATC) employs knowledgeable individuals to serve as hutkeepers and *AT* monitors to prevent overuse and misuse of the huts and to educate hikers on trail etiquette. Users of these huts are asked to pay a small fee to help cover the expenses of the hut managers. In addition to the Park huts a covered shelter is available for backpackers at the Tom Floyd Wayside just north of the Park. A new shelter for *AT* hikers has been constructed (1984) on Calf. Mtn.

AT distances between shelters. Listing is from north to south.

From U.S. 522 to Tom Floyd Wayside (just north of Shen. Pk.)	3.1 miles
Tom Floyd Wayside to Gravel Springs Hut (0.2m.)	9.9
Gravel Springs Hut (0.2) to Pass Mtn. Hut (0.2)	13.3
Pass Mtn. Hut (0.2) to Rock Spring Hut (0.2)	15.0

Rock Spring Hut (0.2) to Bearfence Hut (0.2)	11.4
Bearfence Hut (0.2) to Hightop Hut (0.1)	12.5
Hightop Hut (0.1) to Pinefield Hut (0.1)	8.3
Pinefield Hut (0.1) to Blackrock Hut (0.2)	13.1
Blackrock Hut (0.2) to Calf Mtn. Shelter (0.3)	13.2
Calf Mtn. Shelter (0.3) to U.S. 250 at Rockfish Gap	6.9

Cabins

The PATC operates six locked cabins in the SNP. These cabins are the property of the National Park Service and are operated by the PATC under permit. Each cabin is attractively located in the center of good hiking country. Four of them are located near both the *AT* and Skyline Drive.

The cabins are designed for either overnight or longer use and make excellent bases for stays of several days while exploring the surrounding country.

A moderate fee is charged for use of the cabins. Details are available from the Potomac Appalachian Trail Club Headquarters, 1718 N St., N.W., Washington, D.C. 20036, open from 7pm to 10pm Mondays through Fridays: not open Saturdays, Sundays or holidays. Cabin reservations must be made in advance for their occupancy; keys are obtained from PATC Headquarters. The cabins are available both to members and to responsible non-members. Members may make reservations one month in advance, once per year; they otherwise follow the three-week-ahead limitation imposed on non-members. Non-members making a reservation for the first time must be properly identified and will be required to fill out a responsibility statement.

The cabins are equipped with all necessary items except food, personal bedding, flashlight, and firewood. There is an inside wood stove and fireplace (some inside, some outside) for cooking, plus all necessary pots and pans, plates, cutlery, cups, saucers, glasses, etc. Also provided are bunks, mattresses, and blankets (one per occupant) up to the stated capacity of the cabin. It is advisable to bring one's own sleeping bag, lanterns and fuel for them. Broom, ax, saw, first-aid kit, and other items necessary for good housekeeping are provided. There is a latrine near each cabin.

Soap, toilet paper, tea, coffee, sugar, salt and pepper are sometimes available at the cabins. Users may add to the stock of these items if they have any of their own supply left over; they should be placed in the proper containers. No "strike anywhere" matches are to be left at the cabins. (Rodents may gnaw on them.) No unused food other than the items already mentioned should be left in the cabins and campers should take such items back to town with them. Remnants, including buried food, attract vermin to the cabin areas.

The number of occupants of a cabin may not exceed the stated capacity of the cabin. The maximum stay by one party at one or a succession of cabins is 10 days, including only one weekend. Because of the popularity of the cabins, only one reservation may be in process at one time. The cabin reservation period runs from 4 pm of the first date stated to 4pm of the day succeeding the last date. If a reservation is to be cancelled it must be cancelled for the entire period and a new application filed if reservation for a shorter period is desired.

Range View Cabin is located in the Northern Section of the Park; Corbin, Rock Spring, Pocosin and Jones Mtn. Cabins in the Central Section; and Doyles River Cabin in the Southern Section. All are shown, along with their trail and road approaches, on the appropriate PATC maps.

Detailed Description of Cabins

Range View Cabin

This is a one-room stone cabin built in 1933 by members of the PATC. It is equipped with four double-decked, single-width bunks, an inside cooking stove and an outside fireplace under eaves of the cabin. The cabin looks out across an area cleared of trees and tall brush toward farms in the valley below. Campers from Mathews Arm Campground and hikers along the *AT* often visit the cabin area, especially on weekends, so it is somewhat lacking in privacy.

Parking for this cabin is at the Rattlesnake Point Overlook on the Skyline Drive, SDMP 21.9. From Washington, D.C. the shortest driving route is via Front Royal. To reach the cabin from the parking area follow the *AT,* which crosses the Drive just south of the overlook, south for 0.7m., then turn left onto the spur trail that leads 0.1m. to the cabin.

Corbin Cabin

This is an old mountaineer's cabin, restored by PATC volunteers in the early 1950s. (See Alvin Peterson's article in the July-September 1954 PATC Bulletin.) It is a solidly built, two story cabin with sleeping quarters on both floors. There is a fireplace in the living room, wood stove in the kitchen, and an outside fireplace. It is to be nominated to the National Register of Historic Places.

The cabin is located in Nicholson (Free State) Hollow beside the Hughes River, a pleasant mountain stream. Water is obtained from this stream.

One may approach the cabin either from the east (for a shorter driving distance but a much longer hike-in) or from the Skyline Drive. Most cabin users prefer to drive to the Shaver Hollow Parking Area on the Skyline Drive, SDMP 37.8. They then follow the rather steep Corbin Cabin Cut-off Trail for 1.4m. to reach the cabin. This route is also the shortest approach from the *AT*. (There is a short spur trail connecting the *AT* and the parking area.) Some cabin users prefer to park at the Hughes River Gap Parking Overlook, SMP 38.6, and hike down the Nicholson Hollow trail 1.9m. to the cabin.

To reach the cabin from the Piedmont, turn west from Va. 231 at a point (about 10m. south of Sperryville) just south of the highway bridge over the Hughes River onto Va. Sec. 602. Continue up the south side of the river on paved road. (It will first be Rt. 602, then 707, and then 600.) In 4.3m. from Va. 231 where road turns sharply to the left, park car and follow up the Nicholson Hollow Trail on foot for 4.0m. to reach the cabin.

CABINS

Rock Spring Cabin

This cabin, built of squared logs, looks out across the valley to the Massanutten range behind. The view from the cabin is excellent during the day but at night the twinkling lights of Stanley and Luray add a magical touch to the landscape. The cabin is equipped with enough bunks to sleep 12 persons, an inside wood stove and outside fireplace. It can be kept cozily warm in winter. There is a spring 50 yds. north of the cabin.

Warning: There is an extremely sharp drop-off in front of the cabin which can be dangerous for small children.

Parking for this cabin is just north of the Spitler Knoll Overlook on the Skyline Drive, SDMP 48.1. A short spur trail leads from the Rock Spring Parking Area to the *AT*. Follow the *AT* north for 0.6m., then turn left onto the spur trail leading 0.2m. to the cabin.

Jones Mountain Cabin

This cabin was originally the home of mountaineer moonshiner Harvey Nicholson. It was unoccupied from the 1930s when the SNP was established until recently and was falling into ruins. Then members of the PATC, with the Park Service Administration's permission, restored the cabin, making every effort to retain those parts of the original structure that were still serviceable and to replace damaged material with handcrafted replacements. In 1975 the restored cabin, which now presents a fine example of early cabin workmanship, became available for campers. For some history of this area read *Lost Trails and Forgotten People* by Tom Floyd (a PATC publication). A person may not reserve the Jones Mountain Cabin, however, unless he has previously held and used cabin reservations elsewhere without evidence of cabin abuse.

To reach the cabin from Skyline Drive is difficult. The shortest route (about 5 miles) would be to start at Bootens Gap, follow the *AT* north for 0.6m., then descend the Laurel Prong Tr. to Laurel Gap. Turn right onto the blue-blazed Cat Knob Tr. and follow 0.5m. to its upper end on the Jones Mtn. Trail. Follow the latter out to Bear Church Rock; then descend to the cabin.

To reach the cabin from the Piedmont, turn west onto Va. 230

from U.S. 29 just south of Madison. Follow Va. 230 for 4 miles to Wolftown, then turn right onto Va. Sec. 662. Continue on Rt. 662 taking the right fork, still Rt. 662 but a dirt road, at Graves Mill and continuing up the Rapidan River, soon entering the SNP where it becomes the Graves Mill Fire Rd. At 2.0m. beyond Graves Mill reach the junction of the Staunton River with the Rapidan. A few feet up the old road to the left of the fire road there is a special parking area for cabin users. From this parking area it is 3.0m. by foot to the cabin, following the Staunton River Tr. for 2.0m., then the Jones Mtn. Tr. for 0.8m., and finally the short trail to the cabin.

The cabin is equipped with mattresses to sleep 10, a wood stove for heating, and both inside and outside fireplaces. There is a spring about 75 ft. from the cabin. There is a large front porch high above the ground. *Warning: While double railings have been built along the edges of the front porch and inside the cabin along the edge of the open-ended loft used for sleeping quarters, this cabin is not recommended for families with small children; the long hike-in is also difficult for such families.*

Pocosin Cabin

This cabin is a one-room squared log structure located in a pleasant area with a good view toward the Piedmont. There are a number of excellent hiking possibilities in the area for both the experienced and novice hiker. The cabin is furnished with three double-deck double-width bunks with foam mattresses. A wood stove is provided for cooking and heating inside and there is also a fireplace outside under the cabin eaves.

Parking for this cabin is about 0.1m. along the Pocosin Fire Road from the Skyline Drive, SDMP 59.5. The hike-in is another 0.2m. along the fire road. A short (0.1m.) connecting trail leads between the cabin and the *AT*. This cabin is recommended for families with small children as there are no hazards near the cabin such as steep embankments; also the hike-in is short and easy.

Doyles River Cabin

This cabin, constructed of squared logs, sits above a cliff near the head of the Doyles River. It overlooks a picturesque valley with views of Cedar Mtn. and Via Gap. Sunsets are often spectacular as viewed from the cabin. There are bunks enough to sleep 12 persons. An inside wood stove and outside fireplace are available. The spring is 350 ft. downhill from the cabin.

Warning: Because of the cliff face in front of the cabin, it is not recommended for families with small children.

Parking space is provided at the north end of the Doyles River Trail on the east side of the Skyline Drive, SDMP 81.1. Hike-in distance (via the Doyles River Trail) is 0.4m.

SUMMARY OF CABIN INFORMATION

Cabin	Capacity	Recommended for families with small children	Driving distance from D.C. to parking area (mi.)	Hike-in distance from parking area (mi.)	Hike-in distance from *AT* (mi.)	SDMP at or near parking area	PATC map
Range View	8	Yes	93	0.8	0.1	21.9	9
Corbin	12	No	93	1.4	1.5	37.9	9
Rock Spring	12	No	103	0.8	0.2	48.1	10
Jones Mtn.	10	No	106	3.0	-	-	10
Pocosin	12	Yes	114	0.2	0.1	59.5	10
Doyles River	12	No	129	0.3	0.3	81.1	11

INDEX
of Place Names along the Trails

Abbott Ridge	248
Appalachian Trail Conference (ATC) (Harpers Ferry)	15
AT Mileage Summaries	45, 67, 83, 100, 119, 131
Austin Mtn., Austin Mtn. Tr.	27, 241, **242**, 244, 248
Bacon Hollow	72, 98
Baldface Mtn.	65, 105
Barking Dog Spring	37
Beagle Gap	82, 88
Beahms Gap, Beahms Gap Overlook	44, 122, 159, 257
Beahms Gap Spur Tr.	44
Bear Church Rock	221, 222
Bear Den Mtn.	82, 88
Bearfence Mtn. Hut	60, 63, 104, 106, 107, 224, 225, 257
Bearfence Mtn. Loops	63, 107, **224**
Bearfence Mtn.—Bearfence Mtn. Parking	63, 107, 225
Bearwallow	161
Beecher Ridge Tr.	**164**, 165, 168
Beldor, Beldor Hollow	230
Berry Hollow Fire Rd.	193, 195, **196**, 197, 198, 205
Bettys Rock Tr.	57, 113, **208**
Big Bend Fire Rd.	229
Big Blue Trail	40, 42, 121, 124, **160**, 163, 165
Big Branch, Big Branch Falls	253
Big Devils Stairs	146, 148, **150**, 151
Big Flat Mtn.	75
Big Meadows Area—Wayside, Picnic Grounds, Lodge, Campground (See also Byrd Visitor Center)	5, 47, 55, 60, 61, 104, 109, 110, 207, **209**, 210, 211
Big Rock Falls	218
Big Run Loop Tr., Big Run Overlook	76, 94, 236, **237**, 238, 241, 244
Big Run, Big Run Portal Tr.	235, **236**, 237, 238, 240, 241
Blackrock, Blackrock Tr. (Central SNP)	61, 108
Blackrock, Blackrock Spur Tr. (Southern SNP)	78, 92, 245, **247**, 249
Blackrock Gap	79, 91, 248, 249, 252
Blackrock, Blackrock Hut	77, 79, 89, 92, **257**
Blakey Ridge	217
Bluff Mtn.	222

INDEX

Bluff Tr. 39, 91, 125, 147, **148,**150, 151
Bootens Gap 62, 107, 218, 219, 261
Bolen Cemetery 154, 159, **184**
Broad Hollow Tr. 181, 183
Brokenback Run 178, 199, 202
Brown Mtn. Overlook 239
Brown Mtn., Brown Mtn. Tr. (See also Rocky Mtn.—Brown Mtn. Tr.) 27
Browns Gap, Browns Gap Fire Rd., Browns Cove 76, 92, 93, 94, 234, **235,** 238, 242, 244
Browntown Tr. 39, 125, 127, **144**
Broyles Gap 214, 215
Buck Hollow Tr. 51, 118, **173**, 174, 180
Buck Ridge Tr. 173, **174**, 181
Bucks Elbow Mtn., Bucks Elbow Mtn. Fire Rd. .. 80, 81, 82, 89, 90, **254**
Buracker Hollow 190
Bush Mtn. 63
Bushytop 190, 191
Buzzard Rock Peak 246, 248
Byrds Nest #1 .... 56, 111, 198, 204, 205, **257**
Byrds Nest #2 .... 56, 57, 111, 113, 208, **257**
Byrds Nest #3 .... 51, 115, 118, **257**
Byrds Nest #4 .... 44, 122, 123, 171, **257**
Byrd Visitor Center 50, 55, 108, 110, 209, 210
Calf Mtn., Calf Mtn. Shelter 69, 82, 88, **257**
Calvary Rocks, Calvary Ridge, Chimney Rocks 79, 250
Camp Hoover 22, 49, 62, 108, **209**, 216, 218, 220
Cat Knob, Cat Knob Tr. 107, **219**, 220, 222
Catlett Mtn. Trail 179, 181, **186**, 187
Catlett Spur Tr. 179, 181, **187**
Cedar Falls 229
Cedar Mtn. 76, 94, 263
Cedar Run Tr., Cedar Run Falls 57, 193, **195**, 196, 198, 203, 207
Cedar Run/Whiteoak Canyon Link Tr. 194, 196
Chapman Mtn., Chapman Mtn. Rd. 216, 217
Charlottesville Reservoir 253
Chester Gap 141, 145, 146
Cold Spring Hollow 250

INDEX

Comers Deadening 198, 199, 206
Compton Run 168
Compton Gap, Compton Gap Fire Rd./Tr. (and Va. Sec. 610) 37, 38, 124, 140, 141, **145**
Compton Mtn., Compton Mtn. Springs 26, 38, 128
Compton Peak East Tr. 38, 128
Compton Peak West Tr. 38, 128
Conway River, Conway River Fire Rd., Conway Valley .. 62, 107, **224**, 225
Copper Mine-Dark Hollow Loop Tr. (See Dark Hollow Falls-Rose River Loop Tr.)
Corbin Cabin 50, 115, 117, 177, 178, 182, 202, **260**
Corbin Cabin Cut-off Tr. 52, 117, 176, 178, **182**, 260
Corbin Hollow, Corbin Hollow Tr. 198, 199, 201, **202**
Corbin Mtn. Corbin Mtn. Tr. 178, 186, 199, **201**, 202
Covington River 153
Cresent Rock Overlook 26, 57, 113, 207, 208
Crescent Rock Tr. 200, **207**
Crimora Fire Rd. **244**, 250, 251
Crimora Lake, Crimora Manganese Mines 250, 251, 252
Crusher Ridge Tr. 53, 116, **174**, 177
Dale Spring 177
Dark Hollow Falls, Dark Hollow Falls Parking, Dark Hollow Falls—Rose River Loop Tr. ... 33, 58, 109, 207, 210, **211**, 214
David Spring 60, 109
Deadening Nature Trail 75, 95, **233**
Dean Mtn. 65, 105
Devils Ditch 225
Dickey Hill 140, 141, 142
Dickey Ridge Tr. 38, **129**, 142, 143, 145
Dickey Ridge Visitor Center, Dickey Ridge Picnic Grounds .. 5, 141, 142
Dorsey Hangar Hollow 250, 251, 252
Doubletop Mtn. 62, 108
Doyles River Cabin, Doyles River Cabin Parking .. 69, 73, 76, 86, 94, 234, 235, **262**
Doyles River Overlook 76, 94
Doyles River Tr., Doyles River Falls 33, 75, 78, 92, 94, **233**, 263
Dripping Spring 171

INDEX

Dry Run Falls, Dry Run Falls Fire Rd. 65, 105, **229**
Dry Run, Dry Run Hollow 191
Dundo, Dundo Hollow, Dundo Picnic Grounds/Group Campground 5, 69, 77, 78, 86, 89, 92
Elkwallow Area—Wayside, Picnic Grounds, Spring, Gap .. 5, 41, 43, 122, 123, 169, 170
Elkwallow Tr. 49, 123, **169**
Fishers Gap, Fishers Gap Overlook ... 58, 59, 109, 110, 207, 210, 212, 213
Flattop Mtn. 71, 72, 98
Fork Mtn., Fork Mtn. Rd. (Central SNP) . 62, 216, 219, **220**, 221, 222
Fork Mtn. Tr. (Central SNP) 219, **221,** 222
Fork Mtn. Tr. (Northern SNP) **158**, 159
Fort Windham Rocks 38, 129, 140, **141**, 145
Four-Way 152
Fox Hollow Tr. 140, 141
Franklin Cliffs, Franklin Cliffs Overlook 21, 58, 112
Free State Hollow (see Nicholson Hollow) . 52, 117, 177, 189
Front Royal Entrance Station 140
Furnace Mtn. Tr., Furnace Mtn. Summit Tr. .. 244, 245, 246, **247**
Furnace Spring 54, 115, 116
Furnace Spring Tr. 54, 115, 190, **191**
Gap Run, Gap Run Tr. 231
Gas Line Road 255
Gendarmes, The 171
Gimlet Ridge 145
Ginger Spring 37, 130
Gordonsville Pike (See Rose River Fire Rd. and Red Gate Fire Rd.) 59, 111, 210, 212
Gravel Springs Gap 39, 126, 144, 146, 148, 151
Gravel Springs Hut . 36, 40, 41, 122, 125, 127, 148, 151, **257**
Graves Mill Fire Rd. 216, 217, **219**, 262
Half-Mile Cliffs 195, 196
Hall Mtn. 248
Hangman Run 241
Hannah Run, Hannah Run Tr. 176, 178, **179**, 187
Harmony Hollow 37, 130, 141, 143, 146
Harris Hollow, Harris Hollow Tr. .. 39, 41, 125, 127, 145, 148, 150, **151**

INDEX

Harry F. Byrd Sr. Visitor Center (See Byrd Visitor Center)
Hawksbill Gap, Hawksbill Gap Overlook .. 26, 57, 112, 195, 208
Hawksbill Mtn., Hawksbill Tr. ... 55, 57, 101, 110, 112, 189, **208**, 257
Hazel Mtn., Hazel Mtn. Tr. ... 118, 173, 174, 175, **180**, 183, 186, 187, 188
Hazel River, Hazel River Tr. 180, 181, **183**, 188
Hazel School 183, 184
Hazeltop Mtn. 62, 101, 107, 108, 218
Hazeltop Ridge Overlook 223
Heiskell Hollow Tr. 164, 165, **167**
Hickerson Hollow Tr. 141, **143**
Hightop Hut, Hightop Hut Tr., Hightop Hut Fire Rd. 70, 71, 97, 99, **230**, **257**
Hightop Mtn. 71, 99
Hogback Peaks #1, 2, 3 & 4 .... 41, 42, 124, 125, 145
Hogback Spur Tr. 42, 125, **160**
Hogcamp Branch 211, 212, 214
Hogwallow, Hogwallow Gap, Hogwallow Flats, Hogwallow Spring 38, 39, 128
Hoover Camp (See Camp Hoover)
Hot-Short Mtn. Tr. 178, 181, **186**
Hughes River 178, 182, 197, 201, 204, 260
Hughes River Gap, Hughes River Overlook .53, 116, 176, 260
Hull School Tr. 152, 154, 157, 158, **159**, 171, 172
Ida Valley 57, 112, 113
Indian Run Maintenance Bldg., Indian Run Spring, Indian Run Access Rd. 38, 129, 145
Indian Run Tr. 178, 199, 201, **202**
Ivy Creek, Ivy Cr. Maintenance Bldg., Ivy Cr. Service Rd. 73, 74, 95, **233**, 237
Ivy Creek Overlook 74, 96
Jarman Gap 38, 81, 89, 90, 252, 254
Jenkins Gap, Jenkins Gap Tr., Jenkins Gap Overlook 38, 128, **143**, 144, 146, 147
Jeremys Run, Jeremys Run Tr. .. 43, 123, 166, 167, **169**, 171
Jewell Hollow, Jewell Hollow Overlook 52, 117
Jinny Gray Fire Rd. (see Keyser Run Fire Rd.)
Jones Mtn. Cabin, Jones Mtn. Cabin Tr. .. 60, 104, 219, 220, 221, 222, 223, **261**

INDEX

Jones Mtn. Tr. 219, 220, 221, **222**, 223
Jones Run, Jones Run Parking 33, 78, 92, 234
Jordan River Tr. 147, 149
Kemp Hollow 44
Kettle Canyon 189, 190, 191
Keyser Run Fire Rd. 41, 125, 152, **153**, 155, 159, 160
Kites Deadening 64, 105
Knob Mtn., Knob Mtn. Tr. 44, **166**, 167, 168, 169, 170
Knob Mtn. Cut-off Tr. 167, **169**, 170
Lake Front Royal 35, 36, 130
Lands Run Gap, Lands Run Fire Rd. 140, 141, **142**, 143
Laurel Gap 107, 219
Laurel Prong Tr. 62, 107, **218**, 220, 221
Leading Ridge Tr. 52, 117, **174**
Lefthand Hollow 247
Lewis Mtn. (Southern SNP) 241
Lewis Mtn. (Central SNP), Lewis Mtn. Campgrounds .. 5, 47, 60, 63, 70, 97, 104, 106, 224, 229
Lewis Mtn. East Tr. 64, 106, 224, 225
Lewis Mtn. West Tr. 64, 106, **229**
Lewis Peak Tr. 27, 241, **243**, 245
Lewis Run Fire Rd. 244
Lewis Spring Falls, Lewis Spring Falls Tr. 33, 61, 108, 109, **211**
Lickinghole Hollow 81, 194, 199, **200**, 207
Limberlost Tr. 192
Little Devils Stairs Tr. 152, 153, **154**, 155
Little Hogback Mtn., Little Hogback Overlook .. 41, 125, 154
Little Roundtop Mtn. 71, 98
Little Stony Man Mtn. 116
Little Stony Man Tr. 53, 116, **189**
Little Stony Man Parking 26, 53, 116
Loft Mtn. 74, 75, 95, 233
Loft Mtn. Campground 5, 69, 73, 75, 86, 93, 95, 233
Low Gap 140, 141
Madison Run Fire Rd. 76, 94, 235, 238, 243, **244**, 247
Madison Run Spur Tr. **238**, 244
Marys Rock 27, 51, 108, 257
Massanutten Range 40, 121, 244
Mathews Arm, Mathews Arm Campground .. 5, 40, 122, 127, 161, 164, 165, 166, 169

INDEX

Mathews Arm Tr. 161, **164**, 168
McCormick Gap 82, 88
McDaniel Hollow Tr. 220, 221, 222, **223**
Meadow School Fire Rd. 63, 107, 223, 224, 225
Meadow Spring, Meadow Spring Parking 51, 108, 174, 176, 180
Milam Gap 62, 108, 217
Mill Prong Horse Spur Tr. 62, 108, 216, **217**, 219
Mill Prong Tr. 62, 108, **217**, 218
Millers Head Tr. 56, 113, **190**
Monkey Head 61, 109
Moore's Run 37, 130
Moormans River Fire Rd. 79, 80, 81, 90, **252**, 253, 254
Mount Marshall 118
Mt. Marshall Tr. 38, 128, 143, 146, **147**, 148, 149
Nakedtop, Nakedtop Tr. 57, 58, **112**, 113, 208
National Zoological Park Conservation Center 38, 130
Negro Run 194
Neighbor Mtn., The 44, 123
Neighbor Mtn. Parking 44, 123, 171
Neighbor Mtn. Tr. 44, 123, 170, **171**
New Market Gap 53, 116
Nicholson Hollow 52, 175, 250
Nicholson Hollow Tr. . . 53, 116, 174, **177**, 179, 182, 186, 201, 202
Nicholson Moonshine Tr. 219, **223**
Northern Virginia 4-H Educational Center 37, 130
North Fork Rd. 159
North Marshall Mtn. 39, 127, 128
Old Hazel Tr. 188
Old Rag Fire Rd. 192, 193, **198**, 200, 201, 202, 206
Old Rag Mtn., Old Rag Circuit .. 27, 117, 188, 198, **203**, 257
Old Rag Shelter 111, 198, 204, 205, 257
Old Rag Valley, Old Rag Post Office 193, 197, 198, 205
Old Skyland Road Tr. 54, 116, **191**
Onemile Run, Onemile Run Tr. 74, 96, **232**
Oventop Mtn. 118, 172
Overall Run, Overall Run Falls 33, 162
Overall Run Tr, (see also Big Blue Tr.,) .. 42, 124, 161, **163**, 164

INDEX

Overall Run—Beecher Ridge Connector Tr. 164
Page Valley 208
Paine Run, Paine Run Tr. 79, 245, 246, 247, **248**
Panorama, Panorama Restaurant, Panorama Parking 5, 41, 50, 51, 115, 118, 122
Pass Mtn. Hut 40, 44, 122, 172, **257**
Pass Mtn., Pass Mtn. Tr. 44, 122, **172**
Passamaquoddy Tr. 53, 116
Pasture Fence Mtn. 253
Patterson Field 75, 95
Patterson Ridge Tr. 237
Peak, The 146, 147, 148, **149**
Phils Arm Run 144
Pinefield Gap, Pinefield Hut 73, 74, 94, 96, **257**
Pine Hill Gap Tr. 180, 181, **185**
Piney Branch River, Piney Branch Tr. 43, 124, 152, 155, **156**, 157, 159
Piney Ridge Tr. 43, 123, 152, **157**, 158
Piney River Ranger Station 43, 123, 152, 156, 157
Pinnacles, The, Pinnacles Overlook ... 51, 117, 176, 179, 257
Pinnacles Picnic Grounds 5, 52, 117
PLD Tr. 159
Pocosin Cabin 60, 64, 104, 105, 225, 226, **262**
Pocosin Fire Rd. 64, 106, **225**, 228, 262
Pocosin Hollow Tr. 64, 106, **226**
Pocosin Horse Tr. 64, 105, 106, **226,** 228
Pole Bridge Link 152, 154, **155**, 156
Pollock Knob 56, 113
Portal, The 236
Possums Rest, Possums Rest Tr. 37, 129
Potomac Appalachian Trail Club (PATC) 18
Powell Gap 71, 98
Powell Mtn. Tr. 223
Ragged Run Rd. 205
Range View Cabin 40, 43, 122, 123, **151**, 152, 156, **259**
Rapidan River, Rapidan Valley .. 28, 209, 219, 220, 224, 262
Rapidan Fire Rd.—Va. Sec. 649 ... 209, 214, **215**, 216, 217, 218, 220
Rattlesnake Point, Rattlesnake Point Overlook .. 42, 124, 152, 156, 161, 260

INDEX

Red Gate Fire Rd. 58, 60, 109, 111, 210, 213
Ridge Tr. (see also Old Rag Circuit) 198, 203
Riprap Parking 79, 91, 245, 249, 250, 251
Riprap Tr., Riprap Hollow 79, 91, **249**, 250, 251
Roach River Valley 71, 98
Robertson Mtn., Robertson Mtn. Tr. 186, 198, 199, **202**
Robinson River 193
Rockfish Gap 69, 83, 86, 87
Rockfish Gap Entrance Station 83, 88
Rockfish Spur Tr. 83, 88
Rock Spring Cabin 56, 58, 111, 112, 261
Rock Spring Hut 56, 58, 111, 112, **257**
Rock Spring Parking 261
Rocky Branch Tr. 44, 122, 172
Rocky Mount, Rocky Mt. Tr. 74, 96, **231**
Rocky Mtn., Rocky Mtn.—Brown Mtn. Tr. ... 236, 237, 239
Rocky Mtn. Run Tr. **237**, 239
Rockytop, Rockytop Tr. ... 27, 236, 238, **240**, 242, 243, 244
Rose River 33, 111, 207, 211, 213
Rose River Fire Rd. 58, 60, 107, 207, 210, 212, **213**, 214, 215
Rose River Loop Tr. (see Dark Hollow Falls—Rose River Loop Tr.) 58, 109, 111, 212, 214
Roundtop Mtn. 71, 98
Rush River 150
Saddle Tr. (see also Old Rag Circuit) 198, 203
Saddleback Mtn. Tr. 65, 104, **228**
Sag, The 219, 220, 221, 222
Sams Ridge Tr. 181, **182**, 184, 185
Sawmill Ridge, Sawmill Run Overlook 80, 90, 252
Scott Mtn. 81
Shaver Hollow, Shaver Hollow Parking, Shaver Hollow Spring 52, 116, 176, 182, 260
Shenandoah National Park Headquarters 11
Signal Knob 140
Simmons Gap, Simmons Gap Fire Rd. 72, 73, 96, 97, 98, **230**
Simmons Gap Ranger Station 72, 96, 98
Skyland Area ... 5, 47, 50, 54, 102, 113, 114, 115, 188, 190, 192
Skyland—Big Meadows Horse Tr. ... 56, 113, 192, 196, 199, 203, **206**

INDEX

Skyland Fire Rd. (see Old Skyland Road Tr.)
Skyline Drive Mileage Summaries 46, 68, 85
Slaughter Tr. 63, 107, 224, **225**
Sloan Creek 36, 130
Smith Roach Gap, Smith Roach Gap Fire Rd./Tr .. 71, 98, 99, **230**
Snead Farm Loop Tr. 141, **142**
Snead Farm Rd. 141, **142**
Sours Lane 53, 116
South Marshall Mtn. 39, 127
South River Cemetery 226
South River Falls, South River Falls Tr. 33, 65, 105, **227**, 228
South River Fire Rd. 64, 65, 105, 226, **228**
South River Maintenance Bldg. 65, 104, 105, 226, **228**
South River Picnic Grounds 65, 105, 227, 228
Spitler Hill 207
Spitler Knoll Overlook 58, 112, 261
Spotswood Tr. 69
Springhouse Road Tr. 37, 129, 141, 145
Staunton River, Staunton River Tr. ... 28, **220**, 222, 223, 262
Stony Man Horse Tr. 115, **190**, 191
Stony Man Mtn. 53, 116, 189, 190, 216
Stony Man Mtn. Overlook 53, 116
Stony Man Nature Tr. 54, 116, **189**
Stony Mtn. Tr. 115, 116, **214**, 215
Story of the Forest Tr. 61, 109, 207, **210**
Stull Run, Stull Run Fire Rd. **244**, 245
Sugarloaf 42, 124
Swift Run Gap, Swift Run Gap Ranger Station 47, 66, 69, 70, 86, 99, 101, 103, 104
Tanners Ridge Fire Rd. 62, 108, **215**
Tanners Ridge Horse Tr. 61, 108, **215**
Thompson Hollow Tr. 162, **163**
Thornton Gap 35, 47, 49, 101, 118, 120, 121
Thornton Hollow Tr. 44, 123, 152, 153, **158**, 159
Thornton River 173
Thorofare Gap (Northern SNP) 149
Thorofare Mtn. (Central SNP) 199, 201
Timber Hollow, Timber Hollow Overlook 57, 113, 208
Tom Floyd Wayside 36, 37, 127, 130, **257**

INDEX

Traces Interpretive Tr. 161, **165**
Trayfoot Mtn., Trayfoot Mtn. Tr. . 78, 92, **245**, 247, 248, 249
Turk Branch Tr. 80, 90, 91, 253, **254**
Turk Gap, Turk Gap Tr. 80, 90, 91, 250, **251**, 252
Turk Mtn., Turk Mtn. Tr. 27, 80, **252**
Tuscarora Tr. 160
Twomile Ridge, Twomile Run Overlook 74, 96, 232
Upper Dark Hollow Tr. **214,** 216
Upper Hawksbill Parking 57, 113, 208
Upper Lewis Run 244
U.S. 522 .... 35, 130, 141, 145, 146
U.S. 211 .... 44, 47, 49, 118, 120, 122
U.S. 33 .... 66, 69, 99, 101, 104
U.S. 250/I-64 .... 83, 86, 87, 88
Utz Hightop Tower 217
Via Gap 263
Weakley Hollow Fire Rd. 178, **196,** 197, 199, 202, 204
Weaver Mtn. 74, 96
Weddlewood Tr. 165, **168**
West Naked Creek Fire Rd. 223
Whiteoak Canyon, Whiteoak Canyon Tr. ... 26, 33, 189, **192,** 195, 196, 199, 200, 203, **207**
Whiteoak Fire Rd. 195, **203,** 207
Whiteoak Horse Tr. 190, **192,** 199
White Rocks Ridge, White Rocks Tr. 181, 184, **188**
Wildcat Ridge Tr. 80, 91, **250**
Wilson Run 223

NOTES

NOTES

NOTES